SOCIOLOGY FOR THE NEW TRIBE OF THE DIGITAL AGE

SOCIOLOGY FOR THE NEW TRIBE OF THE DIGITAL AGE

AN INTRODUCTION

FIRST EDITION

Shahid M. Shahidullah, Ph.D.

Hampton University

cognella®
SAN DIEGO

Bassim Hamadeh, CEO and Publisher
Anne Jones, Project Editor
Susana Christie, Senior Developmental Editor
Rachel Kahn, Production Editor
Asfa Arshi, Graphic Design Assistant
Trey Soto, Licensing Specialist
Natalie Piccotti, Director of Marketing
Kassie Graves, Senior Vice President, Editorial
Jamie Giganti, Director of Academic Publishing

3970 Sorrento Valley Blvd., Ste. 500, San Diego, CA 92121

CONTENTS

CHAPTER 1

The Digital Society of the 21st Century

Sociology for the Digital Tribe

CHAPTER THEME

Future historians will probably describe the beginning of the 21st century as one of the most intriguing and enigmatic times in human history. The first two decades of the century have seen the best of times—the emergence of a digital society and the opening of a vast horizon of unfathomable human possibilities for a peaceful and productive social order based on knowledge building and creativity. The first two decades of the century, however, have also seen the worst of times—the rise of right-wing populism, racism, nativism, divisiveness, terrorism, and religious violence and intolerance worldwide. At no stage in American history were these issues as central to political debates and discourses as they were in the 2nd decade of the 21st century. The digital tribe—the leaders and shapers of the coming decades of global events and issues—needs knowledge and skills, not just about social media and digital technology. They need to know the more fundamental forces of social and political transformations—race, class, gender, ideology, and religion. The new digital tribe is already growing up with a vision for positive social change and a world free from racism, sexism, nativism, divisiveness, and bigotry. Indeed, the new digital tribe is the new generation of "sociologists" in the making for the 21st century.

Introduction

Different generations think differently, face unique challenges, and need additional knowledge and skill sets. America's baby boom generation (born 1946–1964) was different from Generation

X (born 1965–1980), and Generation X was different from the Millennial generation (1981–1994). The Millennial generation is again somewhat different from today's Generation Z (born 1995–2005)—the generation born in the wake of the 21st-century birth of the digital age. The generation born in the middle of the 1990s, those who are now about 20–25 years of age, is sometimes described as "digital native." This generation can also be described as a new digital tribe. In 2019, the digital tribe comprised about 28% (92 million) of America's 327 million people. "Recent research from Bloomberg predicts that Gen Z-ers will account for 2.47 billion people of the 7.7 billion inhabitants of the planet by 2019—that is 32%, and surpass the 2.43 billion figure for Millennials for the first time" (Wood, 2018, p. 1).

What is the nature of the emerging digital society of the 21st century, and what possibilities does it bring for the digital tribe? What are the social, political, and economic challenges that have accompanied the growth of the digital age, and what do those challenges mean for the digital tribe? What are the unique worldviews and personalities of the digital tribe, and how are they different from the earlier generations? What forms of new knowledge and skill sets do the digital tribe need to explore and advance the possibilities of the digital society and to overcome global social, political, and economic challenges? Moreover, how is sociology relevant to the new knowledge and skills needed for the digital tribe? These are the themes that are expanded in this chapter.

The Digital World and the Emerging Possibilities

Future historians will probably describe the 21st century as one of the most creative times in human history. Human knowledge and creativity have always been the driver of human civilization. Humanity has progressed from the Iron Age to the Bronze Age, from the Bronze Age to the birth of the agricultural civilization, and from an agricultural to industrial civilization primarily through the discovery of new knowledge and technology. In every step of civilization's progress, human social order and mechanisms were radically transformed in the face of many unseen social and political challenges, and humans have vastly widened their adaptive abilities through the development of new knowledge and creativity.

In the 21st century, the best of humanity came about through the birth of the internet and social media, inventions through which society seems to have reached the pinnacle of human knowledge and creativity. The internet and social media have brought unprecedented social and economic transformations unknown throughout the evolutionary history of human experience (Table 1.1). The digital age brings enormous possibilities for the expansion of new knowledge, unknown creativity, and unique innovations.

Age of the Internet and the Internet of Everything (IoE)

There are two remarkable ways these possibilities are emerging: The birth of the age of the Internet of Everything (IoE) and the expansion of cloud computing. The IoE is fundamentally transforming the connectivity between and among people, processes, data, and things. The nature, power, functions, and designs of future machines and materials will be radically altered by integrating computers, artificial intelligence, and the internet. This is what is described as the age of the Internet of Everything.

The IoE is the coming of a new age that "is bringing together people, process, data, and things to make networked connections more relevant and valuable than ever before—turning information into actions that create new capabilities, richer experiences, and unprecedented economic opportunity for businesses, individuals, and countries" (Bradley et al., 2013, as quoted in Banafa, 2016, p. 1). In the future world of the IoE, billions of things and billions of people will be connected through the internet. Bradley et al. (2013) estimated that in 2013 about 10 billion things were related to the IoE. In 2020, it's believed the IoE connected about 50 billion things to the internet (Bradley et al., 2013, p. 2). The emerging world of IoE will mostly be invisible. Many of the future digital technologies will not be visible through human eyes. Today, a computer the size of a grain of salt includes a solar cell, thin-film battery, memory, pressure sensor, and wireless radio and antenna. Cameras the size of a grain of salt now have a 250 x 250-pixel resolution. And sensors the size of a speck of dust detect and communicate temperature, pressure, and movement (Bradley et al., 2013, p. 3).

FIGURE 1.1   Baby Girl with Computer

TABLE 1.1 The Nature of the Expanding Cyberspace, 2019

Global Cyberspace	Nature of Penetration	American Cyberspace	Nature of Penetration
Total global population	7.67 billion	Total population	3.27 million
Total internet users	4.38 billion	Total internet users	312.3 million
Active social media users	3.48 billion	Active social media users	230 million
Mobile social media users	3.28 billion	Active social media users	200 million
Annual digital growth	367 million (9.1%)	Internet users a percentage of total population	95%

Annual growth of mobile social media users	297 million (10%)	Mobile internet users	82%
Mobile internet users as a percentage of the total global population	52%	Most active social media Platforms	YouTube (82%) Facebook (80%)
World's three most visited websites	Google, YouTube, and Facebook	Used a social media network in the past month	97%
Watch videos online	92%	Three most visited websites	Google, YouTube, Facebook
Total number of world's people purchasing consumer goods via e-commerce	2. 81 billion	Total number of Americans purchasing consumer goods via e-commerce	258.5 million

Source: www.hootsuite.com

FIGURE 1.2   Internet of Things

The Birth of Cloud Computing

The second remarkable way in which the internet and social media have been opening a vast trajectory of possibilities for new knowledge and creativity is through the invention of cloud computing. Humans have always been separated by time and space dimensions. The internet and social media have removed the constraints of time and space differences and remarkably widened the scope of human connectivity. The birth of cloud computing through which data and information can be accessed, organized, manipulated, synthesized, shared, and stored from any smart device, and from any location and at any time, has been bringing an entirely new horizon of creativity and innovations.

In 2020, there were about 59 zettabytes of data created and stored in cyberspace. In 2025, the global data creation is expected to reach 163 zettabytes (one zettabyte is equal to one billion terabytes of data, and one terabyte is equal to one thousand gigabytes or one million megabytes, or one billion kilobytes of data) (Holst, February 2020, p. 1). In 2018, 19.01 exabytes of data were traveling through cyberspace per month. By 2022, this number is expected to reach 77.5 exabytes of data per month (one exabyte of data equals one billion gigabytes of data) (Pensworth, March 7, 2020, p. 1). The digital experts visualized that, by 2020, "private clouds and public clouds will be commonplace, exchanging data seamlessly. There will not be one cloud; rather, there will be many clouds, bounded by geography, technology, different standards, industry, and perhaps even vendor. We may still call it cloud computing, but it will be an interconnected ether" (Gantz & Reinsel, 2012, p. 1). By 2025, "49% of the world's stored data will reside in public cloud environments ... and the Global Datasphere will grow from 33 Zettabytes (Z.B.) in 2018 to 175 ZB by 2025" (Reinsel et al., 2018, pp. 3–4).

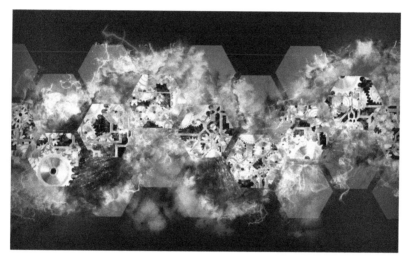

FIGURE 1.3   Cloud Computing

Changing Nature of the Brain, Mind, and Work

The body, brain, and the mind of the digital tribe of the 21st century are profoundly entangled and enmeshed with digital technologies (Table 1.1). In 2020, out of the world's 7.83 billion people, 4.66 billion are connected to the internet, and 5.22 billion are unique mobile phone users. Out of the world's 4.66 billion internet users, 4.2 billion are active users of social media. From January 2020 to January 2021, the global internet users increased 7.3 percent and added 316 million more internet users. If 316 million people are added every year to the Internet, by 2030, most of the world's current population of 7.83 billion will probably be connected to the internet.

Out of the 332 million people in the U.S., 298.8 or 85.5 percent of the population (as of January 2021), are active internet users, 269.5 million are active mobile internet users, 240 million are active social media users, and 233 million are active mobile social media users (Johnson, March 4, 2021). In 2021, YouTube remained the most used social media platform for U.S. adults, followed by Facebook (69 percent), Instagram (40 percent), Pinterest (31 Percent), LinkedIn (31 percent), Snapchat (25 percent), Twitter (23 percent), and WhatsApp (23 percent) (Pew Research Center, April 7, 2021). Among the U. S. teens, however, Snapchat is the most popular platform. A 2020 survey by Statista (Tankovska, January 28, 2021) "found that Snapchat was the most important social network for 34 percent of U.S. teens. The fast-growing social video app TikTok was ranked second with 29 percent of teenagers in the United States stating it to be their favorite, ahead of legacy platforms Facebook and Twitter (p. 1).

The same survey also observed that "some 92 percent of American teens accessed the internet daily, where 56 claimed to connect several times a day, and 24 percent are connected almost constantly to the internet. Furthermore, the move from desktop computers to mobile devices ensured that teenagers would be some of the most fervent users of mobile internet, anytime, anywhere" (Tankovska, January 28, 2021, p. 1). Another survey by Social Media Week (April 20, 2017) shows that "Snapchat is most valued for keeping in touch with friends (89%). 78% of students surveyed said they use Snapchat daily. 76% of students surveyed said they use Instagram daily. 66% of students surveyed said they use Facebook daily. [And] 71% of students surveyed said they use Snapchat more than six times per day" (p. 1). Social media is rapidly and significantly shaping the brain and the minds of the digital tribe. At no stage of civilization has a particular generation of youths been so profoundly affected by technology.

In addition to changing machines and material things, the internet is also fundamentally changing and transforming the nature, design, and functioning of today's social organizations, such as government, business, offices, banks, hospitals, and schools. The internet is fundamentally altering the way we do things, from shopping to dating. It is estimated that "about 40 percent of Americans shop online several times a month, and 20 percent of Americans shop online several times a week. About 140 million Americans monthly shop online by using the Amazon App" (Clement, 2017, p. 1).

The expansion of cloud computing has brought a new trend of working from home for the digital workforce. By 2020, more than 60 million of the new digital tribe were believed to have entered the U.S. workforce. A significant part of this generation will work from home and join the emerging workforce trend described as Bring On Your Device (BOYD). High-tech companies are creating innovative digital platforms, such as CICSO Meraki, that can facilitate virtual work from home with the aid of digital workers' laptops, smartphones, iPads, and tablets. According to a survey conducted by Global Workplace Analytics (2017), based on data from American Community Survey (U.S. Census Bureau), "Regular work-at-home, *among the non-self-employed population*, has grown by 140% since 2005, nearly 10x faster than the rest of the workforce or the self-employed. 80% to 90% of the U.S. workforce says they would like to telework at least part-time. Fortune 1000 companies around the globe are entirely revamping their space around the fact that employees are already mobile" (pp. 1–2).

Birth of the Digital Tribe: The Emerging Challenges

Future historians will probably describe the 21st century as one of the most intriguing and enigmatic times in human history. The first 2 decades of this century have seen the best of times—the emergence of the digital society and the opening of a vast horizon of unfathomable human possibilities for a productive civilization based on knowledge building and creativity. Alas, the first 2 decades of the century have also seen the worst of times. The arrival of new technology in every stage of human history gave birth to new social and political organizations and created a unique cultural landscape.

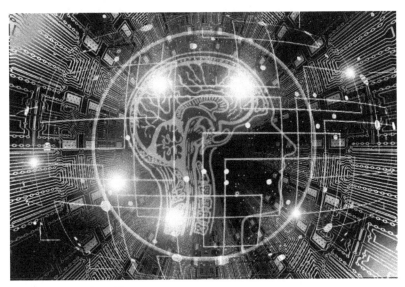

FIGURE 1.4   Artificial Intelligence

The advent of industrialization created new cities and urbanity, new classes and politics, and a new culture of modernity. The social and political order of age, however, also shapes and molds progress in knowledge and technological innovations. Digital technology in the 21st century is expanding when the world is politically, socially, and culturally in turmoil. The first 2 decades of 21st the century have seen almost all significant social and political achievements of the 20th century—such as democracy, equality, secularism, inclusivity, modernity, and globalization—challenged and vilified, and deliberately destroyed.

Digital Tribe and the Emerging Political Challenges

These challenges are happening in front of the eyes of the digital tribe, but to its members, they are ungraspable (Table 1.2). Perhaps they are too young and too busy traveling to the new world of fun and entertainment brought by the new age of social media. They may be too "green" to read big pictures and larger trends. They are, of course, not responsible for the emerging chaos and crisis. But they need to grasp the depth and meaning of the emerging social and political challenges because today's digital tribe will lead the world in the coming decades in politics, economics, professions, and culture. The world's present crisis is not a crisis of the economy or a crisis of knowledge and technology. It is a crisis much bigger and more global in nature. For the last 250 years, the world, under the leadership of the West, particularly American leadership, was engaged in building a global liberal social order, or a global liberal civilization. For nearly 1,000 years, throughout the Middle Ages and in nearly all regions and civilizations of the world, humanity lived under a social system of divisiveness, exploitation, domination, and dehumanization.

THE PROFILE OF THE DIGITAL TRIBE—GENERATION Z

Born between 1995 and 2012, making up 24.3% of the U.S. population, and on track to be the most diverse generation in U.S. history by 2024, Generation Z is about to make its presence known in the workplace in a major way—and it's important to understand the differences that sets it apart. Gen Z cannot remember a time before the September 11, 2001, attacks and the War on Terror. Its members were born after the collapse of communism and witnessed the meteoric rise of China in the global economy. It came of age in a world where content and information are increasingly free and shared, where the body of human knowledge has expanded with a mapping of the human genome, and where one-click online purchasing is taken for granted.

Gen Z is the most ethnically and racially diverse generation in history: One in four is Hispanic, 14% are African American, and 6% are Asian, according to studies led by the Pew Research Center (November 15, 2018). And its views on gender and identity are unprecedented and untraditional: Gen Z refuses to turn ethnicity and race into checkboxes on a survey form. Gen Z has arrived replete with a set of stereotypes and generalizations: Gen Zers are tech-dependent; they want to experience new adventures, not just buy things, and they're less loyal to brands. As the first digitally native generation, it's touted that it prefers digital communication to avoid face-to-face interaction, its members are harder to reach because of their short, 8-second attention span, and they're focused on authenticity in a brand. Yet companies and organizations would be wise not to fall for the myths and stereotypes: Whether you're talking about gender and ethnicity or modes of learning, Gen Z refuses to fit into neat little boxes.

Source: Deloitte. (2020). Welcome to Generation Z (NOW-Network of Executive Women). www.newonline.org

TABLE 1.2 New Tribe in the Digital Age: The Conflicting Social and Political Realities

Born (around 1995)	Growing Up (around 2010–2020)
Great global optimism	Increasing global pessimism
Expansion of global democracy	Retreat of global democracy
Expansion of the global economy	Contraction of the global economy
Expansion of globalization	Growth of new nativism and divisiveness
Growth of new inclusivity	New global discourses on exclusivity
Expansion of America's leadership for global modernity	Retreat of America's leadership for global modernity

End of the Cold War	Reincarnation of the Cold War
Birth of the internet	Birth of social media
Glorification of the digital age	Cybercrime and dark side of the digital age

The whole of the medieval era was a time for the celebration and deification of the kings, queens, and popes. The notion of what we call "democracy" was unknown to the medieval world's power elite, despite the fact that Plato and Aristotle, about 1,500 years before the rise of the high Middle Ages, talked about democracy, good society, good governance, ethics, and morality. Medieval humanity was legally stratified and divided, and the notions of humanism, human rights, and individualism were unknown to the era. The institution of patriarchy lawfully and culturally controlled the lives of medieval women. Historians have no clue how many millions of women throughout the Middle Ages were abused, raped, mutilated, and abandoned. Medieval children were chattels of the patriarch. The medieval world had no concept about what we today call "the rights of the children." Torture and exorcism, sanctified by the Church and canon law, defined the medieval criminal justice system. Until the late 18th century, homosexuals in the Middles Ages were publicly burned alive. People who were physically and mentally disabled were described as "sinners" and were left on the streets to die. It was to challenge and destroy the ideology and the worldview of the medieval civilization that a worldview of a global liberal civilization was born in the 18th and 19th centuries.

Birth of the Liberal Civilization

The worldview of liberal civilization is probably one of humanity's crucial discoveries. It is probably more engulfing and more significant than today's discovery of digital civilization. The liberal civilization's worldview is the constellation of a series of new cultural codes and ideologies. The liberal worldview is not the idea of a king, or a queen, or a pope. It is not the idea of a single individual or a single philosopher. The liberal worldview was born and crystallized through some 400 years of new thoughts and ideas about a "good society" germinated by the philosophers of the Renaissance of the 15th century, the Reformation of the 16th century, the Scientific Revolution of the 17th century, and the Age of Enlightenment of the 18th century. The Renaissance's ideas about the role of human reason and humanism brought a new dream for a good society based on human rights, human dignity, and human equality. The philosophy of individualism, theologically germinated and justified by the theologians of the Reformation movement, signified that a good society is possible by freeing individuals from the domination of the state, religion, and culture. The Reformation theologian Martin Luther gave birth to the doctrines of grace alone (*sola gratia*), Scripture alone (*sola Scriptura*), faith alone (*sola fide*), Christ alone (*sola Christus*), and glory to God alone (*soli Deo Gloria*). The Reformation gave birth to a social order based on the principle of church and state separation.

The Scientific Revolution brought discoveries about the mysteries and properties of nature and life. It gave birth to a new naturalistic and empirical frame of reference to human knowledge. The Scientific Revolution brought a message to humanity that a good society is possible not by common sense and bigotry but by applying science-based research, reason, and knowledge. The Renaissance's ideas, the Reformation, and the Scientific Revolution brought a new vision and a new worldview to the 18th century, described by historians as the Age of Enlightenment. Montesquieu, Hobbes, Locke, Rousseau, Comte, Marx, and many other

Enlightenment philosophers created a new model of civilization that is now described as modernity or a liberal vision of culture.

The liberal idea of a society is based on democracy, humanism, universal human rights, equality, the rule of law, equal justice, church and state separation, religious freedom, the sanctity of private property, inclusivity, and globality. Through this vision the idea of modernity was born, modern America was born, the modern West was born, and the modern world was born. For the past 245 years, America remained engaged with the experiment to build a modern liberal society at home and a modern liberal civilization abroad. Today, the American experiment is under severe attack, and the American vision for spreading liberty abroad is being abandoned. A series of new social and political challenges are now engulfing America and the world, and the vision of liberal civilization is being demeaned and destroyed. The new tribe of the digital age must be aware of and knowledgeable about these challenges. Some of the destructive forces of the liberal social order that are now visible may engulf and influence the world of the digital tribe much more intensely in the coming decades.

Challenges to the American Experiment of Liberal Democracy

The foremost challenge of the new digital tribe is the coming crisis of the American experiment for a liberal democratic social order, which reached 245 years in 2021. The American experiment began in 1776 with the promulgation of the Declaration of Independence by Thomas Jefferson: "We hold these truths to be self-evident, that all men are created equal, that they are endowed by their Creator with certain unalienable Rights that among these are Life, Liberty and the pursuit of Happiness."

From George Washington to Barack Obama, every American president, despite different political views and ideologies, strongly defended the American experiment based on the core values of a liberal social order, both at home and abroad. America, by birth, is an open and global society with visions of democracy, equality, religious freedom, and inclusivity. For the past 245 years of the experiment, these visions have been defined, codified, justified, and widened. Every American president from Washington to Obama deeply shared Jefferson's vision of spreading the "Empire of Liberty." In a letter to Joseph Priestly, in 1802, Jefferson stated, "We feel that we are acting under obligations not confined to the limits of our society. It is impossible not to be sensible that we are acting for all mankind" (para. 1). Jefferson believed that as one of the first countries to begin the experiment of modernity and the enlightenment model of civilization, America had a moral obligation to spread modernity to the entire world. In his Cairo speech, in 2009, President Obama echoed the same message to America and the world. Obama (2009) made a valiant declaration: "I've come here to Cairo to seek a new beginning between the United States and Muslims around the world, one based on mutual interest and mutual respect, and one based upon the truth that America and Islam are not exclusive and need not be in competition" (p. 2). Obama (2009) told the young Egyptians that democracy, the rule of law, transparent governance, equality, and religious tolerance "are not just American ideas; they are human rights. And that is why we will support them everywhere" (p. 3).

In 2017, America came to a new turning point in its journey for a modern liberal social order, one that began in 1776. That year in America, 2017, was a time that saw not just the enthronement of the presidency of Donald J. Trump but also the coming to power of a political regime that boldly declared and was firmly dedicated to rolling back the 245-year-old American democracy experiment. America that year entered a new age of nativism, divisiveness, fundamentalism, and localism, as exemplified by President Trump's campaign promise to "Make America Great Again"—a political turn described as the birth of America's "right-wing populism" (Albright, 2018; Boot, 2018; Goldberg, 2018).

America's right-wing populism, however, was not born in 2017. It was the culmination of more than 50 years of struggle by America's ultraconservatives and the antimodernists for a sociopolitical order in America vastly different from the vision espoused by Jefferson and all American presidents who came to power between Washington and Obama (Zito & Todd, 2018). It is probably too early to see how this political transformation and the resurgence of right-wing populism will affect America's core institutions of democracy and an inclusive society's core values. Still, many scholars and intellectuals widely share a view of a significant and entirely new turn in American history. Most likely, violence, conflicts, and confusion in many spheres of life and society will remain endemic in America in the coming decades (Johnston, 2018; Maclean, 2017).

The new digital tribe is excited about the emerging world of digitalization, but a part of the tribe is also becoming confused and concerned. It cannot fathom the meaning and reason for the eruptions of violence, as in the White-supremacist rally in Charlottesville, Virginia, in 2017, the synagogue massacre in Pittsburgh in 2018, and the mass killing at a Walmart in El Paso, Texas, in 2019. The digital tribe cannot connect the dots on why Muslims from some countries are banned from entering America or why children are separated from their parents at the U.S.-Mexico border. It doesn't have a clue on why Russia and some of its authoritarian allies are suddenly becoming America's close friends. Today's digital tribe was born and is now growing up in a very conflicting and confusing moment of American history. Still, it will have to try to understand and grapple with the genesis of these sociopolitical challenges.

But the resurgence of a new age of antidemocracy and antiliberalism—the birth of the age of right-wing populism—is not merely an American phenomenon. It is becoming a global problem. From London to New York, Delhi to Denmark, and Paris to Pakistan, the waves of right-wing populist ideology are rapidly spreading. Democracy has been on the march in the West for more than 250 years. It began symbolically with the promulgation of the Magna Carta in 1215 but progressed more decisively and politically with England's Glorious Revolution of 1688, the American Revolution of 1776, and the French Revolution of 1789.

During the past 250 years, democracy and the liberal social order in the West unceasingly advanced despite the American Civil War of 1861–1865, the First World War of 1914–1918, the Second World War of 1941–1945, and the Cold War decade of the 1960s. During these wars and times of turmoil, America was guided by Thomas Jefferson's vision that the spreading of the Empire of Liberty globally is America's moral responsibility. In the developing world of Asia, Africa, and Latin America, the movement for democracy and a liberal social order began in the wake of decolonization in the 1960s and 1970s. In the 1960s and 1970s, thousands of Americans died during the Cold War and became permanently disabled in different wars, and America spent trillions of dollars. All of these to defend the ideology of democracy and liberal social order both at home and abroad (Shahidullah, 2019a).

The birth of socialism in Russia after the Russian Revolution in 1917 created an alternative ideology of a socialist world system, a system antithetical to democracy and the liberal social order. It was opposed to the doctrines of the Renaissance's humanism and individualism, religious freedom of the Reformation movement, and to democracy and equality of the Age of Enlightenment. The Cold War of the 1960s erupted because of Russia's deliberate move to bring the whole of the developing world and a part of Europe within the socialist world system. The Cold War was formally ended in the 1980s after a new political regime in Russia, under Mikhail Gorbachev, decided to join the camp of democracy and liberal social order. This political revolution in Russia did not last long. After a period of political chaos, Russia, at the beginning of the 21st century and under Vladimir Putin's leadership, decisively went back to its ideology of a world socialist system. Russia now has more than 7,000 nuclear warheads to defend its socialist system. China and North Korea, both with hundreds of nuclear warheads, remain firmly within the world socialist system. For nearly 3 decades, America's engagement with the Cold War was primarily to defend global democracy and the international liberal social order.

Today, the global political history is traveling through an entirely different route, and the ideology of "America first" is deepening along America's political horizon. America's political regime under President Donald Trump deliberately abdicated its leadership for promoting global democracy and the vision of a global liberal social order. The right-wing political regime had a mindset that America's leadership in the past for advancing the cause of democracy abroad was misguided and misleading. In his inaugural speech, President Trump (2017) lamented that "for many decades, we've enriched foreign industry at the expense of American industry; subsidized the armies of other countries, while allowing for the very sad depletion of our military. We've defended other nations' borders while refusing to defend our own" (para. 6). He then further defended his isolationist worldview. He said we (America) "spent trillions and trillions of dollars overseas while America's infrastructure has fallen into disrepair and decay. We've made other countries rich, while the wealth, strength, and confidence of our country have dissipated over the horizon" (Trump, 2017, para. 6).

America's rise and expansion of right-wing populism glorify and justify the global expansion of right-wing populism and lead to the retreat of global democracy (Levitsky & Ziblatt, 2018; Luce, 2017). Global democracy is in retreat, and many are even talking about "the death of democracy" (Levitsky & Ziblatt, 2018). The crisis of democracy and the liberal social order is slowly creeping into the whole world. In Europe, right-wing populism is growing in Germany, England, France, Greece, Italy, Hungary, Sweden, Finland, the Netherlands, and Austria. The World Economic Forum's (2018) report, *Global Risk 2018: Fractures, Fears, and Failures*, observed that the world's geopolitical landscape is rapidly changing. The rise of nationalism and state-centered politics, growing tensions among the world's major powers, and increasing vulnerability among small states create new "fractures" within the global international system and limit the advance of global modernity. The report expressed a huge concern that "the world has moved into a new and unsettling geopolitical phase. It is not just multipolar, but multi-conceptual. There is no longer any assumption—as there had been in the post–Cold War phase, framed by the so-called New World Order. This creates new risks and uncertainties and destabilizing feedback loops between changing international relations and countries' domestic political conditions" (2018, p. 1). This global political scenario is emerging and deepening in front of the digital tribe (Shahidullah, 2019b).

The contemporary trends of divisiveness, isolationism, nativism, localism, conservatism, fundamentalism, and racism in world politics will have serious effects not just on political order and stabilities but also on many realms of culture. Right-wing populism not only sanctifies authoritarianism in power but also fuels the growth of hate, racism, and bigotry. India, the so-called world's largest democracy of 1.3 billion people, is now under the firm grip of a right-wing Hindu fundamentalist regime in which religious violence and intolerance against Christians and Muslims have rapidly grown. In the American homeland, hate crimes against Jews, Muslims, and Mexicans significantly increased after the ascendency of the Trump presidency in 2017. The Federal Bureau of Investigation (FBI) (November 13, 2018) reported in 2018 that between 2016 and 2017, hate crime or bias crime in America increased by 17%. The Southern Poverty Law Center (SPLC) (2017), one of the major think tanks in America, noted that hate crime against Muslims increased 67% in 2015, "the year in which Trump launched his [presidential] campaign. The SPLC found that the number of hate groups [against Muslims] operating in 2016 rose to 917—up from 892 in 2015" (para. 5).

Most of the political regimes dominated by right-wing populism, or the radical right or ultraright, are governed by false and manufactured ideology, and they are profoundly anti-intellectual. Social media contributes more to the spread and the diffusion of false ideologies around the world. Examples of false news and its devastating effects are not few and far between in both America and global societies connected through the internet and social media. Social media is a new digital highway for carrying and spreading hate, racism, violence, and bigotry (Shahidullah & Das, 2019). Cybercrime is not just economically devastating; it is also politically and morally damaging and demeaning. It is widely believed that a future Cold War or even a future "hot war" will be in cyberspace. Today's digital tribe has a compelling reason to be aware of the sociology behind these and other related social, political, and cultural trends and challenges in America and the global society.

New Knowledge and Skill Choices for the Digital Tribe

In every stage in the evolution of human knowledge and technology, there emerged the need for new knowledge and adaptive skills and capabilities. The rise of industrialization in the 19th century gave birth to the need for new knowledge about cities and urban life, class and capitalism, state and citizenship, business and bureaucracy, race and religion, and crime and poverty. These needs for new knowledge and skills gave birth to the modern educational system—a system mostly unseen in the Middle Ages. Different social sciences also emerged in the 19th century to explain and explore the emerging problems of industrialization and urbanization in that century.

With the arrival of a science-based knowledge society in the middle of the 20th century, there again evolved the need for a new set of knowledge and skills compatible with modern science and technology. From the 1970s, in almost all branches of knowledge, from nursing to nanoscience and neurology to sociology, new skills for understanding and applying scientific research and technology began to be taught and learned. By the end of the 20th century, most jobs began to demand college degrees. A study commissioned in 2002 by the American Association of Colleges and Universities (AACU, 2002) found that even at that time, 87% of "elite" job holders and 53% of "good" job holders had more than a high school education. From 1973 to 1998, the percentage of managers and business professionals with only a high school diploma fell by nearly 50% while those with at least some college rose substantially (p. 5). The study also found that "college graduates earn 80 percent more than high school graduates or $1,000,000 over a lifetime" (AACU, 2002, p. 5). With the arrival of the internet and the digital age, there has emerged again the need for more advanced and sustained education for new knowledge and skill sets compatible with the technology and the social and political complexities of the 21st century.

Challenges of the Science-Based Knowledge Society

From the middle of the 20th century, scholars and business and political leaders began to debate the nature of the new knowledge and skill sets needed for the science-based knowledge society. Two competing models began to inform this debate from that time. The first model is to create a new class of technocrats who will develop the expertise to understand and apply the latest technology. This created a whole new generation of technocrats and professionals who earned the expertise in their spheres of science and technology but were mostly devoid of understanding the larger social, political, cultural, and global contexts within which the new knowledge society was born and had grown, and of understanding how the new world was to be led and governed.

From the 1970s and 1980s, a new model of integrated education began to grow and expand within American colleges and universities. This model is a uniquely American innovation in higher education. It is based on the notion that higher education must firmly blend scientific and professional education with the disciplines collectively described as liberal arts, such as sociology, economics, political science, psychology, history, cultural studies, ethics, philosophy, and global studies. In nearly all 4-year colleges and universities in America, from Harvard to Hampton, Pittsburgh to Princeton, this integrated and blended model of education, albeit in varying degrees of emphasis, is the core of the undergraduate curriculum. The need for liberal education and the blending of science and professions with liberal arts knowledge has never been so crucial as in the 21st century. As described earlier, the 21st century is the best of and worst of times. The century brought a new digital society—a society qualitatively very different from the science-driven-knowledge society of the 1970s and 1980s. Modern science does not yet clearly know how this world of digitalization will influence the minds of the new digital tribe and how the globalization of digital technology and social media will affect politics, economy, crime, culture, faith, sex, marriage, and intimacy.

The new digital tribe will have to have a college education and a new set of knowledge and skills that are strongly liberal in spirit—holistic, synthetic, global, historical, cultural, and moral. In 2013, the American Association for College and Universities commissioned another study on employer priorities in college learning and student success. The study surveyed 318 presidents, CEOs, C-suite-level executives, and vice presidents from public- and private-sector organizations. The study found that "nearly all employers surveyed (95%) say they give hiring preference to college graduates with skills that will enable them to contribute to innovation in the workplace" and that more than nine in 10 agree that "innovation is essential" to their organization's continued success (American Association of College and Universities, 2013, p. 1). The study further noted that "nearly all those surveyed (93%) agree, 'a candidate's demonstrated capacity to think critically, communicate clearly, and solve complex problems is more important than their undergraduate major.' More than nine in ten of those surveyed say it is essential that those they hire demonstrate ethical judgment and integrity; intercultural skills; and the capacity for continued new learning" (American Association of College and Universities, 2013, p. 1).

The Centrality of Liberal Education

A more sophisticated version of this argument in favor of an integrated liberal arts education model came from a significant study conducted by the World Economic Forum—one of Switzerland's top global think tanks on development and socioeconomic transformations. In 2015, the World Economic Forum published a

New Vision for Education report, *Unlocking the Potential of Technology*. The study developed a new education model for today's digital tribe, described as Social and Emotional Learning (SEL). The study found that about 65% of children entering grade school "will work in jobs that do not exist today, a transformation that will require social and emotional skills such as creativity, initiative, and adaptability to navigate" (World Economic Forum, 2015, p. 5).

The SEL model of learning is composed of three sets of skills for the 21st-century workplace: foundational literacies, competencies, and character qualities (Table 1.3). According to the SEL model, prominence among the skills needed for the workplace in the 21st century is not the kind of skills that come from basic physics, chemistry, engineering, and mathematics (STEM areas). The STEM areas are needed to build professional knowledge and expertise, but they do not rightly expand the horizon of the mind for creativity and innovations; they do not provide an understanding of scientific reasoning and its difference from the faith, philosophy, and common sense; and they do not help to cultivate a sense of culture, morality, historicity, diversity, and globality. The STEM areas involve the fundamental laws and properties of nature, such as atoms, molecules, lights, forces, gravity, and magnetism. The STEM areas do not address humans and their multifaceted social, economic, political, moral, philosophical, and metaphysical issues. Therefore, the blending of STEM learning with liberal arts is the key, the SEL model suggests, for creativity, innovations, and adaptability in the 21st century.

TABLE 1.3 World Economic Forum, SEL Model: Education for 21st-Century Skills

Foundational Literacies	Competencies	Character Qualities
Literacy Numeracy Scientific literacy Financial literacy Cultural literacy	Critical thinking/problem-solving Creativity Communication Collaboration	Curiosity Initiative Persistence Adaptability Leadership Social and cultural awareness
Source: World Economic Forum (2016).		

Education for the 21st Century

In 2013, Google conducted a critical study to examine the top skills needed in the digital economy of the 21st century based on data collected from its hiring, firing, and promotion practices since 1998. The study made a surprising finding that STEM is the last of the top eight skills of those who succeeded at Google. The top seven skills, the study found, are creative thinking, a sense of cultural empathy, a sense of cultural relativity, the ability for knowledge synthesis, the ability for problem-solving, the ability to work in a team, and a global perspective—a curiosity for cross-cultural understanding. Former Apple CEO Steve Jobs rightly "insisted that STEM would not be enough. The future will require experts in the 'human, cultural, and social as well as computational'" (McGonagle, 2018, p. 8).

It is, therefore, not surprising that some of the top CEOs of Fortune 500 companies came from liberal arts background, such as Starbucks CEO Howard Schultz (BS in communication); Michael Eisner, former Walt

Disney CEO (BA in English); Richard Plepler, HBO's CEO (BA in government); Carly Fiorina, former Hewlett-Packard CEO (BA in medieval history and philosophy); Susan Wojcicki, YouTube CEO (BA in history and literature); and Jack Ma, chairman, Alibaba (BA in English) (Linshi, 2015). The liberal arts knowledge is characterized by certain qualities that make it vital for learning and professions in the 21st century. The liberal arts knowledge is scientific, holistic, synthetic, critical, historical, comparative, global, relativistic, moral, and humanistic (Table 1.4). These different facets of knowledge—learned from other liberal arts disciplines, combined with high science, computers, artificial intelligence, and the internet—are at the core of the evolution, constructions, and transformations of modern digital society.

Sociology and the Knowledge Needs for the Digital Tribe

Profile of the Digital Tribe: Generation Z

Out of all generations of Americans that came since the 1950s—the baby boom generation, Generation X, Generation Y, and the Millennial generation—Generation Z, or the digital tribe of the 21st century, is qualitatively very different in terms of its political visions, social choice, and social responsibility. Its members are racially more diverse, politically more progressive, economically more responsible and global, educationally more ambitious, and religiously more tolerant. A recent report from Deloitte (2020) said, "Generation Z will soon surpass Millennials as the most populous generation on earth, with more than one-third of the world's population counting themselves as Gen Zers. In the US, Gen Z constitutes more than a quarter of the population and, by 2020, will be the most diverse generation in the nation's history" (p. 1).

In 2018, the Pew Research Center conducted a study of 60,000 households based on data collected by the U.S. Census Bureau and the U.S. Department of Labor. The goal of the study was to understand the demographic profile of the postmillennial generation—Generation Z. The study found that nearly half (48% of Generation Z [ages 6–21]) are racial and ethnic minorities in comparison with 18% of baby boomers and 30% of Generation X. In 1968, among baby boomers, 82% were White. In 2018, among Generation Z, 52% were White. In 1986, among Generation X, 44% went to college. In 2017, among Generation Z, 59% went to college. In 1986, among Generation X, 23% lived with college-educated parents (Pew Research Center, November 15, 2018).

Another study conducted by the Pew Research Center (January 17, 2019) on social and political views of the generation Z found that this generation is firmly for widening democracy and the social and political rights of all groups of people in America and the world as a whole. A large part of the generation Z believes that diversity is good for America (62 percent in comparison to 48 percent of Boomers), and this is also true of the generation Z republicans. "Half of Gen Z Republicans (51%) say increased racial and ethnic diversity is a good thing for the country. This compares to 38% of the Millennials, 34% of Gen X, and 30% of Boomers" (Pew Research Center, January 17, 2019, p. 10). The same survey shows that 70 percent of Generation Z members do not approve of President Trump's job performance. Unlike any previous generation, Gen Z is more concerned with the global issues of poverty, inequality, and climate change.

TABLE 1.4 Key Characteristics of Liberal Arts Knowledge

Knowledge Characteristics	Knowledge-Related Ideas and Descriptions
Scientific Reasoning	Understanding of the meaning of scientific inquiry, not just what is astronomy, physics, and chemistry; understanding that scientific inquiry is theoretical, factual, generalizable, and evidence based; scientific theories are changeable and falsifiable; science is a passion for knowledge.
Holistic	Whole-part relationship; systematic knowledge; the idea that the characteristics of a system are different from the constituent parts that comprise the system; the system has structures and functions—examples: general systems theory, quantum physics, planetary system, respiratory system, digestive system, economic system, political system, global financial system, and the global economic system.
Synthetic	Ability to make creative and innovative discoveries or theories by combining knowledge from different disciplines, such as computer and biology and innovations in biometrics; neurology and behavioral science and the birth of the new field of behavioral neurology; Harvard economist Robert Reich described the new generation of experts in the 21st century as "symbolic analysts."
Critical/Analytical	The ability to understand and examine different layers of social realities; many sociologists call it a "backstage" analysis, and many philosophers call it a "hermeneutic understanding" or "destructuration."
Historical	Curiosities about history and evolution of different events such as the history of slavery, the history of women's struggle for voting rights, the history of women's struggle for work and education, the history of civil rights in America; and historical consciousness about the evolution of human cultures and civilizations.
Comparative/Relativistic	Understanding how different societies do things differently or different generations think differently; knowledge of other countries and cultures in terms of their ways of doing things; knowledge of social, religious, and cultural diversities in world societies
Global	Understanding of the world as interconnected and interdependent countries and cultures; knowledge of the world as a system; knowledge of the political, economic, and cultural forces of globalization; ability to analyze local change and transformations in terms of the strengths of globalization
Moral/Humanistic	Understanding the notion of morality; ideas of good society, good governance, and good polity; knowledge about ethics—what is right and what is wrong; defining humans as moral beings; concerns for human issues, such as poverty, global violence against women, global violence against children, global violence against the LGBTQ communities; concerns for development and freedom for all of humanity and the negation of war and violence

The World Economic Forum in 2017 conducted a similar study, titled *Global Shapers Survey 2017*, on the values and beliefs of the global Generation Z, particularly those below age 30. What is sociologically profound about this study is that youths below 30 worldwide (it was estimated that the global population of Generation Z reached 2.56 billion in 2020) share some common values and beliefs on many social and political changes and transformations in the 21st century. The survey is based on respondents from 186 countries and is translated into 14 languages.

One of the curious findings is that most of the respondents said their core identity does not come from their gender, race, religion, or nationality. They see themselves as global citizens. "For a large majority of young people, identity is not about the region, geography, religion, or ethnicity; they simply see themselves as 'human' (40.8%). This is also the most popular answer choice across regions. For them, their race is the human race" (World Economic Forum, 2017, p. 29).

The majority of the respondents also said equality is the foundation of a democratic and free society. They demanded equality for all humans irrespective of gender, race, ethnicity, and religion. The survey found that "when asked what would make them feel freer in their society, 51.4% of young people answered 'equal access to opportunities for all.' This demonstrates that they are a socially conscious group concerned about the well-being and future of others" (World Economic Forum, 2017, p. 29). The survey observed that, "regionally, North America exhibits a spectacular propensity for openness. Over 80% of young people surveyed are comfortable, welcoming refugees in their own neighborhood, showing a readiness to embrace different cultures in their everyday life" (World Economic Forum, 2017, p. 31).

New Sociological Visions for Change and Transformation

What the previous data suggest is that the global digital tribe, particularly the American digital tribe of the 21st century, is growing up with a profoundly different sociological vision for change and transformations. As described previously, the 21st century is seeing not just the best of times—the birth of a global digital society—but also the worst of times—the global spread of racism, nationalism, nativism, authoritarianism, right-wing populism, threats of nuclear war, the specter of cyberwar, and religious intolerance and violence. For today's digital tribe—tomorrow's leaders in politics, business, science, education, and professions—the grasping of sociology's perspective is vital. Sociology is a unique brand of social science that is curiously and ceaselessly concerned about human problems and issues. Sociology is vastly relevant for the digital tribe to understand how social inquiry can be scientific; how holistic and synthetic understanding is possible; why historical, comparative, and global experience is critical; and why a moral and humanistic perspective is vital to understanding the emerging issues and crises of the 21st century.

There are some similarities between the intellectual and social contexts of the rise of sociology in the 19th century and the academic and social contexts of the 21st century. The 19th century in Europe, when sociology was born, was also the best of times and the worst of times. It was the best of the times because it saw the birth of modernity and the birth of the ideas of democracy, equality, freedom, and individualism. The old empires and aristocracies of the medieval world were disintegrating in the 19th century with the advent of modern states, modern capitalism, modern bourgeoise, modern education, modern cities, and modern industrial technology. The 19th century, however, was also the worst of times. The old medieval society was crumbling, but there was no direction about where modernity was leading humanity. New cities were growing with the burst of a new bourgeoisie, but there was no knowledge for urbanity management. New forces of industrialization and urbanization brought optimism about economic prosperity; however, further confusions and uncertainties about the disintegration of old family values and the rise of new urban crimes and poverty also emerged.

THE KEY COMPETENCIES FOR THE DIGITAL TRIBE

The advent of digitalization is fundamentally transforming the nature of work and is bringing many significant challenges for the digital tribe of the 21st century. High school education was competitive in the early phase of industrialization. A college degree was adequate to work in the postindustrial society of the 1970s and 1980s. In the face of advancing digitalization, however, social and collective governance need qualitatively different kinds of knowledge, skills, and abilities. "Over the coming years, technological developments, such as big data, cloud computing, the internet of things, robotics, artificial intelligence, and immersive communications are likely to have a significant impact on the world of work and employment and to trigger far-reaching changes" (Deloitte, 2017, p. 4).

Today's digital tribe needs to be educated and knowledgeable about combining theory and practice. Learning of theory, models, and concepts will be critical for technological innovations and competence for political and corporate governance. In the new age of digitalization, knowledge of mathematics, science, and engineering must be combined with knowledge of the law, public policy, arts, and humanities. The new digital tribe must know the sociology of management, administration, and the sociological profile of the "new clients" and "new customers." The advent of digitalization is also bringing new challenges for skill enhancement. Creativity in problem-solving through knowledge synthesis is now vital for the digital tribe. Its members need content and process skills and critical thinking, social perceptiveness, and the ability for negotiations and persuasions. In the sphere of ability, essential is the need for overall cognitive competence—competence for logic and reasoning, knowledge synthesis, and synergy.

Source: Deloitte. What key competencies are needed in the digital age? The impact of automation on employees, companies, and education. www2.deloitte.com

In this context of both unbounded optimism and unfathomable tensions in the wake of the birth of modernity in the 19th century, sociology was born. Sociology was born precisely with two missions: to provide a scientific analysis of the structure and formation of the society in general and to study the directionality of modernity. At the beginning of this century, the world observed similar predicaments: unbounded optimism and unfathomable uncertainties. An unprecedented amount of optimism is hovering along the horizon of the 21st century in the context of digital society's rise.

After thousands of years, human knowledge and technology seem to have come to a point where humans can achieve a world free of poverty, exploitation, violence, hate, and racism—a world of global liberal civilization. Alas, the 21st century is seeing the resurgence of racism, nativism, nationalism, and religious hate and violence. The hope, however, lies with the digital tribe—a tribe born with a vision for building a world of democracy, equality, globality, and humanism. Sociological knowledge will be precious for this digital tribe to enrich its curiosity and understanding of the social, political, and cultural forces leading the 21st century.

Suggested Questions, Essays, Assignments, and Quizzes

1. The boundaries of the digital world have been reaching almost every country, culture, and corner of the world. It is vital for the digital tribe to know the scope and dimensions of the emerging world that is real but physically unseen and invisible. Visit the website (https://datareportal.com/reports/digital-2020-global-digital-overview) and read and review the document *Digital 2020: Global Digital Overview*. Based on your review of this document, make two charts—one on the global digital profile and the other on the American digital face describing cyberspace's various dimensions (Table 1.1). Based on the data, make a comment at the end of the charts on your understanding of the expanding nature of cyberspace.

2. Sociologists have observed that in all ages, all societies, and at all times, there is a generational divide. Different generations think about and perceive the world differently. Their acts and dreams are different. In America, there has emerged a new discourse on the coming of a Generation Z in the context of the rise of contemporary digital society. Based on class lectures and your own experience, write an essay (two or three single-spaced pages, 12-point font) describing Generation Z's social, political, ideological, and personality profile.

3. The digital society has brought enormous possibilities for growth, change, innovations, and transformations. But it has also brought many significant economic, social, political, and cultural challenges. The first 2 decades of the 21st century have remained engulfed with some of these challenges. Based on your reading this chapter and your internet research, write an essay (three or four single-spaced pages, 12-point font) describing the fragile state of liberal democracy in the wake of the rise of racism, nativism, localism, misinformation, hate, and bigotry in recent politics in America.

4. In the context of the rise of the digital society, what is at stake is the future of liberal democracy and the liberal social order and civilization. The digital tribe is living at a crucial juncture when the progress of liberal social order in America is under severe attack. Based on your reading of this chapter and your internet research, write an essay (three or four single-spaced pages, 12-point font) describing the social, political, and cultural profile of liberal democracy (i.e., core American values).

5. The rise of the digital society and the rise of new social and political forces challenging the roots of liberal democracy will demand new knowledge and skills for the digital tribe. Its members will have to be not only technologically literate but also socially and politically educated. In other words, they will have to combine and synthesize science with liberal arts knowledge. Based on your reading of this chapter and your internet research, write an essay (three or four single-spaced pages, 12-point font) describing liberal arts knowledge (Table 1.4).

6. The digital tribe will make up the future leaders in politics, economics, law, culture, science, and technology. The future directionality of the liberal civilization both at home and abroad depends on today's digital tribe's knowledge and ideological profile. Based on your reading of this chapter

and your internet research, write an essay (three or four single-spaced pages, 12-point font) explaining sociology's role in making the digital tribe in the 21st century.

7. Sociology is described as a science because it applies the rules and canons of science in explaining forms and patterns of social facts and events. Sociology, however, is also described as a humanistic discipline. Sociologists are interested in exploring both the bright and the darker sides of human lives and stories—moral, ethical, and humanistic. Understanding some of the moral issues of American society is imperative for the digital tribe. In the context of these statements, describe the problems and plights of America's transgender community (focus on some related laws and public policy debates and discourses).

8. Curiosities about the history of different social facts and events are an integral part of sociological understanding. Sociological consciousness is both historical and temporal. In the context of the previous statement, write an essay (two or three single-spaced pages, 12-point font) comparing the social and psychological profiles of the baby boom generation and Generation Z (i.e., how you are different in many ideas, values, attitudes, perceptions, dreams, and habits from your parents' generation and why you believe you are so very different from them).

9. Grasping of quantitative reasoning is an essential part of a liberal arts education. The learning of quantitative reasoning does not mean the understanding of math and physics, or chemistry or computers. It means a scientific bent of mind; it means a passion for facts and evidence; it means critically examining the barrage of false information unceasingly unfolding in front of our eyes, mainly through social media. Cite and describe (preferably in the form of a table) five significant sociological data sources, such as poverty, health, demography, work and employment, drug, crimes, and addiction.

10. Global or international understanding is an essential part of a liberal arts education. Sociology is intensely interested in seeing the world as an interconnected and interdependent system of diverse countries and cultures. Sociologists study how the world is going through globalization—intensely social, economic, and cultural connectivity between and among the world's different countries. Today's digital tribe is much more global in comparison with the baby boom generation. In the context of the idea of international understanding and the perception of the growth of globalization, write a personal story (two or three single-spaced pages, 12-point font) about five to 10 people you know from other countries, cultures, languages, and religions (explain how you know them and for how long).

References

Albright, M. (2018). *Fascism: A warning*. Harper Books.

Association of American Colleges and Universities. (2002). *Greater expectations: A new vision for learning as nation goes to college*.

Association of American Colleges and Universities. (2013). *It takes more than a major: Employer priorities for college learning and student success* (research by Hart Associates).

Banata, A. (2016, August). *The internet of everything (IOE)*. Retrieved from https://www.bbvaopenmind.com/en/technology/digital-world/the-internet-of-everything-ioe/ on April 30, 2021.

Berger, P. L. (1990). *The sacred canopy: Elements of a sociological theory of religion*. Anchor Books. (Original work published 1967)

Boot, M. (2018). *The Corrosion of Conservatism: Why I left the right*. Liveright Publishers.

Bradley, J., Barbier, J., & Handler, D. (2013). *Embracing the internet of everything to capture your share of $14.4 trillion*. CISCO. Retrieved from https://www.cisco.com/c/dam/en_us/about/business-insights/docs/ioe-economy-insights.pdf on April 30, 2021.

Clement, J. (June, 2017). *Online shopping behavior in the United States—Statistics and facts.* Retrieved from www.statista.com on April 30, 2021.

Deloitte. (2020). *Welcome to Generation Z* (by K. Gomez, T. Mawhinney, T., & K. Betts). Retrieved from https://www2.deloitte.com/content/dam/Deloitte/us/Documents/consumer-business/welcome-to-gen-z.pdf on April 30, 2021.

Deloitte. (2017). Key competencies are needed in the digital age? The impact of automation on employees, companies and education. Retrieved from https://www2.deloitte.com/content/dam/Deloitte/ch/Documents/innovation/ch-en-innovation-automation-competencies.pdf on April 30, 2021.

Federal Bureau of Investigation. (November 13, 2018). *2017 hate crime statistics released.* Retrieved from https://www.fbi.gov/news/stories/2017-hate-crime-statistics-released-111318 on April 30, 2021.

Gantz, J., & Reinsel, D. (2012, December). *The digital universe in 2020. Big data, bigger digital shadows, and biggest growth in the Far East.* International Data Corporation. Retrieved from https://www.cs.princeton.edu/courses/archive/spring13/cos598C/idc-the-digital-universe-in-2020.pdf on December 20, 2020.

Global Workplace Analytics. (2017). *Telecommuting trend data.* Retrieved from https://globalworkplaceanalytics.com/telecommuting-statistics on April 30, 2021.

Goldberg, J. (2018). *Suicide of the west: How the rebirth of tribalism, populism, nationalism, and identity politics is destroying American democracy.* Crown Publishing Group.

Holst, A. (February 5, 2021). Amount of Information Globally 2010–2024. Retrieved from https://www.statista.com/statistics/871513/worldwide-data-created/ on February 27, 2021.

Jefferson, T. (1802). *From Thomas Jefferson to Joseph Priestly, 19 June 1802.* Founders Online. Retrieved from https://founders.archives.gov/documents/Jefferson/01-37-02-0515 on December 20, 2020.

Johnson, J. (March 4, 2021). *United States: Digital Population as of January 2021.* Retrieved from https://www.statista.com/statistics/1044012/usa-digital-platform-audience/on April 16, 2021.

Johnston, D. C. (2018). *It's even worse than you think: What the Trump administration is doing to America.* Simon and Schuster.

Levitsky, S., & Ziblatt, D. (2018). *How democracies die.* Crown Publishing Group.

Linshi, J. (2015, July). 10 CEOs who prove your liberal arts degree isn't worthless. *Time.* Retrieved from https://time.com/3964415/ceo-degree-liberal-arts/on December 20, 2020.

Luce, E. (2017). *The retreat of western liberalism.* Atlantic Monthly Press-Grove Atlantic.

MacLean, N. (2017). *Democracy in chains: The deep history of the radical right's stealth plan for America.* Penguin Books.

May, E. T. (2011). *America and the pill: A history of promise, peril, and liberation.* Basic Books.

McGonagle, M. (2018, January). Sorry STEM, Google just made the case for more foreign language education. *Transparent Language.* Retrieved from https://blogs.transparent.com/language-news/2018/01/01/sorry-stem-google-just-made-the-case-for-more-foreign-language-education on December 20, 2020.

Obama, B. (2009, June). *Remarks of President Obama at Cairo University.* Obama White House. Retrieved from https://obamawhitehouse.archives.gov/the-press-office/remarks-president-cairo-university-6-04-09 on December 20, 2020.

Pensworth, L. (March 7, 2020). *2019 Internet Statistics, Trends & Data.* Retrieved from https://dailywireless.org/internet/usage-statistics/ on February 27, 2021.

Pew Research Center. (April 7, 2021). *Social Media use in 2021.* Retrieved from https://www.pewresearch.org/internet/2021/04/07/social-media-use-in-2021/ on April 16, 2021.

Pew Research Center. (January 17, 2019). *Generation Z Looks a Lot Like Millennials on Key Social and Political Issues* (by K. Parker, G. N. Graf, and R. Igielnik). Retrieved from https://www.pewresearch.org/social-trends/2019/01/17/generation-z-looks-a-lot-like-millennials-on-key-social-and-political-issues/ on April, 30, 2021.

Pew Research Center. (November 15, 2018). *Early Benchmarks Show 'Post-Millennials' on Track toMost Diverse, Best-Educated Generation Yet.* Retrieved from https://www.pewresearch.org/social-trends/2018/11/15/early-benchmarks-show-post-millennials-on-track-to-be-most-diverse-best-educated-generation-yet/ on April 30, 2021.

Reinsel, D., Gantz, J., & Rydning, J. (2018). *The digitalization of the world: From edge to the core* [White Paper]. International Data Corporation. Retrieved from https://www.seagate.com/files/www-content/our-story/trends/files/idc-seagate-dataage-whitepaper.pdf on December 20, 2020.

Shahidullah, S. M. (2019a). America's global project on modernity: Continuity, change, and challenges in the 21st century. In S. M. Shahidullah (Ed.), *Modernity, modernization, and globalization: Issues and challenges in the 21st century* (pp. 45–80). NOVA Science Publications.

Shahidullah, S. M. (2019b). Modernity, power, and politics: The issues and challenges of democracy in the 21st century (The rise of the ultra-rights in global politics). In S. M. Shahidullah (Ed.), *Modernity, modernization, and globalization: Issues and challenges in the 21st century* (pp. 81–110). NOVA Science Publications.

Shahidullah, S. M., & Das, S. (2019). Modernity and global issues and challenges of religious liberty and tolerance: The case of South Asia. In S. M. Shahidullah (Ed.), *Modernity, modernization, and globalization: Issues and challenges in the 21st century* (pp. 207–238). NOVA Science Publications.

Tankovska, H (January 28, 2021). Most Popular Social Networks of Teenagers in the United States from the Fall of 2012 to Fall 2020. Retrieved from https://www.statista.com/statistics/250172/social-network-usage-of-us-teens-and-young-a on April 30, 2021.

Social Media Week. (April 20, 2017). 15 Stats on How Gen-Z Spends Their Time on Social Media and Mobile Messaging. Retrieved from https://socialmediaweek.org/blog/2017/04/stats-gen-z-social-mobile/ on April 30, 2021.

Southern Law Poverty Center. (2017, February). *Hate groups increase for second consecutive year as Trump electrifies the radical right.* Retrieved from https://www.splcenter.org/news/2017/02/15/hate-groups-increase-second-consecutive-year-trump-electrifies-radical-right on December 20, 2020.

Trump, D. (2017). *Full text: President Trump inauguration speech*. Politico. Retrieved from https://www.politico.com/story/2017/01/full-text-donald-trump-inauguration-speech-transcript-233907 on December 20, 2020.

Wood, J. (2018). *Generation Z will outnumber millennials by 2019*. World Economic Forum. Retrieved from https://www.weforum.org/agenda/2018/08/generation-z-will-outnumber-millennials-by-2019/on December 20, 2020.

World Economic Forum. (2018). *Global risk report: Fractures, fears and failures*. Retrieved from https://reports.weforum.org/global-risks-2018/global-risks-2018-fractures-fears-and-failures/ on December 20, 2020.

World Economic Forum. (2017). *The Global Shapers Survey*. Retrieved from https://www.globalshapers.org/news-updates/the-annual-survey-2017-is-live on April 30, 2021.

World Economic Forum. (2016). *New Vision for Education: Fostering Social and Emotional Learning Through Technology*. Retrieved from https://www.weforum.org/reports/new-vision-for-education-fostering-social-and-emotional-learning-through-technology on April 30, 2021.

World Economic Forum. (2015). *New Vision for Education: Unlocking the Potential for Technology*. Retrieved from https://widgets.weforum.org/nve-2015/index.html on April 30, 2021.

Zito, S., & Todd, B. (2018). *The great revolt: Inside the populist coalition reshaping American politics*. Crown Forum.

Figure Credits

CHAPTER 2

The Sociological Perspective

Society as a Domain of Competing Systems of Knowledge

CHAPTER THEME

The concept of society is born in the human brain, and humans are essentially social. Human society and human social facts and events, hence, are knowledge-based and knowledge-driven. Our understanding of different facets of society, such as race, gender, class, status, age, culture, and politics, and other issues and problems, such as equality, liberty, human rights, discrimination, poverty, and crime, are shaped and formed by certain types of ideas and knowledge. No society is governed by science alone, and no individual is entirely scientific. Religion, philosophy, and common sense also shape the way we make sense of the social world. Our behavior, values, beliefs, and perceptions are significantly influenced by different knowledge systems—religion, philosophy, science, and common sense. Understanding different social facts and events and different social issues and problems in the context of different knowledge systems are, therefore, vital to begin to develop a sociological perspective.

Introduction

Aristotle, in his book *Politics*, surmised that "man is by nature a social animal. Society is something that precedes the individual. Anyone who either cannot lead the common life or is so self-sufficient as not to need to and therefore does not partake of society is either a beast or a god." Since the days of the fifth-century Greek philosopher Hippocrates, humans have been searching for an answer to why humans are social. Hippocrates theorized that the brain is the center of the mind, and hence, the brain and human sociality are connected. About 2,000 years after Hippocrates, Rene Descartes, in 1641, theorized that the brain is the center of the soul and, therefore, the brain and the birth of human sociality are connected. In 1781, philosopher Immanuel Kant, in his *A Critique of Pure Reason*, made an argument that human brains create for humans a set of reasons and logics for the conduct of social life, and those reasons and logics are universal to humans. They are not socially and culturally contingent (Graziano, 2015).

The birth of human sociality, until recently, however, remained a puzzle: How does the human brain construct the phenomenon of human sociality? The modern science of behavioral neurology has discovered that human brains are wired to be social. Human brains are wired to connect to others, be aware of others, and reflect on others. Princeton neuroscientist Michael Graziano recently made a stunning discovery about the way the brain makes us social. In his book *Consciousness and the Social Brain*, Graziano theorized that "consciousness is a key part what us makes socially capable. ... Consciousness is the window through which we understand" (2015, pp. 1–2). Graziano's attention schema theory suggests that human sociality is an external scheme of thought about other human beings, but it is born and processed in the human brain. "The attention schema theory extracts some order out of the chaos. The brain uses the process of attention to sort data—to focus on some signals at the expense of other signals" (Graziano, 2015, p. 182). Through a complex process of information processing about other humans, human brains make us involuntarily and inviolably social.

Knowledge-Society Connections: A Knowledge Typology

The creation of the human domain of the "social"—the social mechanisms and arrangements—is mediated primarily by developing and using different types of human knowledge, such as magic, religion, philosophy, science, and common sense (Table 2.1). The discovery of new knowledge, ideas, and technology has always been a primary human concern. Knowledge and intelligence are the drivers of human cultures and civilizations. Human societies and civilizations have progressed from one stage to another, primarily because of the evolution of human knowledge. In ancient civilizations, magic, mythology, and animism, in addition to common sense, were the primary sources of knowledge for organizing the social order. With the progress of civilization, organized religions, such as Hinduism, Judaism, Buddhism, Christianity, and Islam, became one of the dominant sources of knowledge. With the birth of philosophy, particularly in ancient Greece and Athens of the fifth century B.C.E., human civilization reached a new stage of knowledge production. For about 2,000 years in medieval society, religion was the dominant form of knowledge. In medieval Europe, Christianity defined almost all facets of human social life from birth to marriage to mortality.

With the birth of the scientific revolution and the growth of modern scientific knowledge in the 17th century, human societies and civilizations reached a new phase of modernity. As a science of society, sociology emerged in the backdrop of the scientific revolution and the birth of the modern scientific method. In this chapter, the core learning goal is to understand the characteristics of these different types of knowledge and how they shape and influence social facts and events. Although science is the dominant form of knowledge in modern societies, no modern society is governed by science alone. A 2012 survey of 2,200 people by the U.S. National Science Foundation reported that about 26% of Americans, more than 75 million people, could not correctly answer whether sun revolves around the earth or the earth revolves around the sun (Spector, February 19, 2014). A survey of 1,018 adults by the Gallup Poll (June 7, 2014) found that about

42% of Americans believe in creationism. Most of the social facts and events and social issues and discourses in modern societies are only partly scientific. They are fundamentally religious or philosophical. A genuine understanding of different types of knowledge and their role in shaping social facts and events is the starting point of developing a scientific and sociological eye for making sense of the enormous complexity of the social world (Table 2.1).

TABLE 2.1 Toward a Knowledge Typology: Knowledge-Society Connections

Types of Knowledge	Characteristics	Grounds of Validity	Knowledge Issues
Religious	Divine Godly Faith-based Spiritual Unchangeable Uncritical	Holy texts/scriptures Saints and prophets Religious experts Theological reasons	Abortion Reproductive rights Same-sex marriage Adultery/divorce School prayer Church-state separation Death penalty Right to die Religious tolerance
Philosophical	Normative Ethical and moral Antitheocratic Traditional Authoritative	Philosophical knowledge Logic and reasoning Philosophical texts Values governing human life Values governing human society	Morality Justice and fairness Responsibility/obligation Humanism Equality/natural rights Universal human rights Democracy/rule of law Individualism/privacy Church-state separation
Scientific	Theoretical Observational Empirical Experimental Mathematical Factual Progressive Changeable Falsifiable Social Public	Facts and evidence Testable hypotheses Research and replications Theories, ideas, imaginations Models and paradigms Science-based technology	Structure of DNA DNA mapping DNA and body clock DNA and intelligence DNA and brain functions Electromagnetic waves Food radiation Nuclear power Digital society Internet and cyberspace Artificial intelligence

Common Sense	Experiential Biased Untested Selective observation Based on prejudice Antiscience Anti-intellectual	History, tradition, and wisdom Cultures and customs Religious myth and ideas Collective social experience "Struggle for existence"	Local knowledge Ordinary knowledge Misinformation Falsehood Racism, hate, and bigotry

Nature and Characteristics of Religious Knowledge

Religious knowledge is based on Scriptures and the sayings and sermons of the prophets and saviors. Hinduism, Judaism, Buddhism, Christianity, and Islam are different bodies of knowledge on how human social life has to be organized, controlled, and governed. There are many other faith groups in the world, but the present world's 7.7 billion people are mostly organized by these five great world religions.

Sociologists have discovered that religion is one of the central organizing themes, a "sacred canopy" (Berger, 1967/1990) that is inviolable and indispensable for understanding human sociality and social life. Religious knowledge is sacred, godly, and divine. It is unchangeable and uncritical, and it is based on faith and not on science and rationality. Religious knowledge is justified on the basis of the sacred texts and Scriptures. In the domain of religion, experts are the prophets, popes, cardinals, bishops, rabbis, monks, Brahmins, and imams. Religious arguments are limited to theological reasoning. In all societies, social issues and problems are deeply entangled with the religious views and opinions of the common people. Sociologically, society is not just a territorial boundary, a set of social institutions and organizations, or just a sense of collective solidarity. Society is also a moral community—a community of believers in what is right and what is wrong, what is acceptable and what is unacceptable, and what is ethical and what is unethical.

Core Religious Issues in Politics and Public Policy in America

A significant part of this moral dimension of society is governed by religious knowledge, and this is true even in the most scientifically advanced societies of the West. In America, for example, the social issues of abortion, school prayer, homosexuality, and same-sex marriage are deeply entangled with religious views and opinions (Table 2.2). In 1973, the U.S. Supreme Court, in *Roe v. Wade*, decided that women's access to safe and legal abortion is a constitutional right. In several decisions, the Supreme Court ruled that prayer in public schools is a violation of the Establishment Clause of Amendment 1 and the constitutional principle of church and state separation (e.g., *Everson v. Board of Education*, 1947; *Engel v. Vitale*, 1962; and *Abington School District v. Schempp*, 1963). In *Lawrence v. Texas*, in 2003, the Supreme Court ruled that the criminalization of homosexuality is a violation of the liberty principle of the due process clause of the Constitution's Amendment 14. In 2015, in *Obergefell v. Hodges*, the Supreme Court legalized same-sex marriage in all 50 states (Shahidullah, 2019b). The court held that "the Fourteenth Amendment requires States to recognize same-sex marriages validly performed out of state. Since same-sex couples may now exercise the fundamental right to marry in all States, there is no lawful basis for a State to refuse to recognize a lawful same-sex marriage performed in another State on the ground of its same-sex character" (*Obergefell v. Hodges*, 2015).

These and many other related Supreme Court decisions have had profound effects on the minds of many religious people in the United States, and many far-reaching consequences on American law and politics. A study by the Pew Research Center found that about 60–70% of evangelical Christians in America oppose the legalization of abortion (Wilson, 2018). Among the Catholics, 48% backed legalization, and 47% opposed legalization. A 2019 survey by the Pew Research Center showed that 61% of Americans supported same-sex marriage, and 31% opposed it. The survey observed that support for same-sex marriage had been steadily increasing since 2004, when only 31% of Americans favored legalizing same-sex marriage. The survey also found that support for same-sex marriage is positively connected to religious views and religiosity. "Among people who are religiously unaffiliated, a solid majority have supported same-sex marriage since 2004.

TABLE 2.2 Selected Religious Issues in Politics and Public Policy in America

Religious liberty (First Amendment)
Church and state separation
Abortion
Federal dollars for family planning
Federal dollars to support family planning abroad
Right to die
Reproductive rights
School prayer
Bible reading in public schools
Posting religious symbols in public buildings
Death penalty
Sex education
Rights of the LGBTQ+ communities
State involvement in appointing church ministers
Same-sex marriage
Genetic research
In vitro fertilization
Federal investment for stem-cell research
Human cloning
Role of religious leaders for campaign support
Federal grants for religious organizations

Today, 79% of religious 'nones' say same-sex couples should be allowed to marry" (Pew Research Center, 2019, p. 3). The support for same-sex marriage is lower among those who attend church regularly (39%) than those who are loosely connected to the church (66%). Religious views are also closely connected to political groups and ideologies. About 60% of Republican voters, in comparison with 40% of Democrats, believe it is very significant that the president shares their religious faiths and religious views (Masci, 2016). The entanglement of religion with social and political issues are universal across all countries and cultures. Therefore, one of the core tenets of sociology is to scientifically examine how religious knowledge shapes human sociality, humans' inner sense of attachment and reflexivity, and provides an external glue to groupness by building a sacred canopy.

Nature and Characteristics of Philosophical Knowledge

Since society is a moral community and humans are also moral beings concerned about what is good and evil and what is right and wrong and what is moral and immoral, philosophical issues are also deeply intertwined with human sociality and the construction of human social mechanisms and arrangements. Human ethical concerns have changed from time to time, and vary from society to society, but there is no society without any worries for moral issues.

The body of knowledge that is concerned with human ethics and moralities is described as philosophy. Religion is also a branch of knowledge that is concerned with human ethics and moralities. The Ten Commandments of the Old Testament are the earliest examples of human concerns for what is right and wrong; however, there are some fundamental differences between religion and philosophy. Moral and ethical issues of faith are justified on the grounds of Scriptures. They are seen as sacred, divine, and unchallengeable by human reason and rationalities. Philosophical knowledge, on the other hand, is extrareligious. Philosophical knowledge is not regarded as holy and transcendental. The grounds of knowledge validity in religion are the sacred Scriptures and sacred texts, such as the Old Testament and New Testament, the Qur'an, and the Gita. The grounds of knowledge validity in philosophy are the thoughts, ideas, and writings of the great philosophers.

The World's Great Philosophical Tradition

There is a vast body of philosophical knowledge that has grown since the days of Socrates, Plato, and Aristotle. This body of knowledge is primarily Western, but it has also been enriched by the traditions of Chinese, Indian, Buddhist, and Islamic philosophies. Philosophical knowledge is concerned with human normative and moral issues, such as justice, fairness, equality, goodness, honesty, democracy, responsibility, obligation, duty, loyalty, privacy, power, domination, war, violence, and punishment. Since the days of Socrates, philosophers have been searching for an understanding of what it means to be a "good" human being; what it means to have a "good" society; what it means to have justice and fairness; and what it means to have "good" governance.

Socrates wanted to explore the ideas of ethics and justice on the basis of reason and logic, and he believed that for a human to be able to recognize their own ignorance is the beginning of their search for philosophical knowledge on ethics and morality. Socrates refused to agree that the Athenian state of his time was just and fair because it was ordained by God. Therefore, he was found guilty of treason by both the Athenian court and ruling class and, as punishment, was poisoned to death. The death of Socrates was not the end but the beginning of a great tradition of Western philosophy still shaping the minds of the humanities both in the West and the East.

Since Socrates in the fifth century to the present time, many philosophers, including Plato, Aristotle, Confucius, Al-Farabi, Al-Ghazali, Ibn Rushd, Machiavelli, Leonardo da Vinci, Kant, Hegel, Hobbes, Locke, Rousseau, Voltaire, Beccaria, Comte, Marx, Bentham, Adam Smith, Bertrand Russell, Dewey, Chomsky, and

John Rawls, have vastly enriched our understanding of justice, fairness, democracy, equality, and modernity. The American Declaration of Independence and the Constitution's Bill of Rights, written and crafted by Thomas Jefferson, deeply reflect the philosophies of democracy, good governance, and the religious tolerance of 17th-century British philosopher John Locke. The Bill of Rights, which describes the notions of justice, rights of the accused, and the nature of punishment, was significantly influenced by the philosophical thoughts and writings of Cesare Beccaria, an 18th-century Italian philosopher, contained in his book *On Crimes and Punishments*, published in 1764 (Table 2.3).

TABLE 2.3 25 Great Philosophers and Their Enduring Ideas

Philosophers	Core Ideas
Socrates 399 B.C.E.	What is morality, justice, and ethics?
Plato 428 B.C.E.	How to define good government and the role of king-philosophers
Aristotle 384 B.C.E.	Who should rule in a good government and the origin of empirical research
Confucius 551 B.C.E.	Role of law and learning—family as the basis of civilization
Machiavelli 1469–1527	Role of a good "prince"—a ruler
Leonardo da Vinci 1452–1519	Philosophy of Renaissance—artist and scientist
Calvin 1509–1564	Calvinism and the rise of Protestantism
Kant 1724–1804	Reason and ethics
Montesquieu 1689–1755	Social basis of law and morality
Hegel 1770–1831	Father of modern idealism
Hobbes 1588–1679	Social contract theory/father of modern political science
Descartes 1596–1650	The origin of scientific method
Bacon 1561–1626	Father of empirical research—champion of scientific inquiry
Rousseau 1712–1778	General will and the social contract theory
Locke 1632–1704	Social contract theory and the nature of modern government
Voltaire 1698–1778	Enlightenment philosopher: role of science and reason
Beccaria 1738–1794	Father of modern criminology/*On Crimes and Punishments*
Adam Smith 1723–1790	Father of modern economics/origin of capitalism
Comte 1798–1857	Positivism and the father of sociology
Marx 1818–1883	Capitalism and class struggle; socialism and birth of the Cold War

| Bentham 1748–1832 | Father of utilitarianism |
| Dewey 1859–1952 | Father of modern pragmatism |

Sociology is different from philosophy, but the understanding of how philosophical knowledge is intertwined with policies, debates, and discourses on social issues and problems in society is vital for expanding the sociological eye. The statement in the American Declaration of Independence that "we hold these truths to be self-evident, that all men are created equal, that they are endowed by their Creator with certain unalienable Rights, that among these are Life, Liberty and the pursuit of Happiness" is probably one of the great philosophical ideas of all time. It is also the kernel of modernity. When Abraham Lincoln in his Gettysburg Address said that "four score and seven years ago, our fathers brought forth, upon this continent, a new nation, conceived in liberty, and dedicated to the proposition that all men are created equal," he gave us a philosophy to pursue the path to modernity.

In his 1968 Memphis speech, when Martin Luther King Jr. said that God "allowed me to go to the mountain, I've looked over. And I have seen the promised land," he gave the world a philosophy to rid itself of violence, hatred, and racism. The philosophies of liberty, democracy, equality, respect for the rule of law, respect for diversity, and tolerance of religious differences are at the very core of American polity. America is not just a piece of physical land, a territorial boundary. It is these philosophies that are collectively defined as "American exceptionalism."

People throughout the world came and are still coming to America to be a part of this great journey toward the "promised land" of liberty, equality, and democracy. It is this philosophy of the "Empire of Liberty" that Thomas Jefferson wanted to spread to the world. Jefferson believed that as one of the first countries to begin the experiment of modernity and the enlightenment model of civilization, America had a moral obligation to spread the philosophy of modernity to the world (Shahidullah, 2019a).

This was loudly echoed in our modern time by President Ronald Reagan in his vision of America as a "shining city." In his farewell address to the nation on January 11, 1989, President Reagan said the shining city "was a tall, proud city built on rocks stronger than oceans, windswept, God-blessed, and teeming with people of all kinds living in harmony and peace; a city with free ports that hummed with commerce and creativity" (para. 33). Reagan dreamed that "if there had to be city walls, the walls had doors and the doors were open to anyone with the will and the heart to get here. That's how I saw it, and see it still" (1989, para. 33). Reagan's vision of America as a shining city will probably remain as one of the most powerful philosophies about American exceptionalism (Shahidullah, 2019a).

Core Philosophical Issues in Politics and Public Policy in America

For a sociological perspective of what is occurring in contemporary America, these philosophical notions behind the birth of this nation need to be deeply understood and comprehended. After about 245 years of continuity of the philosophy of American exceptionalism and America's global engagement for spreading the Empire of Liberty, America has come, from the 2nd decade of the 21st century, to a new crossroads of history. Many core American values are now being challenged and castigated.

A society without religion is misunderstood, and a society without science is misdirected. Nevertheless, a society without philosophy is hollow. Many of America's social and cultural issues, such as universal human rights, religious liberty, church and state separation, democracy, gender equality, racial equality, social justice, police brutality, mass incarceration, rights to own a gun, universal access to health care, universal access to education, and cultural diversity, are deeply philosophical. In the arena of public policy and the domain of public opinion, these issues are discussed and debated in terms of competing and conflicting philosophical grounds, and hence, America's contemporary politics and culture are becoming increasingly contentious. There is also growing in America a "culture war" (Table 2.4). This makes a sociological perspective of understanding the nature and the future of America's "exceptionalism" far more significant in the 21st century.

TABLE 2.4 Selected Philosophical Issues in Politics and Public Policy in America

Rule of law (due process law—14th Amendment)
Religious liberty (First Amendment)
Church and state separation (U.S. Constitution—First Amendment)
Democracy (representative government)
Constitutionalism (constitutional laws)
Separation of power (executive, legislative, and judicial)
Checks and balances (i.e., congressional control on the executive)
Protection against unreasonable search and seizure (Fourth Amendment)
Protection against self-incrimination (Fifth Amendment)
Protection against cruel and unusual punishment (Eighth Amendment)
Citizenship and voting rights
Rights of immigrants
Rights of the disabled (Americans with Disability Act of 1990)
Deadbeat Parents Punishment Act of 1998 (parental obligations and responsibilities for child support)
Unborn Victims of Violence Act of 2004 (enhanced punishment for killing a pregnant woman)
Hate crime (Matthew Shepard and James Byrd Jr. Hate Crimes Prevention Act of 2010)
Economic justice (Equal Pay Act of 1963)
Social justice (rights of the LGBTQ+ communities; Hate Crime Bill of 2009)
Social equality (Civil Rights Act of 1964)
Reproductive rights (*Griswold v. Connecticut*, 1965; *Roe v. Wade*, 1972)
Racial equality (Emancipation Proclamation, 1863; *Brown v. Board of Education*, 1954)
Martin Luther King Jr. "I Have a Dream" speech, 1963
Martin Luther King Jr. "Promised Land" speech, 1968
Civil Rights Act of 1964
Environmental ethics
Police ethics
Bioethics (issues related to the beginning and the end of life, right to life, and right to die)

Nature and Characteristics of Scientific Knowledge

When we wear a sociological lens to make sense of the social world, we see that many social and cultural issues are ingrained in religious and philosophical ideas and worldviews. We also see that many social problems and facts and events are influenced by scientific knowledge (Table 2.1). Understanding the nature of science and the characteristics of scientific knowledge, and how science is different from religion and philosophy, also becomes a crucial task for sociology. An understanding of science and scientific knowledge for the lay person or for students of sociology does, of course, not mean an effort to understand the theories of high science, such as Newton's theory of gravity, Einstein's theory of relativity, Heisenberg's principle of uncertainty, or the complex algorithms of modern artificial intelligence. Understanding modern science means grasping the nature of scientific reasoning and the logic of scientific methodology. It also means a sensitivity to decipher the role and the effects of contemporary science on social life (Table 2.5).

TABLE 2.5 The Nature of Science and Scientific Knowledge

Definition: Nature of Science	Examples	Limits
Science as a body of knowledge	Physics Chemistry Biology Neurology Sociology Psychology Economics	This definition correctly describes science as a body of knowledge, but it does not explain how science is done.
Science as a methodology	Theorizing Observation Experiments Replication Mathematization Proofs and evidence	This defines science as a unique approach to knowledge generation. This is more closely related to what science is and how science is done.
Science as a particular philosophy of knowledge	Progressive Changeable Falsifiable Naturalistic Social Public	This defines science as a unique form of knowledge and how it is different from religion, philosophy, and common sense.

The World's Great Scientific Tradition

In 1543, a Polish philosopher named Nicolaus Copernicus made a stunning discovery that the Earth is not at the center of the universe and that the other planets and stars of the galaxies do not circle the Earth. Copernicus discovered (later mathematically proven by Galileo) that the Sun is at the center and the Earth and all other planets circle the Sun. This discovery of the heliocentric model of the universe by Copernicus signified the birth of the modern Scientific Revolution. During the past 400 years, the Scientific Revolution spread from physics to biology to social science, including sociology, psychology, economics, and political science. The birth of the Scientific Revolution in the 17th century brought not only discoveries about the facts of nature (e.g., gravity, magnetism, lights, electricity, atoms, and molecules) and the facts of human biology (e.g., the structure of human cells, DNA, and neurons) but also gave birth to a new epistemology or method of knowing—the naturalistic philosophy (Table 2.6). Science does not deny the values and the role of religion and philosophy. Science did not destroy faith and never ignored the philosophical dimensions of social life. Science only makes a different claim on how knowledge about nature, life, mind, and society must be gained and pursued.

TABLE 2.6 Selected Scientific Theories and Discoveries

Nicolaus Copernicus	The heliocentric model of the universe—*On the Revolutions of the Celestial Spheres*, 1543
Galileo Galilei	Conceptualized the notion of natural philosophy—*Dialogues on the Two Chief World Systems*, 1632
Isaac Newton	Theory of gravitation; laws of motion; father of modern physics and optical science—science of lights
Albert Einstein	Theory of relativity, 1905; father of modern nuclear physics
William Harvey	Functions of the heart and the discovery of blood circulation
Alexander Fleming	Discovery of penicillin, 1928; new antibiotics
James Watt	Invention of modern steam engine, 1917
Louis Pasteur	Pasteurization: killing microbes in food and drinks
Faraday and Franklin	Discovery of electricity, 1735 and 1758
Charles Darwin	Evolutionism—*The Origin of Species*, 1859
Jean-Martin Charcot	New developments in brain science and neurology
Michael Merzenich	Neuroplasticity; the brain can change in response to thinking and emotions
Jeffery C. Hall	Genetic basis of the body clock; 2017 Noble Prize winner in physiology
R. Kahn and V. Cerf	Invention of the internet
Steve Jobs and Wozniak	Invention of social media: Apple Computers
Mark Zuckerberg	Invention of social media: Facebook
Systrom and Krieger	Invention of social media: Instagram
Abraham Maslow	Hierarchy of human needs
Jean Piaget	Evolution of intelligence

Lawrence Kohlberg	Evolution of morality
Sigmund Freud	Evolution of the mind: id, ego, super ego—father of modern psychology

Religious knowledge is based on the grounds of received wisdom from the Scriptures and the divine. Spiritual knowledge is a matter of faith, and it cannot be empirically verified and challenged, such as the existence of heaven, hell, and angels. Religious knowledge is based on certainty, and there is no scope for doubts. The scientific methodology begins with doubts and skepticism, and falsifiability is at the core of scientific methods (Popper, 2002). Science is a search for the truth, but the truth is never attainable once and for all. Science is like a "black cat in a dark room"; we know it's there, but we do not know precisely where it is (Holzner, Campbell, and Shahidullah, 1985). Science is, therefore, a continuous process of theorizing about the attainment of the "truth" in the realm of nature, life, body, mind, and society.

Science advances not because of the mere collection of facts and data. Facts and data form the basis of theorizing and validating scientific theories or paradigms (Kuhn, 2012). At a given stage of development, each domain of science is dominated by a core set of theories and assumptions, described by Thomas Kuhn as paradigms. As scientific theories advance, old paradigms are questioned and refuted, and new paradigms emerge to be dominant. The new paradigms again become old when new ideas emerge. Scientific advancement, thus, means advancements in theories and paradigms (Kuhn, 2012). Scientific knowledge is changeable and progressive. We, for example, now know more about the constitution of human DNA and its role in the development of the human brain and behavior than we knew 50 years ago. Modern psychology began with the Freudian paradigm on the role of the unconscious in shaping our minds and behavior. With the rise of behaviorism (e.g., work of John B. Watson and B. F. Skinner) or the learning paradigm (e.g., work of Albert Bandura) in psychology in the 20th century, the Freudian paradigm began to be seriously reexamined.

Unlike religion and philosophy, the grounds of validity in science consist of data, empirical evidence, experiments, and mathematization. The understanding of scientific reasoning and the conducting of scientific research demands applying the canons of scientific inquiry—theorizing, experimentation, mathematization, generalization, prediction, and falsifiability. Religion is based on the authority of the Scriptures and the divine, and philosophy is based on the knowledge and authority of the great philosophers. Scientific knowledge is not justified on the basis of power and authority. The grounds of knowledge validity in science are empirical data, empirical evidence, and empirical experiments. In the Middle Ages, people with physical deformities were seen as sinners and described by the idea of monstrosity. Modern biology and genetic science have discovered that all physical and mental disabilities are rooted in human genes and neurodevelopmental disorders. The rationale of scientific methodology or the naturalistic inquiry is that the facts of nature, body, mind, and society follow specific laws, rules, forms, and patterns, and they must be explained in a naturalistic way without any reference to God, the divine, or the Scriptures.

Sociology and the Knowledge Typology

The crux of sociology—the science of socialness—is that social facts and events are intertwined with religion, philosophy, and science. Natural properties, such as atoms, molecules, light, and gravity, are not intertwined with religion and philosophy. The natural properties do not have values and moralities, and they do not search for meanings and salvations. In so far as their objects of scientific theorizing are concerned, the physicists or the geneticists do not need to explore the relevance of religion and philosophy. The facts of the social world, however, are unintelligible without any reference to how they intersect with human faiths and philosophy.

In America, abortion and women's reproductive rights, for example, converge with science, philosophy, and religion. The advent of birth control pills by Gregory Goodwin Pincus in 1954 and John Rock in 1953 (Eig, 2015; May, 2011), and approved by the FDA in 1957, created a new phase of liberation for human sexuality, particularly for women. Since then women began to organize for the legalization of their reproductive rights, including abortion (i.e., a philosophical demand). The U.S. Supreme Court in *Roe v. Wade*, in 1973, legalized and decriminalized abortion. The legalization of abortion and women's other reproductive rights (e.g., *Griswold v. Connecticut* in 1965 and *Eisenstadt v. Baird* in 1972) created, in turn, new religious tensions in America for those who believe in the biblical definition of the role of sex and reproduction. For the past 50 years, abortion has remained one of the most contentious issues in American politics, courts, and culture (Shahidullah, 2019b).

Similarly, the U.S. Supreme Court in a number of decisions in recent years (i.e., *Romer v. Evans* in 1996; *Lawrence v. Texas* in 2003; the *United States v. Windsor* in 2013; and *Obergefell v. Hodges* in 2015) decriminalized homosexuality and same-sex marriage primarily on the grounds of the philosophical principles of human rights and privacy. In *Lawrence*, the court held that two consenting adults have the right to engage in private conduct under the due process clause of the Constitution's Amendment 14. In delivering the court opinion, Justice Kennedy said liberty protects a person from unwarranted government intrusions into a dwelling or other private place. In our tradition, the state is not omnipresent in the home. "Freedom extends beyond spatial bounds. Liberty presumes an autonomy of self that includes freedom of thought, belief, expression, and certain intimate conduct" (*Lawrence v. Texas*, 2003).

In 2015, in *Obergefell v. Hodges*, the court held that "the Fourteenth Amendment requires a State to license a marriage between two people of the same sex and to recognize a marriage between two people of the same sex when their marriage was lawfully licensed and performed out-of-state." The decriminalization of homosexuality and the legalization of same-sex marriage in America since then has remained politically and culturally highly divisive and contentious. Here again, conflicts between philosophy (issues of rights and privacy) and religion (issues of the biblical meaning of sex and marriage) created huge effects on America's politics, courts, and culture.

In the late 20th and early 21st centuries, particularly with the birth of the computer and the internet, modern science has brought us to a new world of digitalization. The science of modern biology, modern genetics, modern social and behavioral neurology, modern cognitive psychology, and modern artificial intelligence have brought many great hopes and optimism. But modern science and science-based technology also brought many problems and concerns for a stable social and political order. The effects of the internet and social media on intelligence, brain development, personality, morality, marriage, sex, intimacy, family, politics, and culture are yet mostly unknown (Table 2.7). Thus, the appreciation of scientific reasoning is an invaluable and inviolable part of modern sociological consciousness.

Spread of nuclear weapons
Control of global warming
Medical advances and rise of the aging society
Ethics of new reproductive technology
New era of science and religion conflicts
Family, marriage, children, and the new reproductive technology
Social equality and science-based professions
Rise of a new technocratic class
Skilled versus unskilled workforce and the search for a balance
New challenges of gender equality
Need for work-family balance and rise of the digital workforce
Online shopping and emerging changes in the economy
Online shopping and new consumerism
Spread of cybercrime
Spread of cyberterrorism
Possibilities of global cyberwar
Cyber espionage and the future of democracy
Social media and teen brains
Cyberbullying, cyberstalking, and teen depression
Effects of virtual sex, dating, marriage, and divorce
Internet and the spread of hate and racism
Social media and false news
Globalization, the internet, and the rise of a new global culture
Poverty and the effects of the digital divide

Nature and Characteristics of Common-Sense Knowledge

On August 4, 2019, a mother named Jordon Anchondo was killed while shielding her 2-month-old baby from a mass shooter in El Paso, Texas. Both the mother and the shooter were human beings, but two very different human beings. All humans are not the same. They think, act, and behave differently.

Sociologists make no illusions that a society is only a domain of human achievements and discoveries, human creations and innovations, and human peace and prosperity. Sociologists are also curious about the darker side of society—about the problems of hate, racism, sexism, bigotry, violence, and xenophobia (Shahidullah & Das, 2019). The darker side of humanity is governed primarily by common-sense knowledge based on prejudice, misinformation, and false information. Common-sense knowledge has a brighter dimension based on collective wisdom; folk knowledge; and societal norms, customs, rituals, and traditions. But the common-sense knowledge that governs the dark side of the social world is manufactured based on prejudice, hate, and bigotry, not based on science, philosophy, nor the sacred knowledge of the Scriptures. Understanding the nature of common-sense knowledge that controls society's darker side is also one of the real facets of sociological consciousness.

Social and behavioral neurologists have found through their research based on brain imaging that knowledge about racism, hate, and bigotry are processed and stored in different parts of the brain based on false imaginations, illusions, stereotypes, threats, and fears (Amodio, 2014). The development of this biased and unproven common-sense knowledge is particularly hard to control in "a cultural milieu that constantly reinforces racial prejudices and stereotypes" (Amodio, 2014, p. 679). The 2019 El Paso shooter's manifesto, described as "inconvenient truth," contained a series of lies and false information about the Hispanic invasion and destruction of "White America." It reflected the same false ideology that was behind the Christchurch shooting in New Zealand (the theory of "great replacement") and the synagogue shooting in Pittsburgh.

For sociologists, what is particularly intriguing is how this type of common-sense knowledge is in a rapid process of globalization with the aid of the internet and social media. The 20th century was an excellent time for the triumph of science, philosophy, and humanism. It was a time for destruction of the false knowledge and ideologies of Nazism and fascism. The 21st century, however, began with dooms and destructions by global terror and the demeaning of science, intellectualism, philosophy, and humanism by many new proponents of the ultraright ideology (Shahidullah & Das, 2019). Global religious hate and violence are growing both in the East and the West. Racism and bigotry are now at the center of political discourses in the heartlands of liberty and democracy on both sides of the Atlantic. The significance of a sociological eye to make sense of the emerging world of racism, hate, bigotry, nativism, and common sense has never been so great as it is in this 2nd decade of the 21st century.

Suggested Questions, Essays, Assignments, and Quizzes

1. Sociologists assume that humans are knowledge-creating beings, and human society is a knowledge-containing and knowledge-utilizing system. There are various forms of knowledge, but most sociologists believe in a four-fold typology of knowledge. Develop a chart or table describing the four-fold typology of knowledge and explain their significant characteristics.
2. There are five great religions in the world—Hinduism, Judaism, Buddhism, Christianity, and Islam. The world's 7.7 billion people are divided in terms of these great religions, and their religious knowledge significantly shapes the way they act, think, and behave. Develop a table describing the significant doctrines (core divine or sacred themes) of each of these world religions.
3. What are the significant characteristics of religious knowledge? How is religion different from science as a body of knowledge? Answer this question by developing a table or a chart and providing examples.
4. What are the characteristics of philosophical knowledge, and what are the crucial differences between philosophy and religion? Develop a chart describing some of the significant philosophical issues debated and discussed in American politics and public policy.
5. What are some of the significant religious issues central to politics and public policy in America? Make a chart or a table describing five significant religious problems and controversies decided by the U.S. Supreme Court in recent years (read and review the decisions from the internet).
6. The American republic was founded 245 years ago based on core philosophical values and ideals. These values and standards are enshrined in the American Constitution and the Bill of Rights. Describe and explain some of those core values and ideals for which many sociologists describe America as an "exceptional" nation.
7. It is vital for a sociology student to understand the meaning of science and scientific reasoning and

how science is different from other forms of knowledge. Based on your reading of this chapter, related class lectures, and your internet research, write an essay (two or three single-spaced pages, 12-point font) describing the significant characteristics of science as a particular methodology and a unique form of knowledge (you can add a table or chart to write this essay).

8. In politics and public policy, religion, philosophy, and science are entangled in many complex ways. For developing critical thinking ability, students of sociology should be able to disentangle these various forms of knowledge in public discourses. In the context of this statement, write an essay (two or three single-spaced pages, 12-point font) on the influence of religion on voting behavior, focusing mainly on the presidential elections of 2016 and 2020.

9. What are some of the significant philosophical issues that became prominent in debates and discourses during the American presidential elections of 2016 and 2020? Write an essay (two or three single-spaced pages, 12-point font) describing some of the philosophical issues and controversies that probably were responsible for President Trump's (and the Republican Party's) defeat in 2020.

10. Science as a form of knowledge is qualitatively different from politics based on common sense. The validity of scientific knowledge does not depend on politics, and political authority must not intervene in science affairs. Write an essay (two or three single-spaced pages, 12-point font) explaining how the relationship between science and religion and science and politics in America became overtly confusing and controversial in the context of the containment of and vaccination for COVID-19.

References

Amodio, D. M. (2014). The neuroscience of prejudice and stereotyping. *Nature*, 15, 670–682. Retrieved from https://doi.org/10.1038/nrn3800 on December 20, 2020.

Association of American Colleges and Universities. (2002). *Greater expectations: A new vision for learning as nation goes to college.* Washington D. C.: AACU.

Association of American Colleges and Universities. (2013). *It takes more than a major: Employer priorities for college learning and student success* (research by Hart Associates). Washington D. C.: AACU.

Banata, A. (August, 2016). *The Internet of everything (IOE)*. Retrieved from https://www.bbvaopenmind.com/en/technology/digital-world/the-internet-of-everything-ioe/ on December 20, 2020.

Berger, P. L. (1990). *The sacred canopy: Elements of a sociological theory of religion.* Anchor Books. (Original work published 1967)

Bradley, J., Barbier, J., & Handler, D. (2013). *Embracing the Internet of everything to capture your share of $14.4 trillion.* CISCO. Retrieved from https://www.cisco.com/c/dam/en_us/about/business-insights/docs/ioe-economy-insights.pdf on December 20, 2020.

Clement, J. (June, 2017). *Online shopping behavior in the United States—Statistics and facts.* Retrieved from https://www.statista.com/topics/2477/online-shopping-behavior/ on December 20, 2020.

Eig, J. (2015). *The birth of the pill: How four crusaders reinvented sex and launched a revolution.* W. W. Norton.

Gallup Poll. (June 7, 2014). *Evolution, Creationism, and Intelligent Design.* Retrieved from https://news.gallup.com/poll/21814/Evolution-Creationism-Intelligent-Design.aspx on December 20, 2020.

Gantz, J., & Reinsel, D. (December, 2012). *The digital universe in 2020. Big data, bigger digital shadows, and biggest growth in the Far East.* International Data Corporation. Retrieved from https://www.cs.princeton.edu/courses/archive/spring13/cos598C/idc-the-digital-universe-in-2020.pdf on December 20, 2020.

Global Workplace Analytics. (2017). *Telecommuting trend data.* Retrieved from https://globalworkplaceanalytics.com/telecommuting-statistics on December 20, 2020.

Graziano, M. (2015). *Consciousness and the social brain.* Oxford University Press.

Holzner, B., Campbell, D. T., and Shahidullah, M. (1985). Introduction: The Comparative Study of Science and the Sociology of Scientific Validity. *Knowledge: Creation, Diffusion, and Utilization*, Vol. 6 (4), pp. 307-328.

Kuhn, T. S. (2012). *The structure of scientific revolutions* (4th ed.). University of Chicago Press.

Lawrence v. Texas, 539 U.S. 558 (2003). Retrieved from https://www.law.cornell.edu/supct/html/02-102.ZO.html on December 20, 2020.

Linshi, J. (July, 2015). 10 CEOs who prove your liberal arts degree isn't worthless. *Time*. Retrieved from https://time.com/3964415/ceo-degree-liberal-arts/ on December 20, 2020.

Masci, D. (January, 2016). *5 key findings of faith and politics in the 2016 presidential election*. Pew Research Center. Retrieved from https://www.pewresearch.org/fact-tank/2016/01/27/key-findings-faith-and-politics-in-2016-presidential-race/ on December 20, 2020.

May, E. T. (2011). *America and the pill: A history of promise, peril, and liberation*. Basic Books.

McGonagle, M. (January 3, 2018). Sorry STEM, Google made a case for more foreign language education. *Transparent Language*. Retrieved from https://blogs.transparent.com/language-news/2018/01/01/sorry-stem-google-just-made-the-case-for-more-foreign-language-education/ on December 20, 2020.

Obergefell v. Hodges, 576 U.S. (2015). Retrieved from https://www.supremecourt.gov/opinions/14pdf/14-556_3204.pdf on December 20, 2020.

Pew Research Center. (May, 2019). *Attitudes on same-sex marriage*. Retrieved from https://www.pewforum.org/fact-sheet/changing-attitudes-on-gay-marriage/ on December 20, 2020.

Popper, R. K. (2002). *Conjectures and refutations: The growth of scientific knowledge* (2nd ed.). Routledge.

Popper, R. K. (2002). *The logic of scientific discovery* (2nd ed.). Routledge.

Reagan, R. (1989). *Farewell address to the nation*. Reagan Library. Retrieved from https://www.reaganlibrary.gov/archives/speech/farewell-address-nation on December 20, 2020.

Reinsel, D., Gantz, J., & Rydning, J. (2018). *The digitalization of the world: From edge to the core* [White paper]. International Data Corporation. Retrieved from https://www.seagate.com/files/www-content/our-story/trends/files/idc-seagate-dataage-whitepaper.pdf on December 20, 2020.

Shahidullah, S. M. (2019a). America's global project on modernity: Continuity, change, and challenges in the 21st century. In S. M. Shahidullah (Ed.), *Modernity, modernization, and globalization: Issues and challenges in the 21st century* (pp. 45–80). NOVA Science Publications.

Shahidullah, S. M. (2019b). Modernity, power, and politics: The issues and challenges of democracy in the 21st century (The rise of the ultra-rights in global politics). In S. M. Shahidullah (Ed.), *Modernity, modernization, and globalization: Issues and challenges in the 21st century* (pp. 81–110). NOVA Science Publications.

Shahidullah, S. M., & Das, S. (2019). Modernity and global issues and challenges of religious liberty and tolerance: The case of South Asia. In S. M. Shahidullah (Ed.), *Modernity, modernization, and globalization: Issues and challenges in the 21st century* (pp. 207–238). NOVA Science Publications.

Southern Law Poverty Center. (February, 2017). *Hate groups increase for second consecutive year as Trump electrifies the radical right*. Retrieved from https://www.splcenter.org/news/2017/02/15/hate-groups-increase-second-consecutive-year-trump-electrifies-radical-right on December 20, 2020.

Spector, D. (February 19, 2014). *Here's the basic science questions the 1 in 4 Americans got wrong*. Retrieved from https://finance.yahoo.com/news/heres-basic-science-1-4-180551784.html on December 20, 2020.

Wilson, W. (July, 2018). *Pew Research reveals stark differences in abortion among religious groups*. Illinois Family Institute. Retrieved from https://illinoisfamily.org/life/pew-research-reveals-stark-differences-on-abortion-among-religious-groups/ on December 20, 2020.

Wood, J. (2018). *Generation Z will outnumber millennials by 2019*. World Economic Forum. Retrieved from https://www.weforum.org/agenda/2018/08/generation-z-will-outnumber-millennials-by-2019/ on December 20, 2020.

CHAPTER 3

The Science of Sociology

History, Nature, Scope, and Significance

CHAPTER THEME

Sociology was born in the middle of the 19th century in the context of the birth of modern science in the 17th century and the rise of the Age of Enlightenment and modernity in the 18th century. It was born with two missions: to create a science of society and to examine the nature and the directionality of the emerging modern urban and industrial society. Much like physics and biology, sociology is a universal science—a science of society in general. Sociology is not a European science or American science; it is a science of understanding the nature of human society in general. Sociology has made an important place within the family of social sciences and within the arena of governance and policymaking in modern societies, primarily because of its unique perspective of looking at the social world. The sociological perspective's core is that social and group phenomena have significant influence in shaping human behavior and forming a human society. The famous sociological dictum is that a social fact must be explained by another social fact. Modern sociology even explores how many facets and problems of our body, biology, and the mind are shaped and formed by social facts and forces. Sociology is a peculiar form of "consciousness" with a boundless "imagination" about how human social facts and forces grow, evolve, and shape the way we are. Understanding the science of sociology is hugely significant for today's digital tribe, not just because it teaches us how social facts and forces shape our mind and behavior but also because of the centrality of holistic, synthetic, comparative, and historical knowledge for comprehending the larger and global social forces that form the meaning and the moments of the digital age in the 21st century.

Introduction

Auguste Comte, a French philosopher of science, is widely regarded as the father of sociology. The word "sociology" was first used at the beginning of the fourth volume of Comte's six volumes of work, titled *Course of Positive Philosophy* (1830–1842). Comte was so proud of his discovery of sociology that he argued sociology represented the end of the evolution of human knowledge. He placed sociology at the end of the development of six categories of sciences—mathematics, astronomy, physics, chemistry, biology, and sociology. This classification of science remained very simplistic, but his idea that a science of society is possible was a remarkable discovery of that time.

Although sociology as a science of society was discovered in the middle of the 19th century, human curiosities about human issues and problems did not begin in the 19th century; they are as old as human society. Archeologists have discovered that the earliest code of laws was written about 4,500 years ago during the time of King Ur-Nammu in the ancient Sumerian civilization (2047 B.C.E.–2030 B.C.E). King Ur-Nammu was probably the earliest king to think about the notion of the consent of the governed. He believed that governance of a kingdom should be based on the consent of the governed. His code of law prescribed capital punishment for murder, rape, incest, robbery, and adultery (adultery was only punishable by death when committed by women).

In 1901, archeologists discovered the code of laws of King Hammurabi in which he also described in detail the profile of criminal justice in his Babylonian kingdom that existed about 3,700 years ago. The Old Testament and the Hebrew Bible are about 3,500 years old. The Old Testament and New Testament and the Ten Commandments surmised how to lead a balanced social life based on the divine's pearls of wisdom. Historians described Hinduism as an organized religion that is about 5,000 years old. Historical records suggest that Bhagavad Gita, the ancient text of the Hindus, was written about 2,500 years ago. The Gita described how material life could be balanced with the knowledge of spirituality and devotion. The Qur'an is about 1,500 years old. Muslims believe there is scarcely any social issue that has not been revealed by the Qur'an. All organized religions—Hinduism, Judaism, Buddhism, Christianity, and Islam—are the earliest sources of human social thoughts and ideas.

With progress in human civilizations and the growth in human knowledge and intelligence, philosophy as a branch of knowledge was born in ancient Greece and Athens about 2,400 years ago. With the birth of philosophy, particularly of Socrates, Plato, and Aristotle, humans began to become enlightened enough to think about humanity in terms of human reason and rationality. Socrates, Plato, Aristotle, and the whole generation of Greek philosophers explored the meaning of justice, fairness, ethics, morality, and goodness in politics and governance. A good polity, Plato believed, must be governed by a king-philosopher—a ruler who is knowledgeable not just about the art of governance but also about the principles of justice, ethics, and morality. Aristotle believed that a good ruler is one who comes from the middle class and can balance between the two extremes of the excess and deficiency of virtuous qualities.

Around the same time as the rise of Greek philosophy, there emerged another great philosophical tradition in China known as Confucianism. Confucianism became a state philosophy in China about 2,200 years ago, and it is still an essential part of the Chinese culture. Confucius believed that humanity's realization begins in the family, and knowledge and learning are the key ingredients for good governance. Crime control, Confucius said, is not just a matter of more law and incarcerations; it is also a matter of informal control based on family, parents, neighbors, and a culture of shaming. From the fifth to the 15th century, the world saw a great disconnect of humanity from the sources of ancient knowledge and philosophy. For about 1,000 years, the world was under the dominance of medieval civilizations, not just in Europe but also in almost all regions of the world. Historians described this period in human history as the advent of the Dark Ages because there was a great eclipse of human knowledge and enlightenment for more than 1,000 years.

Then from the days of the Renaissance of the 16th century, the Reformation of the 17th century, the Scientific Revolution of the 17th century, and the Age of Enlightenment of the 18th century, human enlightenment began to widen. From the 16th century, new philosophical ideas began to crystalize a new human-centered worldview based on the notions of humanism, individualism, equality, democracy, and science (Table 3.1). The birth of the human-centered worldview led to the disintegration of the God-centered worldview that was at the core of medieval civilization in the Dark Ages. Under the influence of the new worldview and the Scientific Revolution, the social and economic foundations of medieval society began to crumble. The birth of the new human-centered worldview and the rise of industrialization, urbanization, and the growth of new cities, commerce, and bourgeoise led to the birth of the beginning of a new age in the 18th and 19th centuries described as "modernity." The advent of modernity led to the birth of sociology. Auguste Comte believed the advent of industrialization was the end-stage of human social evolution. The science of sociology was the end of the development of human knowledge and intelligence. The core of the idea was that he was supremely proud to have fathered the science of sociology, which he initially described as "social physics."

Sociology Within the Family of Sciences

All of the modern discoveries are the contributions of modern science. Nevertheless, modern science itself is one of the unique human discoveries. The discovery of science is the discovery of the possibility of naturalistic knowledge of nature, life, mind, and society. For thousands of years, human knowledge of nature, life, mind, and society was intertwined with the divine and scriptural knowledge. The possibility of human knowledge without any reference to Scriptures was seen by the birth of Greek philosophy in the fifth century B.C.E. But for the next 2,000 years, until the advent of the Renaissance in the 16th century and the Scientific Revolution in the 17th century, the human search for knowledge was primarily based on the Scriptures.

In the 16th century, Nicolaus Copernicus, through his discovery of the heliocentric model of the universe, created a unique notion that human knowledge can be independent of Scriptures. Humans are capable of knowing the world in a naturalistic way. Humans alone are capable of exploring the laws, patterns, and forces behind the formation of the universe, earth, life, and society. The Copernican Revolution spread from astronomy to physics in the 17th century, physics to biology in the 18th century, and biology to social science in the 19th century. By the time of the advent of modernity and the Age of Enlightenment in the 18th century, the discovery of modern science as a unique form of human knowledge was firmly established. The birth and the spread of modern civilization during the last 300 years were possible primarily for the advent of modern scientific knowledge. The digital society of the 21st century is just a new phase of the spread of contemporary science and science-based technology.

TABLE 3.1 Transformation from Medieval to Modern Worldview

Medieval World View (500 C.E.–1800 C.E.	Modern World View (1800 C.E.–2020 C.E.)
Geocentric worldview	Heliocentric worldview
Dominance of faith and belief	Dominance of reason and rationality
God is supreme and autonomous.	Humans are supreme and autonomous.
Dominance of the church	Church-state separation
Dominance of the pope and priesthood	Dominance of secular intellectuals
Dominance of the sacred	Dominance of the secular
Religion as the dominant source of knowledge	Science as the dominant source of knowledge
Political system—monarchy and aristocracy	Political system–democracy
Dominance of control and authority	Dominance of liberty and freedom
Hereditary and legal inequalities	Legal equality
Collectivism	Individualism
Traditionalism and conservatism	Modernity and liberalism
Intellectual and Social Forces Responsible for the Transformation From Medieval to Modern Worldview	
Intellectual Forces	**Social Forces**
Renaissance (16th century)	Glorious Revolution of England, 1688
Reformation (17th century)	American Revolution, 1776
Scientific Revolution (17th century)	French Revolution, 1789
Age of Enlightenment (18th century)	Industrial Revolution, 1800

How Science Is Defined

Science can be defined in three ways: science as a body of knowledge, science as a unique methodology, and science as a unique philosophy of knowledge. Most commonly, science is defined as a body of knowledge as astronomy, physics, chemistry, biology, psychology, economics, and sociology. If science is defined as a body of knowledge, it nonetheless does not tell us how science is done and how science is different from other forms of knowledge. Religion is also a body of knowledge, and philosophy is also a body of knowledge. The second most common perspective is to look at science as a methodology based on theorizing, observation, facts, evidence, mathematization, and experiments. The scientific method and the canons of science are different from other branches of knowledge; however, science is not just a unique methodology. It is also a unique philosophy or a unique perspective about knowledge.

Unlike religion and philosophy, scientific knowledge is progressive and changeable. Science is characterized, unlike religion, by a sense of uncertainty, skepticism, and falsifiability. Scientific validity does not depend on Scriptures or the power of political authority, and science is a social enterprise. Scientific knowledge is public property, and science, unlike technology, is never patented. Einstein's theory of relativity does not belong to Germany or America. It belongs to the whole of humanity. Science advances because of advances in scientific theories and scientific paradigms (Kuhn, 2012). To comprehend the meaning of scientific reasoning and scientific rationality, understanding the unique features of science is crucial. It is more critical in the digital age when there is a massive proliferation of fake science, false information, and false ideologies with the help of the internet and social media.

Various Domains of Science

There are four distinct domains of science: nature, life, mind, and society. Related to each of these domains, there are multiple branches of science. Related to the domain of nature, for example, there are some core sciences such as astronomy, physics, chemistry, and geology. These branches of science study and theorize about different properties of nature, such as the constitution of the galaxy, formation of the earth, and the nature and forces of lights, electricity, gravity, and magnetism. Related to the domain of life, the major branches are biology, biochemistry, neurology, genetic science, and other agricultural sciences. The life sciences study the constitution and the evolution of life. Concerning the domain of the mind—an invisible entity—the main branches are psychology, cognitive science, and artificial intelligence. These sciences study the structure and the functions of the mind and how the mind grows and evolves. Related to society's domain, there are three core branches of science: economics, political science, and sociology. These branches study the nature and the evolution of economic, political, and social structures.

All of these branches of science are defined as basic sciences. The goal of basic science is the discovery of theories, models, and concepts. The scientists pursuing basic science are remotely concerned with their applications and utility. Related to each group of sciences, there are multiple science-based professions that grew and evolved based on the application of scientific theories and models. The field of electrical engineering, for example, is based on the theories of physics; bioengineering is based on many discoveries in biology and genetic science. The field of business draws ideas from economics; the specialties of law and public policy are based on knowledge from political science; and the areas of criminology, criminal justice, education, counseling, and social work evolved borrowing ideas from sociology. The new computer and information science field emerged based on knowledge from physics, chemistry, biology, psychology, and artificial intelligence (Table 3.2).

Recent years have seen the growth of numerous hybrid areas of science that evolved by borrowing knowledge from multiple areas such as biophysics, neurobiology, behavioral neurology, robotics, artificial intelligence, criminal justice, and cybersecurity. Many fundamental sociological discoveries are used in behavioral neurology, health and medicine, nursing, counseling, social work, law, business, education, criminology, and public policy. The understanding of the location of sociology within the family of sciences is, therefore, significant for understanding the crosscutting effects of the sociological perspective in shaping different branches of knowledge and professions.

TABLE 3.2 Different Branches of Science: Sociology Within the Family of Sciences

Domains of Science	Branches of Basic Sciences	Areas of Scientific Research	Science-Based Professions
Nature	Astronomy Physics Chemistry Geological sciences Material sciences	Planetary system Earth system Atoms and molecules Gravity, laser, and lights Magnetism, mass, inertia Air, winds, and forces	Electrical engineering Chemical engineering Material engineering Environmental engineering Computer engineering
Life	Biology Biochemistry Molecular biology Botany Zoology	Evolution of life Cells and molecules DNA Human physiology Neurology/brain development	Medicine Psychiatry Bioengineering Bioinformatics Genetic engineering
Mind	Psychology Cognitive science Artificial intelligence	Intelligence Personality Motivation Attitudes Perceptions/Depression	Clinical psychology Experimental psychology counseling Software Engineering
Society	Economics Political science SOCIOLOGY Anthropology	Production of goods and services Market structure Government and constitutions Social groups and institutions Family and religion Mores and moralities Culture and values	Law Business Education Criminal justice Journalism Public policy Social work Cybersecurity

Sociology: A Universal Science of Society

The Boundaries of Sociology as a Science

When sociology is defined as a science of society, it does not mean that sociology is the science of a particular society or a country, such as America, Canada, China, or Japan, but society in general. We have many sociological studies in America, Canada, Japan, and many other societies. That does not, however, make sociology the science of a particular society. The universality in defining, understanding, and exploring the nature of modern society, in general, is one of the first discoveries in sociology. Sociological theories, models, and concepts such as physics, chemistry, and biology do not have any national boundaries or any civilizational boundaries. Many, particularly in the developing world, misleadingly view sociology as primarily an American or European science. As a science, the goal of sociology is to understand the nature, structures, and the evolution of society in general, and modern society in particular. As a science, sociology seeks to explore why humans, in general, behave the way they do, think the way they think, and value the things they love. The exploration of scientific theories and concepts universal to modern societies and modern human personalities was the mission at the core of the birth of sociology in the 19th century.

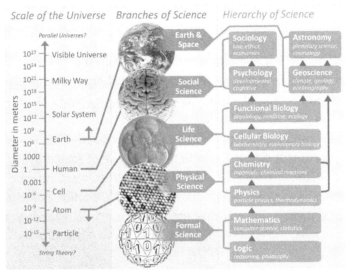

FIGURE 3.1   Branches of Science

August Comte theorized that the evolution of knowledge is the driver of the evolution of society and that humanity has reached, with the birth of industrialization, a positive stage of scientific knowledge. He did not mean that this was true about French society. He made a universal statement about the evolution of human knowledge. When French sociologist Emile Durkheim theorized that suicide is not psychological but social in origin, he did not mean that suicide is social in origin only in France. He made a universal theoretical statement about the role of human attachments to groups and their influence in shaping human behavior. When American sociologist Peter Berger theorized that religion is like a sacred canopy and a glue that binds a group together, he made a universal theoretical statement about the role of religion in society in general. The specific examples to support or replicate a particular sociological theory may come from some particular societies and cultures. Still, sociology is a body of universal ideas, models, and concepts about humanity in general.

The Nature and Typology of Society

This notion of sociology as a science of society, in general, leads to the need for understanding how society is defined and described: what the different types of societies are, how they are formed, and what needs to happen for a collection of people to create a society (Table 3.3). The idea of society is easy to understand but hard to describe, or easy to explain but hard to understand.

The word "society" is used to describe a number of different human groups and collectivities. Most commonly, different countries are described as different societies, such as American society, Canadian society, or Japanese society. Society can be used to describe the collectivity of billions of people, such as the Chinese society, which has about 1.3 billion people, and Indian society, which has about 1.2 billion people. Society can also be used to describe even the collection of two people—a dyadic society. Society can be used to describe a family consisting of a husband and wife, or a group formed by boyfriend and girlfriend, or two intimate partners of same-sex orientations. How different groups are formed and structured, and on what basis, is an essential puzzle for sociological theorizing.

Sociologists explore the puzzle of understanding the idea of a society in multiple ways. They define four main types of societies. The first is a territorial society in which a collection of people has a definite territorial boundary, such as the American society, Canadian society, or German society. The second is a symbolic society in which a collection of people form a community based on shared goals and interests, such as the American Jewish Society, the Evangelical Theological Society of America, the Muslim American Society, or the American Cancer Society. The third is a natural society—societies in which people are born and naturally become a part of that collectivity with a deep sense of solidarity and national pride, such as China, India, Japan, or the United Kingdom. The fourth is a constructed society—societies formed as a result of civilizational transformations and human migrations. America is a prime example of a created culture or civilization. A constructed community may or may not have a territorial boundary, such as Black people in America; Muslims in India, China, and Europe; Christians in Asia and Africa; or Jews in America and Europe.

TABLE 3.3 What Is Society, and How Is a Society Possible?

Nature of Society	Types of Societies	Basis of Society	Functions of Society	Structures of Society
Society is a moral and symbolic boundary. Society is a territorial boundary. Society is an objective entity. Society is a subjective entity.	Territorial societies Symbolic societies Natural societies Constructed societies	Demography—a collection of people Group solidarity Shared values and morality A shared history, language, and symbols	Order and stability Resource generation Recreation of group solidarity Change management: pattern maintenance	Social institutions Roles and status Groups and organizations

Sociologists have found that for a collection of people to form a society, they need a shared sense of goals, interests, values, authority, and solidarity. For example, a collection of people at an airport does not form a society because they do not have shared goals, norms, values, and interests. The sociologists observe that society is both an objective and a subjective reality for an individual. Objectively, we all belong to different kinds of societies or social arrangements, such as family, work, and school, and they shape and control our behavior. Society is external to us. Society, however, is also internal. It resides in our minds and shapes the way we are. In a family, we know the norms and expectations of parents; at work, we see the nature of control and hierarchy; and in a country, we know the laws that define and control our behavior.

One of the significant sociological understandings of a society is that it is not only a set of rules and institutions, and a form of power and authority, or a territorial boundary but also a moral community—a society is symbolic and invisible. The visible properties of society are just a collection of people. Nevertheless, when and whether that collection of people form a society depends on their shared sense of values, morality, interests, goals, authority, solidarity, and even territory. The puzzle of defining society and developing universal theories about how it is formed and evolved, and how it shapes and molds our behavior, is always a genuine sociological curiosity.

Sociology: A Science of Human Groups

Humans as Social Beings

Sigmund Freud, one of the founding fathers of modern psychology, argued that humans are antisocial. Human nature, he believed, is primarily driven to satisfy humans' instinctual gratifications. Since humans are driven merely for the pleasure of instinctual gratifications, it's intrinsically damaging for them to belong to a group.

Some 300 years before Freud, British political philosopher Thomas Hobbes made a similar argument that humans are inherently selfish, greedy, and competitive. They cannot form societies and groups without the help of a strong political authority. Without a strong political power to control the individuals, Hobbes surmised, life will be "nasty, brutish, and short."

FIGURE 3.2   World Population

Sociologists love to read Freud and Hobbes, but they significantly differ in their ideas of humans as intrinsically antigroup and antisocial. Sociology begins with the assumption that humans are, by nature, social. Humans are born in groups, they live in groups, and they die in groups. French sociologist Durkheim said—as did Aristotle about 2,500 years before him—that if someone does not belong to a group, that person is either a "beast" or a "superman." Humans not only belong to groups but also see others as belonging to different groups. In any society, there are numerous groups (Table 3.4). Humans have an insatiable thrust to define other humans in terms of their visible and invisible group characteristics. Sometimes, group definitions and group characteristics are deliberately constructed. How humans develop, define, and deify the phenomenon of human groups and grouping is a significant aspect of sociological theorizing.

Human Sociality and Human Groups

There are some groups to which we belong by our birth, such as our family, race, ethnicity, religion, and nationality. One may get converted into a different religion or may take a different nationality, but one is always born into both a family and a nation. There are other groups to which we belong by our achievements, intelligence, and creativity, such as the groups described as college educated, corporate elites, or political elites. Human social groups are also divided in terms of human actions and attachments. Some groups, described by sociologists as primary groups, such as family, are based on love, emotion, attachments, and intimacy. There are other groups, such as work or school, that are based on rational, measured, and calculated actions and behavior. Unlike the family, the workplace is governed by rational goals and pursuits and not by the pursuit of emotions, love, and intimacy (Table 3.4). Humans belong to human groups, but humans also reflectively make sense of the meaning of those groups and collectivities. We belong to a class based on our incomes.

Human groups are, therefore, intersubjectively understood, defined, and perceived. When we belong to a group or some groups, those groups become the boundary of our actions, solidarity, and pursuit of happiness. Sociologists call these "in-groups" that are uncritically accepted, obeyed, and deified. Most humans live within their in-groups. This is true of a family, true of religion, and even true of a nation. The groups to which we do not belong are at the periphery of our actions and interests, and sociologists call them "out-groups." The out-groups for us remain mostly unknown, uninteresting, and unexplored. The out-groups generate a sense of fear and prejudice, and prejudice sometimes leads to hate and xenophobia.

TABLE 3.4 Examples of Some Groups in America (327 Million People—2019 Estimate)

Men and women	Upper class	North Americans
Married and unmarried	Middle class	South Americans
Transgender people	Lower class	Europeans
Intersex people	Working class	Asians
Two-parent family	Underclass	Latin Americans
Single family–mother dominated	Homeless	Urban-rural
Single family–father dominated	Christians	College educated

Stepfamily	Protestant and Catholics	Noncollege educated
Gay family	Jews and Muslims	Literate and illiterate
Blended family	Hindus and Buddhists	Liberals and conservatives
Young and old	Atheists	Democrats and Republicans
Baby boom generation	Evangelical Christians	Voters and nonvoters
Generation X	Citizens and noncitizens	Employed and unemployed
Millennial generation	Citizens and permanent residents	Political elite
Generation Z	Citizen by birth—by naturalization	Governmental elite
Black and White	Biracial Americans	Military elite
Hispanic and non-Hispanic	Multiracial Americans	Corporate elite
Asian Americans	Italian Americans	Media elite
Pacific Islanders	Polish Americans	Gun rights advocates
Native Americans	Arab Americans	Gun control advocates

The tolerance and respect for group diversity are among the central sociological issues in modern society, particularly in America, built by people from different cultures, civilizations, races, ethnicities, religions, languages, and nationalities. The idea that society is governed by the dynamics of relations, domination, competition, and conflicts between and among its different human groups is a significant sociological discovery (Table 3.5).

TABLE 3.5 Differences Between Primary and Secondary Groups

Key Dimensions	Primary Groups (Family, Relatives, Friends, Communities)	Second Groups (Work, Office, School, Business)
Relationship	Emotional attachment; emotional bonding; relations of love and intimacy; face-to-face relations; enhanced by social media	Rational attachments; diffused bonding; goal-oriented; voluntary; virtual relations; improved by social media
Power	Informal power and authority; informal rules, norms, and mores; nonhierarchical; no legally enforceable chain of command; informal control	Formal power and authority; formal and written rules and laws; enforceable hierarchy and chain of command; formal control
Work	No formal and defined division of labor; collaborative work environment; nonmonetary rewards	The formal division of labor and formal specialization; roles and status are clearly defined; based on formal reward and compensation structures

Time	Time-neutral; open access to all actors irrespective of time and space; relatively stable and permanent structures	Time-bound; defined and time-bound access to all actors; temporal structures
Solidarity	High solidarity based on love, emotion, and intimacy; based on common faith and shared tradition; the dominance of community spirit	Diffused and low solidarity based on formal goals and interests; high level of individualism
Knowledge	Mostly based on religious knowledge and common sense; the dominance of customary and folk knowledge	Dominance of science and professional knowledge; the reward is based on productivity and performance
Space	Predominantly space-neutral; the emergence of new virtual primary groups	Predominantly space-bound; growth of new virtual networks of secondary groups

Sociology: A Science of the 'Social': Sociology as a 'Form of Consciousness'

Sociality as a Human Phenomenon

Sociologists' search for the meaning and typology of society and their curiosity about human groups and group diversities are connected to their discovery that sociology is primarily a science of the "social." The concept of "social" means something that we do together, think together, follow together, and believe together. It is our collective ways of acting and behaving. It is our collective hopes, dreams, choices, and preferences. It is our joint problems, concerns, and anxieties.

FIGURE 3.3   Human Groups—Buddhist Monks

Sociology is the science of everything we do as social beings, as a part of our group existence. Social phenomena do not describe the peculiarity of an individual. For example, if a woman is a victim of intimate partner violence (IPV), that is not within the range of sociological interest. But if millions of women are victimized by intimate partner violence, that is a genuine sociological problem—a problem social in nature. A study conducted by the Centers for Disease Control and Prevention (2010) on intimate partner violence in America observed that "more than 1 in 3 women (35.6%) and more than 1 in 4 men (28.5%) in the United States have experienced rape, physical violence, and/or stalking by an intimate partner in their lifetime" (p. 2). The study further noted, "More than half (51.1%) of female victims of rape reported being raped by an intimate partner and 40.8% by an acquaintance; for male victims, more than half (52.4%) reported being raped by an acquaintance and 15.1% by a stranger" (p. 2).

FIGURE 3.4   Stop Bullying

Therefore, sociologists are genuinely interested in exploring and theorizing about the nature and effect of the social phenomenon of intimate partner violence. Suppose a man or a woman decides to delay marriage. In that case, that is a specific individual choice, and sociologists will not be curious about why a man or a woman is delaying marriage. In America, however, there is a growing trend of delaying marriage, and it has become a genuine sociological curiosity. A recent study by the U.S. Census Bureau (2018) found that "the median age at first marriage in the United States has continued to rise in recent years from 27.1 and 25.3 years in 2003 for males and females, respectively, to 29.8 and 27.8 years in 2018. In 2018, 29 percent of young adults ages 18 to 34 were married, a decrease of 30 percentage points when compared to 59 percent of young adults being married in 1978" (p. 1). In 2018, "there are 35.7 million single-person households, comprising of 28 percent of all households. In 1960, single-person households represented only 13 percent of all households" (U.S. Census Bureau, 2018, p. 1). The rising trend of single-person households in America is no longer a unique phenomenon; it is a growing social phenomenon. Sociology is the science of these kinds of social attributes of human groups and societies.

Sociologists discovered that social facts and phenomena are not rooted in human psychology or ingrained in human genetic peculiarities. Social facts and phenomena are social in origin. Social factors cause human social facts and phenomena. The problem of intimate partner violence, for sociologists, for example, is not genetic in origin, and the role of sociology is to explore the social factors related to intimate partner violence. There are numerous sociological hypotheses about IPV, which could be related to income, education, parental educational background, growing up in a violent home, or drug and alcohol addiction.

The new American trend of delaying marriage is also, for sociologists, not a genetic issue nor a peculiar psychological mentality. Sociologists find that concerning love, sex, emotion, marriage, children, and family, America—since the 1970s, particularly since the rise of the internet and social media in the late 1990s—has been undergoing a major cultural shift. More men and women, particularly women, are increasingly becoming more educated and career-oriented. They have a new sense of freedom, individualism, openness, globality, and adulthood. American society also has become much more tolerant of cohabitation and unwed motherhood. The postmillennials and Generation Z are also concerned about declining marital stability and a high rate of divorce. The social problem of delaying marriage is related to these and other related social factors. The art of explaining a social fact by another social fact, said Emile Durkheim, is the crux of sociology. Almost the whole body of sociological research shows how a social fact is caused by another social fact and how social facts are hugely consequential and meaningful.

As a science of the social, sociology applies all the canons and science methodologies. A sociologist is not a journalist, nor a community organizer, nor a social advocate. Sociology is not social work or socialism. Sociology is a pure and basic science; however, sociology, as sociologist Peter L. Berger (1963) so eloquently described, is also a peculiar "consciousness"—a unique passion for making sense of the social world, a distinctive form of devotion to understanding the vastness and complexity of human social affairs (Table 3.6).

TABLE 3.6 The Four Facets of Sociology as a Form of Consciousness

Debunking Motif	Unrespectability Motif
To look beyond common sense Seeing through Deep structure analysis Backstage analysis	"Hidden injuries" "Other America" Underclass Crime and corruptions Underprivileged
Relativizing Motif	Cosmopolitan Motif
Cultural relativism Value relativism Cultural conversion	Modernism Globalism Humanism

Source: Berger, P. L. (1963). Invitation to Sociology: A Humanistic Perspective.

As a science of the social, Berger described, sociology is intensely and shameless curious about the breadth and depth of human social facts and events. The sociological perspective, for Berger, is that it is a science of seeing through the social reality—a reality that has multiple layers of meanings and a reality that is mostly hidden from the external and formal dramatization of the social world. The sociological perspective, Berger explains, demands a vast curiosity of understanding the life events not just of the elites but also of the disadvantaged and the socially "disrespected" groups of people, such as people experiencing homelessness or drug addiction and sex workers. Berger (1963) said, "Unrespectability, whatever its ramifications in the emotions and the will, must remain a constant possibility in the sociological mind" (p. 47). The sociological perspective, according to Berger, is also a unique bent of mind that explores the enormous diversities and relativism in the unfolding of modern cultures, creeds, and consciousness.

The birth of modernity has set in motion within world societies many significant trends of social change and transformations. The spread of modernity has also created much social chaos, crisis, and confusion by bringing forth the new values of democracy, individualism, secularism, and universal human rights. Sociology, therefore, "is in tune with the temper of the modern era precisely because it represents the consciousness of the world in which values have radically relativized" (Berger, 1963, p. 48).

Sociality and Human Biological Properties

Sociology, from another dimension, has discovered that the notion of the "social" deeply enters into our biology, body, brain, and mind. It is not just a social fact that is affected by another social fact such as the relationship between IPV and growing up in a violent home or the relationship between high school dropout and juvenile delinquency. Social phenomena—factors of the sociogenic system—deeply enter the human brain and influence its growth, structures, and functions. Social phenomena profoundly penetrate the human body and affect human endocrinological and cellular processes.

Equally, social phenomena intensely shape the human mind, motivations, perceptions, attitudes, and emotions. A human belongs not only to a social and cultural system but is also a part of interconnected biogenic and psychogenic systems. A human being is composed of trillions of cells, and genetic science has discovered there are about 25,000 human genes in those trillions of cells. These trillions of cells and the thousands of genes make up the human biogenetic system, making humans a biological being. As part of this biological being, there also exists a psychological system involving the structure and functions of the mind. Sigmund Freud was the first psychologist who discovered that the mind has some definable structures and functions. Sociologists observed that both biogenic and psychogenic systems are greatly affected by human social phenomena.

The effect of the social on biogenic and psychogenic systems is now being extensively studied by biologists, neurologists, psychologists, and the professions of medicine and psychiatry. There is a wide consensus that social factors such as family structure, socioeconomic status (SES), poverty, divorce, parenting, racial disparities, racial victimization, economic disparities, and powerlessness are positively connected to many biogenic conditions such as brain development, hypertension, obesity, dementia, cancer, and Alzheimer's disease. Research has also confirmed that social factors are positively connected to depression, sleeplessness, eating disorders, drug and alcohol addiction, violent behavior, and suicide.

Recently, many neurologists and medical specialists conducted significant scientific studies on the effect of poverty on brain development (Mani et al., 2013; Shah et al., 2012; Noble et al., 2012). A group of researchers from nine hospitals in 2015 conducted a study on the relationship between poverty and brain development. They collected data from DNA samples, MRI scans of the brain, family income, educational background, and test scores on reading skills and memory. The study found that "more educated families produced children with greater brain surface area and a more voluminous hippocampus. However, income had its distinct effect: living in the lowest bracket left children with up to six percent less brain surface area than children from high-income families" (as quoted in Ostrander, 2015, p. 23). Poverty and low socioeconomic status have long-term consequences on behavior and cognitive development. Research on fetus development shows that the fetuses of mothers who are stressed out and smoke cigarettes have "delayed nervous-system development" (Ostrander, 2015, p. 23).

Another group of neuroscientists has found, based on brain scans of a group of 24-year-olds, that "in those who had lived in poverty at age nine, the brain's centers of negative emotion were more frequently buzzing with activity, whereas the areas that could rein in such emotions were quieter" (Ostrander, 2015, p. 23). It was also established by many researchers that dementia and Alzheimer's disease are positively linked to low socioeconomic status. A study from the University of Wisconsin found that "people in the most disadvantaged neighborhoods had markedly worse cognitive performance in all aspects measured (working memory, immediate memory, speed and flexibility of cognition, and verbal learning), even after adjusting for age and education. They also had disproportionately higher levels of one Alzheimer's disease biomarker in their spinal fluid" (Seegert, 2017, p. 2). The study further noted that "living in a neighborhood challenged by poverty, low education, unemployment, and/or substandard housing may increase risk of Alzheimer's disease, and may account for some of the observed differences in Alzheimer's disease risk among people of different racial backgrounds and income levels" (Seegert, 2017, p. 2).

Sociality and Human Psychological Properties

A vast amount of scientific research also reveals that social factors are positively connected to many psychogenic abnormalities in humans. Recent research has shown that family structure is positively connected to children's biogenic and psychogenic spheres of life. "Nearly three decades of research evaluating the impact of family structure on the health and well-being of children demonstrates that children living with their married, biological parents consistently have better physical, emotion, and academic well-being" (Anderson, 2014, p. 1). Research studies by the Centers for Disease Control and Prevention (CDC) found that "Children living with one biological parent were between 3 and 8 times as likely to have experienced neighborhood violence, caregiver violence, or caregiver incarceration or to have lived with a caregiver with mental illness or an alcohol or drug problem" (as cited in Anderson, 2014, p. 6).

About 100 years ago, sociologist Emile Durkheim conducted empirical research on suicides in France and observed that unmarried men are more vulnerable to committing suicide. Many recent research studies have confirmed that unmarried and divorced individuals, particularly divorced men, are more susceptible to committing suicide. A recent study, based on a meta-analysis of research studies published between 2000 and 2016, confirmed that "non-married men exhibited a greater risk of suicide than their married counterparts. … The suicide risk in divorced individuals was higher than for non-married individuals in both men and women … non-married individuals have an aggregate higher suicide risk than married ones" (Kyung-Sook et al., 2018).

In the early 1940s, Abraham Maslow became a pioneer in the study of human motivation by developing a theory of human needs. His approach was based on an interconnected understanding of relationships between and among humans' biogenic, psychogenic, and sociogenic needs. Maslow (1943/2018) theorized that the self-actualization of a human being (needs for family, community, faith, power, status, honor, and respect) is intimately connected to the fulfillment of their basic biogenic requirements (need for food, air, and water) and psychogenic needs (need for economic security, physical security, love, friendship, and intimacy). Maslow prioritized meeting the social conditions at the top of the pyramid of his theory of human needs and motivation. Almost the whole body of sociological research shows how a social fact is caused by another social fact and how social facts are also hugely significant, consequential, and meaningful for the human biogenic and psychogenic domains of life. The art of explaining the social, so said French sociologist Emile Durkheim, is the crux of the science of sociology.

Sociology: A Historical and Comparative Science

Both the comparative and historical perspectives are embedded into the very nature of sociology as a universal science of society and the universal science of human behavior. Natural and biological phenomena are generally invariant. The nature of gravity in America is the same as it is in Egypt, India, or Russia. The natural properties of light and lasers behave in America the same way as they do in Canada or Germany. The nature of blood circulation of an American person follows the same character and rhythms found in a Japanese or Chinese person.

The core functions of the heart are invariant across racial and cultural groups of the world. The historical and comparative perspectives, however, are not unknown in physical and biological sciences. Astronomers compare the nature of different planets and galaxies; physicists compare the nature of different atomic particles; biologists compare the genetic composition of different species; neurologists compare the functions of the other regions of the brain; epidemiologists compare disease patterns in different countries, races, and ethnic groups; and psychologists compare human and animal behavior. Charles Darwin, in his *Origin of Species*, published in 1859, empirically established his theory of natural selection by comparing the genetic composition and the adaptive capacity of different species.

The Historicity of Social Facts and Phenomena

The social phenomena, however, are qualitatively very different, and they widely vary across time and space. Generation Z, born in the late 1990s, for example, as we discussed earlier, does not think in the same way about many social issues as the baby boom generation of the 1950s and 1960s. The issues surrounding women's rights in the 21st century are very different from those of the early 20th century. Our perception of disability today is very different from what it was in the 19th century.

In the same way, social phenomena also vary across societies and cultures. People in most societies of the world do not perceive gun rights in the same way that most Americans perceive them. The American system of the presidency is different from that of France, China, and India. Human values, beliefs, and perceptions about gender, class, race, religion, age, love, sex, intimacy, and marriage widely vary from culture to culture. The human global social world is a vast, chaotic complexity characterized by enormous diversities in human values, choice, and preference. As a science of society, sociology searches for common patterns in the organization of human societies and the invariable principles that govern human behavior. It is for this reason that comparative and historical studies are intrinsic to the perspective of sociology. The historical and comparative studies compel sociologists to explore human societies from global, relativistic, and holistic perspectives.

Sociologists have discovered three major ways of dealing with this problem of the chaotic complexity of the human social world. The first can be described as a snapshot approach. In such an approach, sociologists understand the nature of a society or a particular form of human action and behavior at a given point in time and space. A snapshot approach, however, does not make a sociological theory universal. The second approach is described as "social dynamics," which is like watching a streaming video. Through the social dynamics approach, sociologists seek to understand how the nature of the social organization and social facts and events change over time, how they are differently defined and perceived from one age to another age and from one society to another society. The third approach is comparative and historical. Through this approach, sociologists seek universal validation and justification for their theories of social structures and social dynamics.

The major sociological theories of almost all great sociologists since classical time are based on historical and comparative perspectives. In his *Spirit of Laws*, published in 1734, French sociologist Montesquieu argued that the systems of law and justice are socially contingent, vary from cultures to cultures, and hence, a comparative method is crucial for understanding the patterns in the evolution of law and justice. Auguste Comte, the father of sociology, coined the term "social dynamics." Comte theorized that human societies have progressed from the theological stage, through militarism, to industrialization in the 19th century based on advances in human reason and intelligence. German sociologist Karl Marx examined how human societies progressed from slavery to feudalism to capitalism based on advances in the organization of economic production and human economic relations. German sociologist Max Weber undertook a global study on the economic role of different world religions. He theorized that except for the Protestant sect of Christianity, no world religions, including Hinduism, Judaism, and Islam, played any significant role in advancing rational capitalism. This was because most of those religions, he contended, were theologically organized around the theme of "otherworldliness" in contrast to "this-worldliness." Emile Durkheim conducted a study on the evolution of human solidarity and theorized that social solidarity was relatively strong in premodern societies because of the vital role of family, religion, and repressive law. Durkheim was concerned that social solidarity might become fragile in modern societies because of the declining role of religion and the rise of individualism. He further theorized, based on his comparative study of solidarity across time, that fragility in social solidarity in modern societies might lead to an increase in suicide, crime, and social anarchy.

In the 20th century, the comparative and historical perspectives in sociology were more vigorously studied by sociologists to theorize about the rise of modernization, secularization, democracy, and globalization (Parsons, 1966; Moore, 1966; Bellah, 1967; Skocpol, 1979; Geertz, 1971; Wallerstein, 1979; Tilly, 1984). In the 21st century, a historical and comparative understanding of the chaotic nature of the world social order has become more compelling and significant because of the global expansion of digitalization, the rise of global terrorism, growth in cybercrime, retreat in a liberal democracy, and the advent of the radical right in international politics.

The Peculiarity of 'Sociological Imagination'

The essential nature of historicity in the understanding of sociology and the social world has been very passionately described by the dictum "sociology as an imagination," coined by sociologist C. Wright Mills (1959/2000). Like Peter L. Berger, Mills believes the understanding of the social is not just the act of gathering and analyzing data. Sociology, Mills argues, is a peculiar form of imagination that explores how individual life events at a given point of time are shaped, formed, and patterned by a host of external and larger historical facts and forces of society, which are mostly unseen and uncontrollable. The act of doing sociology as a science, for Mills, is to examine and explore how these unseen and uncontrollable larger social facts and forces shape the peculiarity of individual lives and make up their unique biographies (Table 3.7).

TABLE 3.7 Sociological Imagination: The 'Big Picture'

Birth of the internet	Rise of global terror
Birth of social media	Rise of the global war on terror
Birth of mobile internet	Rise of a new culture war in America
Advent of the global cyberspace	Rise of right-wing populism in America
Advent of 5G connectivity	Rise of nativism and antiglobalism in America
Advent of IoE	Stagnant American middle class
	Slowing of intergenerational mobility
	Birth of the #MeToo movement
	Politics and birth of new feminism in America

Sociology: Scope and Significance

The Scope of Sociology

Sociologists define society in multiple ways. This is because, as the novelist Oscar Wilde once said, "Society exists only in concept; in the real world, there are only individuals." Irrespective of the nature of boundaries and the nature of bonding, sociologists define society as a structure and a process. As a structure, society is a set of roles and statuses, actors and actions, goals and functions, and values and meanings. As a structure, a society is a power game and an arena of conflicts, cooperation, competition, domination, and exploitation. As a process, a society is an ongoing reality in a continuous process of creation and recreation. As a process, society is characterized by change, movements, evolution, and revolutions.

Social structures and processes are human creations and, hence, are also characterized by problems of crime, poverty, violence, and war. As a structure and a process, society shapes and controls individuals, but in shaping and controlling individuals' lives, it often destroys the human self, human pride, and human lives. Sociologists study everything that pertains to society and that concerns human lives (Table 3.8).

Significance of Sociology: The Enlightenment Role

Sociology is significant for its role in building an enlightened mind and refining our understanding of the nature of social factors and their relationships with different facets of life—biogenic, psychogenic, and sociogenic. Sociology is the child of the Enlightenment. Sociology was born through the ideas on the role of reason and humanism that came from the Renaissance, the ideas of freedom and the dignity of an individual that came from the Reformation, the centrality of naturalistic knowledge discovered by the Scientific Revolution, and the philosophies of democracy and equality from the Age of Enlightenment. Sociological thinking is holistic, synthetic, global, relativistic, historical, and comparative.

Sociology is a unique science. Sociologists are keen to discover the universal patterns, structures, and models of social arrangements by following the scientific method's fundamental canons. At the same time, they are also curious about society as a moral entity. Sociologists are concerned with examining how social inequality, social deprivations, human exploitations, and human dominations are physically, psychologically, and socially harmful and destructive. Sociologists are keen to reveal not just the good and elitist dimensions of society. They are also equally intrigued to explore the nature and the creation of the social world of "disrespectability."

It is no wonder that in the 1960s and 1970s, during the Cold War, scores of sociologists became attracted to the ideas of socialism and communism. Many misleadingly branded these sociologists as "communists" or "radicals." From the beginning of classical sociology in the 19th century, sociologists thought that complete equality, defined as an age of communism by Karl Marx, was a myth. At the same time, however, sociologists were drawn to be critical about human exploitation, degradation, and dehumanization. Sociological explanations are never complete without revealing the moral dimensions of human existence and humanity's moral failing. Because humans are not only natural and biological beings, they are also moral beings.

Sociology is vastly significant for the digital tribe growing up in an age of hyperconnectivity. It is substantial for the digital tribe, not just because sociological thinking can lead to skill enhancement and make its members more analytical, critical, holistic, and global in thinking but also because it will help generate a new sense of curiosity about the complexity and the chaotic nature of the emerging digital world. The advent of digital society brought many new social anxieties about family, marriage, divorce, sex, love, and intimacy. The digital culture has set in motion a new set of crimes and criminality—cyberterrorism, cyber espionage, identity theft, online child prostitution, cyberbullying, cyberstalking, cyber harassment, and the global spread of hate, racism, and bigotry. There is now a compelling need for knowledge and enlightenment about the sociology of the emerging digital world.

TABLE 3.8 The Scope of Sociology

Sociological Domains of Inquiry	Examples	Sociological Domains of Inquiry	Examples
Social systems	Family Economy Politics Education Religion	Social processes	Urbanization Suburbanization Gentrification Modernization Globalization Digitalization
Social structures	Capitalism Bureaucracy School Company Government	Social change and trends	Individualism Multiculturalism Single motherhood Same-sex marriage Professionalization Rise of Gen Z

Social actions, cultures, symbols, and meanings	Parenting Leadership Love and friendship Identity and stigma Hate and bigotry Values and norms Cultural Diversity	Social inequality and diversity	Race and gender Nationality Ethnicity Class and class conflict Exploitation Discrimination
Social actors	Dominant elite Corporate elite Political elite Scientific elite Professional elite	Social problems	Crime and violence Drugs and violence Teen suicide Aging society School shootings Mass shootings Obesity Teen dating violence
Social conditions	Demography Residential patterns Poverty	Social movements	Civil rights movement Feminist movement #MeToo movement Black Lives Matter Rise of the radical right

Significance of Sociology: The Instrumental Role

The instrumental role of sociology comes from sociology's primary scientific mission: to understand and theorize about the nature of social phenomena and assess their multifaceted effects on body, mind, brain, and behavior. Sociology has recently become directly relevant to several human-centered professions, such as medicine, psychiatry, brain science, nursing, counseling, law, business, education, journalism, management, criminal justice, and social work. Some of the oldest sociology fields include the sociology of medicine, of law, of modern complex organization, of education, of science, and of crime and deviance. Some of these subspecializations have their own academic organizations and academic journals.

In many U.S. medical schools, the sociology of medicine is an established part of medical education. In the Vanderbilt School of Medicine, for example, the medical sociology curriculum is made up of six courses: Social Capital and Health; Society and Medicine; Gender, Sexuality and the Body; Social Dynamics of Mental Health; Race, Gender, and Health; and Sociology of Health and Environmental Sciences. The U.S. Medical College Admission Test includes many sociological learning objectives, such as social structure and stratification, social interactions, social thinking and attitudes, and social processes and behavior.

In recent years, the General Medical Council of the United Kingdom, the United Kingdom's leading accrediting body for medical education, mandated that sociology be included in the medical curriculum of all U.K. medical schools. It is required that all medical curriculum have at least six sociological learning objectives: a sociological perspective, social patterning of health and illness, sociological knowledge about health and disease, sociological research on health and illness, healthcare policy, and experiences of health, disease, and disability (Collett, 2016). In most modern professions, from law to social work and nursing to criminal justice, sociology forms an essential part of the curriculum.

The greater significance of sociology owes to sociology's focus on training in research and data analysis. There are scarcely any federal departments and agencies where sociologists are not employed for research and policy analysis. One of the earliest examples is the employment of two sociologists, Charles Galpin and Carl Taylor, in the U.S Department of Agriculture in 1919. From 1919–1953, these two sociologists were responsible for researching transformations in rural social structures in America (Larson & Zimmerman, 2003). Within the federal government, sociologists are employed in areas of data analysis, research analysis, policy analysis, program analysis, and program evaluation. The 2018 U.S. Department of Labor *Occupational Outlook Handbook* noted that "employment of sociologists is projected to grow 9 percent from 2018 to 2028, faster than the average for all occupations. Sociologists (median pay $85,052 per year) can expect strong competition because sociology is a popular field of study with a relatively small number of positions" (p. 1).

The *Occupational Outlook Handbook* further added that sociologists typically work in the following areas: "design research projects to test theories about social issues, collect data through surveys, observations, interviews, and other sources; analyze and draw conclusions from data; prepare reports, articles, or presentations detailing their research findings; collaborate with and advise other social scientists, policymakers, or other groups on research findings and sociological issues" (U.S. Department of Labor, 2018, p. 1). The National Science Foundation (NSF), the National Institutes of Health (NIH), and the Centers for Disease Control and Prevention (CDC) are the three apex research organizations of the federal government. The bulk of the billions of dollars spent by the federal government on scientific research every year, basic and applied, is consumed by these three organizations.

Sociology plays a prominent role in all three organizations. There is a sociology program within the NSF's Division of Social and Economic Sciences. The sociology program supports data-based theoretical research on such areas as "organizations and organizational behavior, population dynamics, social movements, social groups, labor force participation, stratification and mobility, family, social networks, socialization, gender, race and the sociology of science and technology" (National Science Foundation, 2019, p. 2). Sociological research also plays a vital role within several research centers and institutes of the NIH that are concerned with social and behavioral issues of health and well-being, such as the National Institute of Mental Health (NIMH), National Institute on Minority Health and Health Disparities (NIMHD), National Institute on Drug Abuse (NIDA), and the National Institute on Aging (NIA). The Centers for Disease Control and Prevention regularly researches issues involving teen drug use, teen violence, and teen suicide. Sociology is relevant for providing a sociological analysis of these and other related issues.

Another arena for significant application of sociological knowledge is international or global development. There exist a large number of international organizations—the United Nations, United Nations Development Program (UNDP), United Nations Children Fund (UNICEF), International Labor Organization (ILO), World Health Organization (WHO), United Nation Office for Drugs and Crime (UNIDO), United Nations Educational and Cultural Organization (UNESCO), International Organization for Migration (IMO), and the World Bank—that play a crucial role in social change and modernization in developing countries. These organizations conduct research and policy analysis on several sociological issues related to development, including women's empowerment, urban sprawl, management of megacities, child labor, democratization, political participation, growth of the middle class, women's rights, crime and justice, human trafficking, cybercrime, terrorism, migration, and internet child pornography. By training, sociologists are superbly competent to work in these areas, and they do work in several international organizations.

Sociology and Other Social Sciences

The birth of modern scientific methods in the 17th century, the advent of modernity, and the Age of Enlightenment in the 18th century led to the birth of social science in the 19th century. The whole of the 19th century was a time of explosion of scientific knowledge, and not just in physics, chemistry, medicine, and biology. It was also a time of many remarkable discoveries in social science, especially in the fields of economics, political science, sociology, anthropology, and psychology. These basic and specialized fields of social science deal with the same phenomena of human society and human behavior, and they apply the same canons of the scientific method; however, they study different aspects of human behavior and various facets of society with different perspectives and through different lenses.

For a student of sociology, understanding the similarities and differences between and among the various branches of social science is vital. In global social science, economics, political science, sociology, and psychology are prominent. There is scarcely any major university in North America and Europe, and the world as a whole, where these basic branches of social science are not academically established and are not taught and learned. The understanding of the perspectives of these social sciences is now of more significance because of the rise of a new generation of applied and professional fields of social science, including business management, data analytics, public administration, public policy, international studies, global studies, women's studies, criminology, criminal justice, and counseling.

Sociology and Economics

Since the days of the beginning of organized human life in ancient times, production, consumption, and distribution of material goods and services have remained at the core of work and organization in human societies. These economic functions are essential for meeting the basic needs of humans. Until the advent of the capitalist system of economy in the 18th century, and more precisely, until Adam Smith, a Scottish philosopher, wrote a treatise titled *An Inquiry into the Nature and Causes of the Wealth of Nations* (1776), there was no significant scientific clue about the nature of humans' economic behavior. Publication of *The Wealth of Nations* signified the birth of the modern science of economics. Smith's (1776, 2018) discovery of the theory of "rational economic man" and a "rational economic market" driven by "invisible hands" provide the foundation for the science of economics.

The idea of rational economic man suggests that human behavior, primarily economic behavior, is driven by rational calculation of economic cost and benefit and financial profit and loss. The sense of this algorithm, the relations between cost and benefit, the economists argue, is innate and intrinsic to human nature. It is socially and culturally invariant, particularly within the modern capitalist system. A rational economic man in America, the economists would say, will behave the same way as a rational economic man in China, India, or Kenya. The rational pursuit of economic behavior is universal.

At the core of the concept of rational economic man is the notion that a rational individual is competent and free to conduct their own economic behavior based on their own volition. A rational economic man, the economists also contend, is not merely a selfish and self-seeking individual. A rational economic man, as Adam Smith argued, even has an "impartial spectator" in their inner mind to reason about the need for "common good." From this notion of a rational economic man free to conduct their own economic behavior, the economists came to the collective idea of an "economic market." The space of human economic behavior that is defined as an economic market, Adam Smith theorized, is fully capable of running on its own. It is governed by an "invisible hand"—the natural forces governing rational human calculation between cost and benefit. The market should not be controlled and dominated by external forces, particularly by centralized planning and centralized government.

During the past 245 years, a considerable body of economic theories, models, and concepts has emerged based on the assumption of the rational economic man discovered by Adam Smith. Modern economists theorize, based on modeling and mathematization, on how different facets of the economic behavior of individuals and different conditions of the economic market (e.g., demand, supply, pricing, investment, money supply, taxation, interest rate, inflation, and recessions) are shaped and formed.

The basic assumption of a rational economic man has remained central to the science of economics. Still, many economists have different views on the self-regulating nature of the market and its role in advancing the common good or general economic welfare. The Keynesian school of economic thought, named after the British economist John Maynard Keynes, is based on a theory that an economic market left alone to be controlled by humans' "invisible hands" may generate an economic crisis. The Great Depression of the 1930s that brought a huge economic collapse in the West's economic system, many economists believe, proved that the free-market economy's classical theory has some severe limitations. The microeconomic behavior of "rational economic man" does not clearly predict the macroeconomic behavior of the free market. The modern science of economics is guided by two leading schools of thought—the classical school of a free-market economy, described as supply-side economics, and the Keynesian school of the need for governmental control and regulations of the market, described as demand-side economics.

For sociologists, the assumptions of rational economic man and rational financial market are hugely problematic. The rational calculation of cost and benefit, for sociologists, is probably an essential aspect of human nature, but it is not socially and culturally invariant. The sociologists assume that human social behavior, including human economic behavior, is socially contingent based on such factors as gender, age, race, class, status, power, and culture. Economic sociology is one of the essential branches of sociology that goes back to Karl Marx and Max Weber's writings in the 19th century. Weber theorized that economic evolution is primarily a sociological process influenced by class relations. The notion of class struggle between the capitalists (bourgeoisie) and the working class (proletariat) is central to the Marxian analysis of the modern capitalist system's structure and dynamics. Weber theorized that a rational capitalist system evolved in the West because of the rise of Calvinist theology. The Calvinist doctrine of Protestantism, Weber argued, theologically justified human engagement for "this-worldly" material advancements. By studying different other great religions, including Hinduism, Judaism, and Islam, he argued that those religions did not evolve an inner sense of theological justifications for their believers for this-worldly material advancements. The rational economic pursuit, for Weber, therefore, is socially contingent.

After the Great Depression of the 1930s, American sociologist Karl Polanyi, one of the great proponents of economic sociology, contended that the collapse of liberal capitalism came at that time because of a dangerous decoupling between the economy and society. The school of institutional economics that has grown within economics after the Great Depression of the 1930s is also based on the theory that economic phenomena are socially and culturally contingent. For example, data show that all economically rational humans of the world do not have the same habits of savings (Jahn, October, 24, 2020). Another study has shown that the savings rate, which is a percentage of savings in terms of income, is 51% in China, 28% in India, 28% in Vietnam, and 32% in Switzerland. The economic behavior of savings is a socially and culturally variable phenomenon (Money, 2012, p. 2). Many recent studies have also shown that the trust social factor is positively connected to economic trade and commerce between different world countries and cultures. "When individuals are more trusting, transaction costs and monitoring costs are lower, and property rights are more secure ... greater levels of trust are consistent with greater economic growth and development ... [and] low levels of trust lead to smaller trading networks between individuals due to high transactions and monitoring costs" (Williamson & Mathers, 2009, p. 4).

Until the 1990s, economists measured the economic development of a country in terms of its annual production of goods and services (GNP). In the 1990s, a new generation of economists coined a new concept titled Human Development Index (HGI) to measure economic development. The HDI is an index that measures the economic development of a country in terms of three indices: health, education, and the standard of living. Recently, a group of economists at Oxford University introduced the Multidimensional Poverty Index (MPI) concept as an extension of the HDI to measure global poverty (Alkire et al., 2015). The MPI estimates poverty not just in terms of jobs and employment but also as deprivations in education, health, and standard of living. In terms of the MPI concept, out of the world's 7.7 billion people, 1.3 billion have multiple dimensions of poverty in education, health, and standard of living. For sociologists, human economic behavior, human economic market, and human economic growth and development are socially and culturally contingent phenomena. They are not socially and culturally neutral and invariant. In 2019, three economists at MIT and Harvard University—Abhijit Banerjee, Esther Duflo, and Michael Kremer—received the noble prize in economics for their discovery, based on many social experiments, showing that poverty reduction in developing countries is essentially a sociological process that needs positive interventions in the areas of school education and preventive health care. The whole field of development economics today is deeply intertwined with sociology.

Sociology and Political Science

Political science is a science of human power, politics, and polity. Political power has always been the central dynamic force for the organization of human societies. Anthropologists have documented that even in the most primitive societies thousands of years ago, political power was critical for social order and organizations. Even today, in many tribal societies of Africa, Oceania, and Asia, power is centralized and legitimized by tribal kings. The ideal nature of power and the relations between those who govern and those who are governed have been the central philosophical issues since the birth of Greek philosophy in the fifth century B.C.E. Plato and Aristotle were the first to philosophize about the nature of "good government" and "good polity." Plato surmised that a good polity ought to be governed by those who are knowledgeable about human nature, ethics, justice, and morality—the king-philosophers. Aristotle surmised that a good polity should be governed neither by the wealthiest elites nor someone from the lowest rungs of society; a good polity is a polity of the middle class. Aristotle was the first to discover the significance of scientific research in matters of politics and polity.

The roots of modern political science go back to the political philosophies of Plato and Aristotle, but as an organized science of power and policy, it was, much as sociology, also the child of the Enlightenment of the 18th century. A series of political thoughts and ideas about the nature of political power, the birth of the state, the notion of the separation of power, the nature of law, the issues of religious tolerance, and the ideal relations between the ruler and the ruled were developed by the philosophers of the Age of Enlightenment in the 18th and 19th centuries. The most prominent were Thomas Hobbes, John Locke, Jean Jacques Rousseau, Baron de Montesquieu, and Edmund Burke. In the 20th century, modern political science was built on the backs of many of the great political philosophies from the Age of Enlightenment. With the advent of modernity in the 19th century, one of the central issues in political science has been understanding the nature of democracy and its evolution in different societies of the world. There is, however, a basic difference between political philosophies and modern political science. The political philosophies are the ideal descriptions of the nature of power and the state. Modern political science, on the other hand, is a science of theorizing based on empirical research on how power is actually created, allocated, distributed, and legitimated within the structure of the modern state.

Aristotle's dictum that humans are political animals is at the center of theorizing in modern political science. The economists theorize about how rational economic individuals organize and behave within the space of the "economic market." The political scientists theorize about how rational political individuals organize and behave within the space of the "state." Political scientists assume that power is the central organizing force in human behavior. Political power, as defined by Robert Dhal, one of the great figures in modern political science, is one's ability to get things done in spite of the will of others not to do so. The phenomenon of political power, Dhal argued, is always predicated on the assumption that it indicates a relationship between two people or two groups of people and is backed by the force of law and the instruments of control and coercion.

Political scientist David Easton (1965) defined that a state is a social system designed, organized, and controlled by the dynamics of political power. Traditionally, political scientists try to understand the nature of the power within the structure of the state as a socially and culturally invariant act of the "political animals." A great body of political science knowledge, therefore, is about the constitutions of the state, the issues of the separation of power, the organization of political parties, the role of political ideologies, and the nature of electoral systems and processes. Political science also explores the nature of different political systems and regimes such as monarchies, democracy, dictatorships, and authoritarianism.

One of the key differences between political science and sociology is that sociology looks at the phenomenon of power, and not as an innate and an invariant part of the nature of human political animals. Sociology has discovered that power is a socially and culturally contingent phenomenon. The nature and the legitimacy of political power not only varies across societies and cultures but also varies across different genders, races, religions, and other groups within a society.

Based on this assumption of the social basis of power and the nature of the state, there has emerged a separate field of political sociology whose roots go back to the writings of many classical sociologists in the 19th century. Max Weber was probably the first sociologist to theorize that it is not the economy but political power that is at the core of the organization of modern society. The legitimacy of power and authority are socially contingent phenomena. In modern societies, in contrast with traditional societies, Weber said, power is legitimated based not on charisma but democracy.

There is a considerable body of research and discoveries in sociology on the social basis of power, democracy, and authoritarianism, such as American sociologist Seymour Martin Lipset's *Political Man: The Social Basis of Power* (1960), Barrington Moore's *The Social Origins of Democracy and Dictatorship: Lord and Peasant in the Making of the Modern World* (1966), and Theda Skocpol's *States and Social Revolutions: A Comparative Study of France, Russia, and China* (1976). The sociological turn in understanding the nature of power, state, and democracy is a significant theoretical trend in contemporary political science. This trend came particularly in the context of the rise of comparative politics and comparative modernization in developing societies. During the 1960s and 1970s, when political scientists began to explore the problem of democracy and modernization of the state in developing countries, they began to theorize about the social basis of power and democracy in a more sociological way (Apter, 1965, 1987; Ward & Rustow, 1964).

Sociology and Psychology

Psychology is a science of the mind. A human brain, which weighs about 3 pounds and is less than 3% of a human body, is a physical and an observable entity. The mind, however, is invisible. From the days of the history of discourses on modern medicine among the Greek philosophers about 2,400 years ago, the birth and the constitution of the mind remained a great scientific puzzle.

Hippocrates, the Greek philosopher and the father of modern medicine, said the human brain is an organ of the human body, and it is the center of the birth of the human mind and consciousness (Adler, 2004). In his *Philosophy of Mind*, Aristotle philosophized that a human soul is intimately connected to the human body and the human brain. The human soul, Aristotle argued, is a separate organ of the human body. The soul is the center of human consciousness, intelligence, perception, motivations, and moral virtues. The human soul, for Aristotle, had different parts and regions that performed different functions. The part of the human soul at the center of human reasoning and rationality, Aristotle defined, is the human mind. Aristotle again divided the human mind into two categories, passive and active. The active or the conscious mind, for Aristotle, was the core of human reasoning, and the passive mind was the storehouse of human sensations and speculations. In understanding the science of the mind, one of the core contributions of the Greek philosophers was that they separated the mind from the role of God and Scriptures. One can, therefore, argue that the concept of mind became the subject of naturalist inquiry from the ancient days of the birth of modern medicine by Hippocrates in the fourth century B.C.E.

About 1,800 years after Aristotle, a French philosopher and the father of the modern scientific method, Rene Descartes, brought the problem of the mind within the boundary of modern scientific discourses. Descartes argued that even though the mind is not an observable physical entity, it is different from the human brain. With the birth of modern science in the 17th century, modern medicine and biology became more specialized concerning the human body. Modern psychology began to emerge at that time to specialize mainly in the understanding of the mind. Psychology is based on the assumption that the mind is a separate and autonomous entity in the human brain and body. The crux of the quest in the science of modern psychology is discovering how the mind grows, evolves, matures, and decays. Modern psychologists are engaged in the search for discoveries involving the structures and functions of the mind. They theorize on how the human self grows, how human reason and intelligence evolve, how human emotions are shaped, and how human personalities are formed. They study the roots of human motivations, feelings, perceptions, and prejudice. One of the significant scientific quests in psychology is about the roots of depression, anxiety, fear, isolation, and aggression and how they birth violence, and antisocial behavior.

Modern psychology, as all other branches of science, has different theoretical schools of thought or perspectives. At the beginning of the 19th century, the dominant view developed by German physiologist and physician Wilhelm Wundt was that psychologists needed to theorize—through introspection and experiments—about the birth of human consciousness. In the late 19th and early 20th century, modern psychology entered a new discourse pioneered by Sigmund Freud. Freud, through a series of theoretical discoveries, established a paradigm that the core of the quest of psychology is the understanding of the nature of the unconscious region of the mind. He theorized that the mind has three different regions, or structures—id, ego, and superego. The region of the mind controlled by the id is the unconscious part of the mind. The id is the store and the driver of human inborn passions and instincts. The id is socially blind, and it seeks to pursue a human's "pleasure principle." Based on Freud's discovery of the nature of the mind, modern psychology created the perspective of psychoanalysis, now dominant in the medical field of psychiatry.

From the middle of the 20th century, psychology began to be dominated by a new perspective described as "behaviorism." The perspective of behaviorism, developed primarily by James B. Watson and B. F. Skinner, is based on the assumption that the conscious and unconscious regions of the mind are beyond scientific analysis because they are not observable. The proponents of behaviorism argue that only humans' external behaviors are real and observable. They say the science of psychology should theorize on how external human behavior is shaped, formed, and expressed. The behaviorist school theorizes that human behavior is governed by an algorithm of reward and punishment. This algorithm is an essential part of human nature and is socially and culturally invariant. Humans will continue doing the behaviors that are rewarded, and humans will continue to refrain from actions that are punished. This notion of behaviorism is at the core of the rational choice theory widely used in social science and policymaking, particularly in criminal justice.

In the later part of the 20th century, psychology saw the birth of two more prominent perspectives—cognitive psychology and humanistic psychology. Cognitive psychology theorizes about the evolution of intelligence, and one of the prominent cognitive psychologists is Jean Piaget. Piaget theorized that human intelligence evolves from a lower to a higher understanding through some fixed and socially and culturally invariant stages. He pioneered the growth of what is known as developmental psychology. The proponents of humanistic psychology, on the other hand, are critical of both Freudian psychoanalysis and behavioral psychology. Humanistic psychology's key assumption is that human behavior is driven by the human's inner passions for growth, development, and self-actualization. Human behavior cannot be broken into pieces to search for meanings and expressions. Human behavior, the humanistic psychologists argue, should be seen holistically. This gave birth to the idea of "gestalt psychology." Abraham Maslow, one of the pioneers of humanistic psychology, developed a theory of the hierarchy of human needs in the 1940s. It is still a significant perspective in explaining human behavior and human motivations in organizational settings. In his theory of the hierarchy of human needs, Maslow theorized that humans will always try for self-actualization—to achieve more power, control, and status. But to reach the self-actualization stage, a lower level of basic human needs must be satisfied.

The scientific field of psychology is rich with several theoretical schools and a considerable body of concepts and experiments. The relationship between sociology and psychology, however, is complex and multifaceted. The perspectives of behaviorism and cognitive psychology seek to understand the mind and human behavior in terms of some socially and culturally invariant principles and algorithms. They seek to theorize that the mind, as an autonomous region in the brain, has its own socially invariant laws, patterns, and principles. On the other hand, sociologists theorize that the growth and nature of the mind are socially and culturally contingent. The social basis of the mind is created and mediated by the brain.

Recent brain and neurological research have established that the mind is created by the brain, and the mind and brain are interconnected. A human brain is composed of billions of neurons, which communicate with one another and release chemicals known as neurotransmitters. These neuron communications create trillions of synapses or connections, which, in turn, create the structure of the mind. Different functions of the mind, such as intelligence or the control of emotion, are located in different structures of the brain. Recent neurosurgical research has shown that if a certain part of the brain is damaged, the properties of the mind in that part of the brain are lost. If the damaged part of the brain is repaired, research shows, the same properties of the mind are restored. The neurologists so conclude that "it is the brain that generates perception, cognition, and memory, and it is the brain that houses the specialized circuitry that allows us to make a cup of coffee, catch a ball, or write a note to a friend" (Finger, 2000, p. 2). Recent research from behavioral neurology also shows that the social roots of the mind are mediated by the brain and its role in the evolution of consciousness. The evolution of human consciousness is essentially a sociological phenomenon mediated by trillions of synapses inside the brain, brain chemicals, and different structures and regions of the brain.

In the science of psychology, Freud was the first to theorize about the social roots of the mind. Freud's concept of superego signifies the presence of society, culture, and morality in the human mind. Human society, according to Freud, is not possible with human minds not controlled by the superego. Freud argued that the superego is the foundation of culture and civilization. The social repression of human instincts is a necessary condition for building a social order. Freud theorized that humans in society are continuously depressed and unhappy. Modern psychoanalysis is based on these Freudian assumptions of inherent conflict in the human mind between the id and superego.

The science of understanding the relationships between the brain and the mind, the brain and society, and the mind and society is still evolving. Different social sciences—economics, political science, psychology, and sociology—study the same phenomenon of human behavior, and they apply the same canons of scientific methodology. These branches of social sciences, however, are like competing knowledge tribes (Table 3.9). They have different assumptions on the guiding principles that govern human behavior, and they have their trajectories of interests in scientific inquiry. This division of labor is intrinsic to the progress of modern science and the evolution of different scientific specializations. It is not the weakness of social science that it is compartmentalized into competing specialties. Natural and biological sciences are equally compartmentalized. Human social behavior, however, is affected by a series of crosscutting factors and forces, some of which are economic, some political, some psychological, and some explicitly sociological. Humans do not behave through the lenses of economics alone, or power alone, or psychology alone.

It is these different branches of social science that have different lenses to make sense of human behavior and the social world. In various domains of science—natural, biological, psychological, and social—there is, therefore, a genuine quest for holistic and synthetic approaches. This quest for interdisciplinary knowledge is pursued not just within a scientific domain but also across scientific domains such as physics and biology, biology and chemistry, biology and computer, neurology and sociology, and psychology and genetics. In social science, the quest for holistic and synthetic knowledge is more compelling because of the chaotic complexity and dynamics of the human social world. Thus, in recent years, a new generation of social science professions (e.g., business, education, social work, criminal justice, counseling, journalism, global studies, and public policy) have evolved for a more holistic and synthetic quest for social science knowledge and a better understanding of human society and human social behavior.

TABLE 3.9 Social Sciences: A Comparison

Social Sciences	Core Assumptions	Scope of the Study	Key Figures
Economics	Humans are rational economic beings. Cost-benefit considerations drive human behavior. The economic market is self-governing, does not need to be intervened.	Demand and supply Money supply Capital movement Taxation Pricing mechanism Employment Market behavior Inflation	Adam Smith John Keynes Thomas Malthus Alfred Marshal Milton Friedman Paul Samuelson Joseph Stigler Amartya Sen
Political science	Humans are political beings. Humans are power-seeking individuals. Power is the central driving force behind human behavior.	State and government Constitution Legislatures Types of government Political parties and ideologies International politics Voting behavior	Plato Aristotle Thomas Hobbes John Locke J. J. Rousseau Gabriel Almond Robert Dhal Karl Deutsch
Psychology	The mind is an autonomous entity. The mind has an understandable structure. Psychology is the study of human consciousness. The unconscious part of the mind drives human behavior. Reward and punishment control human behavior.	Evolution of the mind Birth of the "self" Evolution of intelligence Personality Motivation/perception Emotion and attachment Anxiety disorder and PTSD Psychopathic disorder Depression and bipolar disorder	Wilhelm Wundt G. Stanley Hall William James John Dewey E. Thorndike Sigmund Freud John B. Watson B. F. Skinner

Sociology	Humans are social beings. The brain mediates sociality. Sociology is a science of "social." Explain a social fact by another social fact.	Family, marriage, and intimacy Economy and work Politics Religion Culture and society Social inequality Crime and deviance Social movements Social change	Auguste Comte Karl Marx Max Weber Emile Durkheim Talcott Parsons Robert Merton Peter Berger Erving Goffman H. Garfinkle A. Giddens James Coleman

Suggested Questions, Assignments, Essays, and Quizzes

1. Sociology emerged in the mid-19th century as a science of society in a massive historical change and transformation from the medieval worldview to the modern worldview. Based on your reading of this chapter and related class lectures, write an essay (two or three single-spaced pages, 12-point font) describing how the modern worldview is different from that of the medieval worldview (as a part of your paper, reproduce the related table presented in this chapter).

2. Sociology was born in the middle of the 19th century with two missions: (1) to develop a general science of society and (2) to examine the effects and the directionality of modernity. Based on your reading this chapter and related class lectures, write an essay (two or three single-spaced pages, 12 point-font) explaining this statement. What does it mean to say that sociology is primarily a universal science?

3. What are the critical domains of scientific studies? Where does sociology fit in the family of sciences? What are the different science-based professions that borrow knowledge and ideas from social sciences? Explain in this context the relevance of sociological knowledge for law, criminal justice, and public policy (two or three single-spaced pages, 12-point font), and at the end of your essay, reproduce the relevant table presented in this chapter.

4. "The idea of society is easy to understand but hard to describe, or easily describable but hard to understand." In the context of this statement, write an essay (two or three single-spaced pages, 12-point font) describing the four ways that sociologists define a society. What does it mean to say that a society is not merely a territorial boundary but also a moral and symbolic boundary as well (at the end of your essay, reproduce the related table presented in this chapter)?

5. "Humans have an insatiable thirst for belonging to groups and to define other humans in terms of their visible and invisible group characteristics." In this statement's context, name the groups you belong to as a part of your social life and living. Explain how you are seen and perceived by others at different times regarding your various group affiliations (two or three single-spaced pages, 12-point font). You can pick one or two forms of your group affiliations and expand on them (e.g., gender or race).

6. Humans belong to multiple groups, but sociologists define two significant group identities: primary and secondary groups. Based on your reading of this chapter and related class lectures, write an essay (two or three single-spaced pages, 12-point font) explaining how primary groups are different from secondary groups, particularly in terms of relationship dimension and power, and solidarity dimension. Provide examples, and at the end of your essay, reproduce the related table presented in this chapter.

7. What does it mean to say that sociology is a science of the "social"? Discuss in this context the four facets of sociology as a "form of consciousness" as described by Peter L. Berger, focusing mainly on the "unrespectability motif" of sociology as a science (two or three single-spaced pages, 12-point font, and reproduce the related table presented in this chapter).

8. Sociology as a science is significant both for its enlightenment and instrumental roles. Assume that you will explain this to a relative who is curious about taking sociology, either as a major or as a general education elective. Make five arguments or statements to convince your relative or to justify to them that sociology can be of great significance to your college career and your future professions (two or three single-spaced pages, 12 font-point).

9. Social phenomena are qualitatively very different from natural facts and forces, and they widely vary across time and space. The digital tribe does not think in the same way about many social issues as did the baby boom generation of the 1950s and 1960s. The historical and comparative method is widely used in sociological research. Sociologist C. Wright Mills coined the term "sociological imagination" to make sense of the external and more extensive social facts and events that shape the way we are in each generation. Based on your reading of this chapter and related class lectures, write an essay (two or three single-spaced pages, 12-point font) explaining the concept of sociological imagination and describing some of the broader and larger forces of social change and challenges faced by the digital tribe in the 21st century.

10. Sociology is one of the social sciences, including economics, political sciences, and psychology. What are the critical assumptions of economics, political science, and psychology, and how are they different from sociology? What does it mean to say that sociologists believe that economic, political, and psychological factors of life are socially and culturally relative and variant? Give examples, and at the end of the essay (two or three single-spaced pages, 12-point font), reproduce the related table presented in this chapter.

References

Adler, R. E. (2004). *Medical Firsts: From Hippocrates to the Human Genome*. Wiley.

Alkire, S., Foster, J. E., Seth, S., Santos, M. E., Roche, J. M., & Ballon, P. (2015). *Multidimensional poverty measurement and analysis*. Oxford University Press.

Anderson, J. (2014). The impact of family structure on the health of children: Effects of divorce. *The Linacre Quarterly, 81*(4), 378–387. Retrieved from https://doi.org/10.1179/0024363914Z.00000000087 on December 20, 2020.

Apter, D. E. (1965). *The politics of modernization*. University of Chicago Press.

Apter, D. E. (1987). *Rethinking development: Modernization, dependency, and post-modern politics*. Sage Publications.

Bellah, R. N. (1985). *Tokugawa religion: Cultural roots of modern Japan*. Free Press.

Berger, P. L. (1963). *Invitation to sociology: A Humanistic perspective*. Anchor Books.

Centers for Disease Control and Prevention. (2010). *National intimate partner and sexual violence survey*. Retrieved from https://www.cdc.gov/violenceprevention/pdf/nisvs_report2010-a.pdf on December 20, 2020.

Collett, T. (2016). *A core curriculum for sociology in UK undergraduate medical education*. University of Plymouth.

Easton, D. (1953). *The political system. An inquiry into the state of political science*. Knopf.

Finger, S. (2000). *Minds behind the brain: A history of the pioneers and other discoveries*. Oxford University Press.

Geertz, C. (1971). *Islam Observed: Morocco and Indonesia*. University of Chicago Press.

Jahn, M. (October 24, 2020). *10 Countries with Highest Savings rate: Why Some Countries Save More than Others*. Retrieved from https://www.investopedia.com/articles/personal-finance/022415/top-10-countries-save-most.asp on December 20, 2020.

Kuhn, T. S. (2012). *The Structure of Scientific Revolutions*. Chicago: University of Chicago Press.

Kyung-Sook, W., SangSoo, S., Sangjin, S., & Young-Jeon, S. (2018). Marital status integration and suicide: A meta-analysis and meta-regression. *Social Science and Medicine*, 197, pp. 116–126.

Larson, O. F., & Zimmerman, J. N. (2003). *Sociology in government: Galpin-Taylor years in the U.S. Department of Agriculture*. Pennsylvania State University Press.

Lipset, S. M. (1965). *The political man: The social basis of politics*. Johns Hopkins University Press.

Mani, A., Mullainathan, S., Shafir, E., & Zhao, J. (2013). Poverty impedes cognitive function. *Science, 341*(6149), 976–980.

Maslow, H. A. (2018). *Hierarchy of needs: A theory of human motivation*. Wilder Publishers. (Original work published 1943)

Mills, C. W. (2000). *The sociological imagination*. Oxford University Press. (Original work published 1959)

Money, J. (2012, March). *US savings rate vs. the world*. Budgets Are Sexy. Retrieved from https://www.budgetsaresexy.com/united-states-savings-rates-vs-world/ on December 2020.

Moore, B. (1966). *Social origins of democracy and dictatorship: Lord and peasant in the making of the modern world*. Beacon Press. (Reprinted 1993).

National Science Foundation. (2018). Sociology Program: Doctoral Dissertation Research Improvement Award. Retrieved from https://www.nsf.gov/pubs/2018/nsf18577/nsf18577.htm?org=NSF on December 20, 2020.

Noble, K. G., Houston, S. M. Kan, E., & Sowell, E. R. (2012). Neural correlates of socioeconomic status in the developing human brain. *Developmental Science, 15*(4), pp. 516–527.

Ostrander, M. (2015, June). What poverty does to the young brain. *The New Yorker*. Retrieved from https://www.newyorker.com/tech/annals-of-technology/what-poverty-does-to-the-young-brain on December 2020.

Parsons, T. (1966). *Societies: Evolutionary and comparative perspectives* (A. Inkeles, Ed.). Prentice-Hall.

Seegert, L. (2017, August). *Research details how racial disparities, stress, and poverty can affect Alzheimer's risk*. Association of Health Care Journalists. Retrieved from https://healthjournalism.org/blog/2017/08/research-details-how-racial-disparities-stress-and-poverty-can-affect-alzheimers-risk/ on December 20, 2020.

Shah, A. K., Mullainathan, S., & Shafir, E. (2012). Some consequences of having too little. *Science, 338*(6107), 682–685.

Skocpol, T. (1979). *States and social revolutions. A comparative analysis of France, Russia, and China*. Cambridge University Press.

Smith, A. (1776, 2018). *An Inquiry into the Nature and Causes of the Wealth of Nations*. Create Space Independent Publishing Platform.

Tilly, C. (1984). *Big structures, large processes, huge comparison* (reprinted 2006). Russell Sage Foundation Publications.

Wallerstein, I. (1979). *The capitalist world economy*. Cambridge University Press.

Ward, R. E., & Rustow, D. A. (1964). *Political modernization in Japan and Turkey*. Princeton University Press.

Williamson, C. R., & Mathers, R. L. (2009). *Economic freedom, culture, and growth* (Working paper). George Mason University.

U.S. Census Bureau. (2018). *U.S. Census Bureau releases 2018 families and living arrangements tables*. Retrieved from https://www.census.gov/newsroom/press-releases/2018/families.html on December 20, 2020.

U.S. Department of Labor. (2018). *Occupational outlook handbook, sociologists*. Bureau of Labor Statistics, U.S. Department of Labor.

Figure Credits

CHAPTER 4

Socialization and the Birth of the 'Social'

Theories and Research

CHAPTER THEME

One of the puzzles that sociologists have been trying to grapple with since the beginning of sociology in the 19th century is how we humans become social. Society is not just "out there." Society is also inside our mind and consciousness. But how is society internalized in the minds and consciousness of individuals? Sociologists define this process of internalization of the social as "socialization." Since classical times, sociologists have theorized that socialization is primarily a matter of the social—it is mediated by family, parenting, schools, communities, culture, work, law, religion, and morality. Modern scientific research in genetics, neuroscience, and evolutionary psychology has made many significant contributions to our understanding of socialization. This chapter's theme is that human sociality needs to be understood in the context of the evolution of human nature, its heritable traits and attributes, the socially mediated heritable characteristics within the mind and consciousness, and the social context of family and parenting. Humans, in their struggle for survival and natural selection, have genetically acquired traits and attributes that are prosocial and antisocial throughout their evolution over millions of years. Socialization means to control and contain the expression of antisocial characteristics and features. Research on behavioral genetics and social neurological has shown that while there are immutable human genetic traits and attributes, there remains a crucial role of the social—both in mediation on the effect of the genes, and construction of the social mind and social consciousness within the human brain. Therefore, in understanding the idea of socialization, there is needed a more integrated model that can combine and synthesize the knowledge and intricacies of nature and nurture.

Introduction

As a science of the social, one of the critical puzzles sociologists seek to examine is what it means to be social and how we become social. Socialization, the process of becoming social, is one of sociology's core theoretical concerns. Sociological theorizing on socialization has evolved in two directions. First, sociologists theorize that every society represents a realm of a desirable set of human actions and behavior. This desirable set of actions and behavior is collectively created, shared, and justified. Some of these desirable actions are also legally mandated and enforced in all societies, such as the fact that every society has a desirable way of expressing love, sex, and emotions.

In most nations of the world, adultery, for example, is not advisable. In many societies, adultery is legally punishable. In Saudi Arabia, the punishment for adultery is the death penalty. In the United States, adultery violates the law, but legal sanctions are rarely imposed. Sexual harassment, for example, is also becoming increasingly undesirable and illegal in many modern societies of the world.

Sociologists theorize that social life is impossible without individuals conforming to a society's boundary of desirable actions and behavior. The boundaries are not made of rocks and bricks but are social actions and behavior that are binding and constraining. The institutions of family and marriage, states and governments, schools and universities, firms and companies, faiths and religion, and our ascribed boundaries of gender, race, age, and ethnicity all create some boundaries within which we are born, grow, live, and die. The desirable actions and behavior, however, are not the same in all societies. For example, cohabitation is still not desirable and acceptable in most cultures of Asia and the Middle East. But the fact that social life is possible only through creating a collectively shared, legitimated, and enforceable boundary of social actions and behavior is universal.

Noted American sociologist Peter L. Berger (1963) metaphorically likened society to a prison. But we humans build the walls of this prison. This social prison was born before we were born, and it will continue to survive even after we are dead. Berger (1963) said, "Society is external to ourselves. It surrounds us, encompasses our life on all sides. We are in society ... society is the walls of our imprisonment in history" (pp. 91–92). In this sense of society as an external and objective reality, socialization is a lifelong process of learning how to remain within the bounds of the social prison. Socialization is a process through which a series of external social actors and institutions, such as parents, family, school, work, church, and law, make us learn to be social. But humans not only learn to be social but are also controlled and coerced to be social.

As Berger (1963) further noted, "Society as objective and external fact confronts us especially in the form of coercion" (p. 91). A considerable amount of sociological research and theorizing is focused on examining the role of these external agents in the process of socialization. Sociologists also explore how different external social predicaments, such as poverty, dysfunctional family, incarcerated family, alcoholic family, broken neighborhoods, gang-infested neighborhoods, and war and violence, affect socialization—learning the desirable rules of playing the social drama.

Sociologists' second approach to socialization is much more fundamental. Here, they ask, how do we become a social being in the first place? How does society begin to enter the body and the mind of an individual and gradually make them a normal social being? How does a human baby—purely a bundle of biology—evolve into a mature social being capable of playing the role of parents, teachers, bosses, judges, and leaders? How does an individual develop a sense of the "self" and form ideas about "I," "me," "we," and "they"? How does an individual develop a sense of self-perception, self-evaluation, self-reflection, and self-pride? How do individuals form different attitudes, grow diverse personalities, and acquire language and intelligence of different kinds? How does a sense of right and wrong, just and unjust, moral and immoral, shame and guilt, and sympathy and empathy evolve? How does a child begin to learn whether they are a male or a female, White or Black, Hispanic or Asian, Christian or Jewish, Hindu or Muslim, or an American or a Canadian? Closely related to these more fundamental issues of socialization is a curiosity in the role of genetics in shaping social actions and behavior. This chapter will examine some of the theories and research related to socialization as a process of internalizing the social.

Genes and the Basis of Human Nature, Actions, and Behavior

Since the beginning of human social life, humans have been curious about the puzzle of defining human nature. The essence of the great religions of Hinduism, Judaism, Buddhism, Christianity, and Islam is that human socialness is the creation of the divine commandments. The Ten Commandments of the Old Testament are probably the oldest sermons for socialization. Different themes of the great religions, such as devotion and deference to authority in Hinduism, Judaism's more profound sense of communitarianism, Christianity's idea for human love and compassion, Buddhism's sermon for Nirvana, and Islam's injunction for absolute submission to the divine authority of God, indicate some of the earliest models for socialization.

With the birth of philosophy in ancient Greece about 2,500 years ago, nature and nurture debate entered an era of skepticism. Some of the ancient philosophers, such as Plato, believed human behavior was driven by some innate natural forces, even though those forces remained mostly unknown and undefined. Another group of ancient philosophers, such as Aristotle, believed human behavior to be primarily social in origin. In the 18th century, many philosophers of the Age of Enlightenment, such as Locke and Rousseau, also believed that human sociability is a social creation. Thus, human behavior's social origin remained the central focus for theorizing in sociology during the 19th and early 20th centuries.

Genetic Science and the Nature and Nurture Debate

From the middle of the 19th century, the nature and nurture debate began to be recast to favor the role of genetics in shaping human social behavior. More systematically, the perspective of genetics in shaping human behavior was first formulated by British scientist Francis Galton. In his books *Hereditary Genius*, published in 1869, and *English Men of Science: Their Nature and Nurture*, published in 1874, Galton theorized that intelligence is primarily hereditary and genetic. Deeply influenced by Charles Darwin's 1859 publication of *On the Origin of Species*, Galton believed the social world to be a world of the survival of the fittest because human intelligence and creativity are primarily innate. With birth of the modern science of genetics in the

1950s, and in the wake of discovering the structure of DNA (Watson, 1968) in shaping the human organism, the debate over the role of nature in human socialization entered a new phase.

During recent decades, enormous research has grown on the theme that human genetic compositions profoundly affect human nature, actions, and behavior. Sociologists have always assumed there are several dimensions of human life. We are a biological being, we are a psychological being, we are a social being, and we are also a cultural being. American sociologist Talcott Parsons defined these dimensions as different systems of human actions. They are distinct but interdependent and interconnected (Parsons & Shills, 2001). Sociology was born with the core assumption that humanness is a social thing. Sociologist Emile Durkheim theorized that social factors and forces are not biological or psychological but social and cultural. In the wake of discovering the modern science of genetics, the role of social factors in socialization has not been tossed from the debate. Still, research began to explore the mediating role of genetics in shaping human social behavior and the part of human social behavior in mediating the inherent genetic properties of humans (Polderman et al., 2015).

The essence of discovering the modern science of genetics is that human genes are the drivers of human nature, actions, and behavior. An average human body is made up of about 30 trillion to 40 trillion cells, and human DNA drives the life and functions of these cells. The Human Genome Project, initiated in the 1990s, estimated there are between 20,000 and 25,000 genes in a human body. These genes not only form our eye and hair color and tell us about our susceptibility to cancer, Alzheimer's, Parkinson's, obesity, hypertension, and other forms of debilitating diseases but are also the carriers of innate information about our behaviors, attitudes, personalities, intelligence, and creativity. The human traits of competitiveness, aggressiveness, domination, subjugation, control, morality, compassion, love, sex, and emotion are also shaped in many complex ways by human DNA. Many geneticists believe that social preference for specific values, beliefs, and ideology is also genetic in origin.

About 100 years before discovering the DNA structure, Darwin, in 1859, published his *On the Origin of Species*. In this book, Darwin (1859/2008) theorized, based on empirical data collected from his 5-year voyage to South America, about the origin of human life. He theorized that a human being was not "independently created, but had descended ... from other species" (p. 5). According to Darwin, humans evolved from lower species through genetic transformation and natural selection. Darwin had a strong intuition that humans became humans because of genetic evolution and natural selection throughout millions of years. Darwin argued that all animal species struggle for existence in the natural world, and this struggle profoundly shaped and formed their innate nature—their genetic structures and compositions.

Human Nature and Evolutionary Psychology

Darwin's theory of evolution, in the wake of the discovery of DNA structure in the 1950s, brought a new perspective on the genetic basis of human nature's growth, described as "evolutionary psychology." The core of this perspective is the idea that most human traits and instincts are genetic. Anger, competitiveness, sex, greed, deceitfulness, selfishness, boastfulness, jealousy, egocentrism, hate, cruelty, wickedness, and many likewise antisocial traits are common to people of all historical times and all cultures and civilizations. The attributes of love, reciprocity, empathy, sympathy, creativity, intelligence, morality, loyalty, kindness, selflessness, politeness, honesty, compassion, justice, desire for freedom, and sociability are also common to people of all recorded times and all cultures and societies.

Evolutionary psychologists, borrowing ideas from Darwin, theorize that these different positive and negative human traits became a part of the human genetic composition as a result of millions of years of human struggle for survival within the "grand natural system" (Darwin, 1859/2008, p. 467) characterized not only by hostile physical environments but also populated by millions of hostile species. To win the struggle for existence, humans had to be aggressive, selfish, cruel, and dominating. Simultaneously, to win the battle for existence, humans had to have love, empathy, and a sense of caring and compassion. This dualism in human nature, evolutionary psychologists argue, has evolved as an integral part of the human genomic structure.

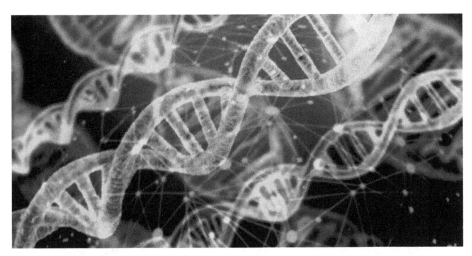

FIGURE 4.1   DNA Genetic Materials

Evolutionary psychologists reject the notion that a human baby is born with a blank slate. In his book *The Blank Slate: The Modern Denial of Human Nature*, Harvard psychologist Steven Pinker (2003) argued that "the dominant theory of human nature in modern intellectual life is based on the doctrines of the blank slate, noble savage, and the ghost in the machine and these doctrines are being challenged by the sciences of the mind, brain, genes, and evolution" (p. 72). The mind, Pinker (1997) argued, is a "system of organ designed by natural selection" (p. 563). Modern cognitive sciences have given us some understanding of the mind, but we may never completely comprehend the mysteries of the brain. Pinker (1997) believes that "our throughgoing perplexity about the enigmas of consciousness, self, will, and knowledge may come from a mismatch between the very nature of these problems and the computational apparatus that natural selection has fitted us with" (p. 565).

Many contemporary behavioral geneticists, behavioral neurologists, and evolutionary psychologists believe the human brain is mostly genetically controlled. Of about 20,000 genes that make up a human body, approximately 6,000 genes control the brain's functioning. The rest of the genes control other organs of the body. "At least a third of the approximately 20,000 different genes that make up the human genome is active (expressed) primarily in the brain. This is the highest proportion of genes expressed in any part of the body. These genes influence the development and functions of the brain, and ultimately control how we move, think, feel, and behave" (National Institute of Neurological Disorders and Stroke, 2010, p. 1). In recent years, a large volume of literature has emerged to examine how human actions and behavior are affected by genes and mediated by the brain.

Genetics and Intelligence

One of the critical areas in the debate between nature and nurture is intelligence (Haier, 2016; Liberman & Long, 2019; Mitchell, 2018; Plomin & Deary, 2015; Plomin, 2018). We are always curious to know why some people are more intelligent than others, why some like mathematics more than music and literature, and why some children are excited to go into the field of medicine. Some feel more attracted to liberal arts and business. Some students who struggle to pass precalculus get the highest grades in sports management or band.

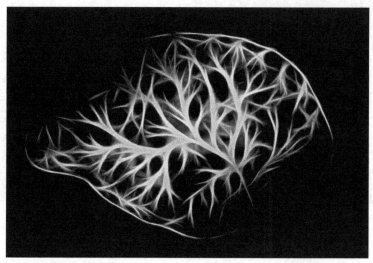

FIGURE 4.2   Brain and Genes

Many recent neuroscientific research studies, based on neuroimaging of brain synapses, circuits, neurons, and networks, observed that intelligence based on genetic traits is mediated by the brain (Haier, 2016). Neurologist Kevin J. Mitchell, in his 2018 book *Innate: How the Wiring of Our Brains Shape the Way We Are*, made a much broader and bolder argument about the genetic basis of intelligence and how the brain mediates it. Mitchell (2018) argues that humans are the product of human DNA: "Simply put, humans have those species-general tendencies and capacities because they have human DNA. If we had chimp DNA or a tiger DNA or aardvark DNA, we would behave like chimps or tigers or aardvarks. Human nature is encoded in our genomes and wired into our brains" (p. 3). Human nature, Mitchell argues, is therefore not a mere philosophical idea. It "is scientifically tractable. We can look, experimentally, at the details of how our species-typical properties are mediated in neural circuitry. And we can seek to uncover the nature of the genetic program that specifies the relevant parameters of these circuits. We are different from each other in large part because of the way our brains get wired before we are born" (Mitchell, 2018, pp. 4–7). Modern MRI data (magnetic resonance imaging) has shown variations among individuals in terms of brain structure and functions. "Collectively, these data show," Mitchell (2018) contended, "that much of the physical variation in brain structure between individuals is attributable to genetic differences. To put more simply, our genes have a big effect—by the far the predominant effect, in fact—on how our brains are wired, very literally" (p. 23).

Most intelligence researchers define that the core of intelligence is "the ability to reason, plan, solve a problem, think abstractly, comprehend complex ideas, learn quickly, and learn from experience" (Plomin, 2018, p. 53). Intelligence has both scientific and social dimensions. Scientifically, "intelligence reflects how the brain works, not as specific modules that light-up in brain-imaging studies, but as brain processes working in concert to solve problems. Socially, intelligence is one of the best predictors of educational achievement and occupational status" (Plomin, 2018, p. 53). British behavioral geneticist Robert Plomin (2018), in his book *Blueprint: How DNA Makes Us Who We are*, made an argument that "inherited DNA differences are the main reason why we are who we are. It is no longer interesting to show that another psychological trait is heritable because all psychological traits are heritable. I do not know of a single psychological trait that does *not* show genetic influence" (p. 6).

In a survey of 5,000 young adults in the United Kingdom, Plomin (2018) observed that reading disability, school achievement, verbal ability, and unique ability are about 60% controlled by DNA. General intelligence (reasoning) is 50% genetic, and personality is 40% genetic. In his research, Plomin observed a huge gap between science and common sense in school achievement. On school achievement, "the average rating in our survey was 29 percent, but genetic research consistently shows that performance on tests of school achievement is 60 percent heritable on average. That is, more than half of the differences between children in how well they do at school is due to inherited DNA differences" (Plomin 2018, p. 10). Plomin (2018), based on his research on the Colorado Adoption Project (CAP) that surveyed children from 250 adopted families, further argued that the "CAP added to the evidence in support of the first law of behavioral genetics, that psychological traits show significant and substantial genetic influence (p. 17). Plomin (2018) observed that during recent decades, genetic research has consistently shown that "genetic differences between people account for about half of the differences in tests of intelligence. This general estimate of 50 percent heritability masks an intriguing finding, which is how heritability changes over the course of our lives" (p. 53).

The geneticists conducting intelligence research have also found that the role of genes in shaping intelligence increases with age, and this trend stays at least up to the age of 70. "The heritability of 50 percent for intelligence is just the lifetime average across all studies. The impressive increase in heritability from 20 percent in infancy to 40 percent in childhood to 60 percent in adulthood stands out from other traits that show little developmental change in heritability, most notably personality and school achievement" (Plomin, 2018, p. 55). The increasing role of genes from childhood to adulthood, according to the behavioral geneticists, is probably because human brains become more complicated with age: "One possible explanation for the increasing heritability of intelligence is that more genes come on line to affect intelligence, perhaps because the brain becomes more complex" (Plomin, 2018, p. 56). Neurologist Kevin Mitchell (2018) similarly observed that twin studies of intelligence have consistently shown that the heritability of intelligence "increases over time. When it is assessed in young children, about 50% of the variance is associated with genetic differences, while the shard family environment also makes a sizeable contribution—30%–40%. However, when assessed in adults, the effect of the shared family environment goes to zero, while the heritability increases to 80% or more" (p. 97).

Genetics and Antisocial Personality Disorder

Genes form, control, and regulate the structures and functions of the brain. The brain forms, controls, and governs the mind. The mind controls and governs our consciousness, thoughts, actions, and behavior (Gazzaniga, 2009, 2015, 2018). The core of socialization is to keep humans within the boundaries of socially desirable and acceptable standards of behavior. But humans cannot be thoroughly socialized. The boundaries of socially desirable actions and behaviors are always fragile and vulnerable. There will always be some people in societies who will cross or break the desirable boundaries of social actions and behavior.

In the literature of sociology and psychology, they are broadly defined as people with antisocial personality disorder, characterized by anger, arrogance, and rebelliousness. Individuals with this disorder display no remorse for cruelty, violence, and destruction and show no respect for right and wrong and justice and morality. They are characterized as being impulsive, deceitful, arrogant, insensitive, and irresponsible. One of the enduring issues in socialization is the understanding of the reasons for antisocial personality disorder, a behavior that geneticists argue is mostly genetic. The characteristics that we define as antisocial are natural in human nature. The behavioral traits that we define as antisocial became a part of human nature through millions of years of human genetic evolution and the human struggle for survival within the "grand natural system" (Darwin, 1859/2008, p. 467).

One of the first systematic scientific efforts to understand the reasons for antisocial personality disorder was made by an Italian physician and anthropologist Cesare Lombroso in the middle of the 19th century. In his book *Criminal Man*, published in 1876, Lombroso theorized that antisocial personality disorder is biological based on the empirical data of dead prisoners. People with this disorder are more likely to have different anatomical structures.

After the discovery of the structure of DNA in the 1950s and 1960s, there has grown a large amount of literature on the genetic roots of antisocial personality disorder based on molecular genetic studies and family, twin, and adoption research (Seo & Patrick, 2008; Reichborn-Kjennerud, 2010; Werner et al., 2015; Ma et al., 2016; Johanson et a., 2019; Lieberman & Long, 2019). Research on neurological sciences and behavioral neurology have shown that different brain regions—including the prefrontal cortex, anterior cingulate cortex, and amygdala—control and regulate our emotional behavior. Imbalance, dysfunctions, and hyperactivity of dopamine hormones and serotonin in these brain regions are positively connected to impulsivity and aggressive behavior (Lieberman & Long, 2019).

In a significant study of the dysfunctional role of the hormones of dopamine and serotonin in producing personality disorder, Seo and Patrick (2008) found that "functional neuroimaging studies have reported associations between hypofunction in the PFC [prefrontal cortex] and aggressive behaviors. A positron emission tomography (PET) study showed that the activity of the orbitofrontal PFC is generally reduced during the expression of aggressive behaviors in healthy individuals" (p. 389). A large volume of literature on genetic and neurological studies on personality disorder, according to Seo and Patrick (2008), "suggests that deficient serotonergic activity in emotion regulation circuitry, such as the prefrontal cortex and the anterior cingulate cortex, may be an important predisposing factor to impulsive aggression. ... Additionally, serotonergic hypofunction may contribute to the hyperactivity of the dopaminergic system, which further promotes impulsive and aggressive behaviors" (p. 395).

Columbia University genetic epidemiologist Reichborn-Kjennerud (2010) conducted a central review of literature on personality disorders' genetic roots. He concluded that "genetic epidemiologic studies indicate all ten personality disorders (PDs) classified on the DSM-IV axis II is modest to moderately heritable. Shared environmental and nonadditive genetic factors are of minor or no importance" (p. 1). He further observed that "molecular genetic studies of PDs ... indicate that genes linked to neurotransmitter pathways, especially in the serotonergic and dopaminergic systems, are involved" (Reichborn-Kjennerud, 2010, p. 1). Johanson et al. (2019) conducted a meta-analysis of 118 neuroimaging studies of psychopathic behavior and found that "psychopathy is linked to biological processes in the brain, and is a highly heritable disorder" (p. 2).

Genetics and Morality

Since the core of socialization is to keep us within the bounds of socially desirable actions and behaviors, the idea of morality—a sense of right and wrong, just and unjust, fair and unfair, and acceptable and unacceptable—and socialization are inseparable. The idea of morality and humanity, indeed, is intimate. Since the beginning of human social life, mainly since the beginning of organized religion about 5,000 years ago and the birth of philosophy about 2,500 years ago, morality has been at the center of debates and discourses on what constitutes a "good" society.

There are two perspectives in the debate and discussions on morality. One view is that morality is primarily a cultural phenomenon. There may be some moral preferences that are universal across cultures and civilizations, but moral codes, thoughts, and ideas are mostly culturally specific. There are no cultures and societies without a set of defined moral laws and injunctions. These moral codes and directives are mostly cultural, such as the codes of Hammurabi and the Chinese codes of Confucianism. They sometimes are also divinely sanctified, such as the Ten Commandments of the Old Testament; the Qur'anic injunctions on rape, incest, theft, and murder; the notion of "karma" in Hinduism; and the idea of "nirvana" in Buddhism. The culturally defined moral codes and injunctions change from time to time with the change of cultures, knowledge, and technology. There are now, for example, worldwide movements against genital mutilation and violence against women, children, and disabled people. There also are now global movements against discrimination against transgender people and people partaking in alternative lifestyles.

The other perspective of morality is about the moral nature of humanity. Are humans intrinsically moral in nature? Is morality an essential part of human life? Is morality innate and genetic? Debates and discourses on the moral character of humanity began with the rise of philosophy in ancient Athens about 2,500 years ago. In the 18th and 19th centuries, Enlightenment intellectuals debated again about the moral nature of humanity in the context of the rise of modern social sciences. Hobbes, Locke, Rousseau, Freud, Marx, Martineau, and Durkheim all reflected and contemplated about human nature and how a good society is possible. Hobbes theorized that humans are inherently evil, and therefore, the birth of a stable state was essential for their socialization. Marx theorized that humans are intrinsically good; it was the birth of class societies that made them worse. After the discovery of the structure of DNA and the resurgence of the Darwinian theory of evolution in the 1950s and 1960s, a genetic interpretation of morality, however, began to become prominent in research and theorizing in behavioral genetics, behavioral neurology, sociobiology, and evolutionary psychology.

Many scholars in these branches of science share the conviction that, like intelligence and the traits of personality disorders, morality is also partly innate and genetic (Wilson, 1975; Ayala, 1987, 2010; Boehm, 2012; Decety & Cowell, 2016; Decety & Wheatley, 2015; Joyce, 2007; Lieberman, 2013; Tomasello, 2016;

Tomasello & Vaish, 2013). A sense of moral judgment is intrinsic to humans. Darwin, in his *Descent of Man, and Selection in Relation to Sex*, published in 1871, wrote: "I fully subscribe to the judgment of those writers who maintain that of all the differences between man and the lower animals, the moral sense or conscience is by far the most important" (p. 67). Darwin believed the evolution of human morality is intimately connected to the evolution of human intelligence. Darwin affirmed that while moral norms are culturally created, human ethical behavior "is biologically determined ... the moral sense is not by itself directly promoted by natural selection, but only indirectly as a necessary consequence of high intellectual powers, which are the attributes that natural selection is directly promoting" (as cited in Ayala, 2010, p. 8).

Darwin also theorized that tribes with a high sense of morality are more likely to be "victorious over most other tribes; and this would be natural selection" (as cited in Ayala, 2010, p. 17). For Darwin, morality was significant for human evolution for two reasons: "First, that morality may contribute to the success of some tribes over others, which is natural selection in the form of group selection. Second, Darwin is asserting a position of moral optimism, namely that the standards of morality will tend to improve over human history precisely on the grounds of group selection" (Ayala, 2010, p. 17). The debate over whether humans are necessarily good or bad, therefore, is misleading. Human traits of aggressiveness, competitiveness, selfishness, cruelty, hate, and violence are genetically a part of human nature. Human traits of morality, reciprocity, gregariousness, empathy, selflessness, and compassion are also genetically a part of human nature. Both these dimensions in human nature have evolved throughout millions of years of human evolution through a process of struggle for survival and natural selection.

Christopher Boehm (2012), an evolutionary anthropologist at the University of Southern California, has been studying primates and the evolution of morality in different cultures for more than 40 years. In his book *Moral Origins: The Evolution of Virtue, Altruism, and Shame*, Boehm contended that conscience began to be a part of human nature probably about 45,000 years ago. He said, "There could be little doubt that humans had a conscience 45,000 years ago, which is the conservative date that all archeologists agree on for our having become culturally modern. Now, if you want to guess at how much before that, the landmark that I see as being the most persuasive is the advent of large game hunting" (as quoted in Gambino, 2012, p. 3). He further argued that when humans began large game hunting, "they had to start punishing alpha males and holding them down. That set up a selection process. Therefore, self-control became an important feature for individuals who were reproductively successful. And self-control translates into conscience" (as quoted in Gambino, 2012, p. 3).

In 2016, renowned evolutionary anthropologist Michael Tomasello published a book titled *A Natural History of Human Morality* (2016). The key argument in the book is that human morality is innate and an essential part of human nature. Hundreds of thousands of years ago, ecological changes, demographic transitions, and the struggles for survival, Tomasello (2016) wrote, "forced early humans to forge together with a partner or else starve. This new form of interdependence meant that early humans now extend their sense of sympathy beyond kin and friends to collaborate partners. To coordinate their collaborative activities cognitively, early humans evolved skills and motivation of joint intentionality" (p. 4). The evolution of joint or shared intentionality is at the core of the development of human morality. "Early humans' sense of mutual respect and fairness with partners thus derived mainly from a new kind of cooperative rationality in which it made sense to recognize one's dependence on a collaborative partner, to the point of relinquishing at least some control of one's actions to the self-regulating 'we' created by a joint commitment" (Tomasello, 2016, p.

5). The core of Tomasello's (2016) argument, therefore, is that because of survival challenges, early humans formed the idea of "we," which led to the birth of human morality and "normatively constituted social order" (p. 5).

A similar argument is made by moral philosopher Richard Joyce (2007) in his book *The Evolution of Morality*. Joyce also observed that morality is one of the inviolable dimensions created in the process of the evolution of human nature. He argued that "natural selection made us sociable, able to enter into cooperative exchanges, capable of love, empathy, and altruism—granting us the capacity to take a direct interest in the welfare of others with no thought of reciprocation—and has designed us to think of our relations with one another in moral terms" (Joyce, 2007, p. 222).

The Biological Basis of Human Nature, Actions, and Behavior

The core of sociology is the discovery that the social—meaning human cultural values, beliefs, and institutions—shape and influence all facets of our humanness, including the social, psychological, and biological. The social facts and forces mold and shape—and not just other social facts and forces, such as politics, economy, marriage, family, divorce, and parenting, but also, in a more fundamental sense, go beneath the skin and shape and mold our body, brain, and mind. The social, cultural, psychological, and biological dimensions of an individual are interconnected and indivisible.

Social discrimination, for example, is mostly universal in human societies. We can think about, as an example, the historical prejudices against the people who are described as "Dalits" or "untouchables" in India. There are about 250 million Dalits in India who are socially discriminated against, disenfranchised, and dislocated because of their peripheral locations within the Indian caste system ingrained in the religion of Hinduism. Because of this phenomenon of social discrimination, the Dalits are not only economically poor and politically marginalized but are also psychologically alienated, disturbed, and distressed. They probably do not even fathom the idea of what it means to have self-pride and self-confidence. The phenomenon of caste discrimination, no doubt, also enters into the body of the Dalits and makes them genetically vulnerable to death and diseases.

This particular framework of exploring the effect of the social and its interconnectedness and integration with psychological and biological dimensions of life has been mainly discovered and developed by Harvard sociologist Talcott Parsons in the 1930s. In his book *The Structure of Social Action*, published in 1937, Parsons theoretically elaborated his notion of an individual's social action as the central locus of sociology and its convergence with their psychological and biological dimensions. Parsons theorized that culture plays a dominant cybernetic role in shaping and molding an individual's social, psychological, and biogenetic action systems. During the 1930s and 1940s, genetic science was in its infancy, and the significant discovery of the genetic structure was yet to be revealed. But sociology since its classical days in the 19th century—more particularly since Parson's discovery of a socially, psychologically, and biologically convergent human action system—has been exploring the notion that culture and biology are deeply interconnected.

Biology and Culture Connections

Biology and culture connections, however, are not alien and unknown to geneticists. Even Darwin thought that human intelligence and morality were crucial for the human struggle for survival and natural selection. Human morality for Darwin was the essential dividing line between humans and animals. Many geneticists, neurobiologists, behavioral neurologists, and evolutionary psychologists believe that millions of years of human struggle for survival progressed not only because of human genetic evolution and genetic mutations but humans also evolved because of their cognitive ability to develop tools, technology, and language. Human cognitive ability gave birth to the organization of tribes, villages, cities, and civilizations.

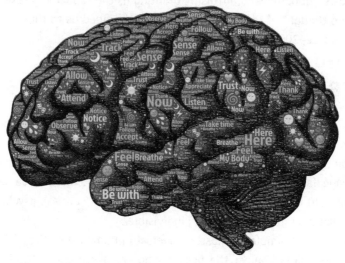

FIGURE 4.3   Brain and Social Consciousness

Humans' cognitive ability made them creative, innovative, and curious. They created the ideas of law, state, government, ethics, philosophy, and science. They developed the institutions of economy, religion, family, and monogamous marriage. Humans discovered not just the internet and social media. They found the idea of writing and a written language and, hence, built the basis of modern civilization. Laland (2017), in his book *Darwin's Unfinished Sympathy: How Culture Made the Human Mind*, contended that it is the culture that tells us "how our ancestors made the journey from apes scavenging a living on ants, tubers, and nuts to modern humans able to compose symphonies, recite poetry, perform ballet, and design particle accelerators" (p. 4).

Human evolution and natural selection, in other words, is not just a process of genetic evolution. It is a process of cultural evolution as well. Recent decades have seen a significant expansion of research on the genetic basis of human behavior (Mitchell, 2018; Plomin, 2018). Those recent decades have also seen the explosion of research on gene-culture connections and the growth of such branches of science as cultural genetics, population genetics, and cultural neurology (Boyd & Richerson, 1985; Durham, 1991; Ehrlich, 2000; Richerson & Boyd, 2005; Gazzaniga, 2009; Laland & Brown, 2011; Narvaez, 2014). Researchers in these other related branches of knowledge "are converging on the view that human evolution has been shaped by gene-culture-connections" (Laland, 2010, p. 1). Their research has revealed that "hundreds of genes have been subject to recent positive selection, often in response to human activities" (Laland, 2010, p. 1). In their *Sense and Nonsense: Evolutionary Perspective on Human Behavior*, Laland and Brown (2011) further observed that "after decades of debate about the relative importance of 'nature' versus 'nurture,' researchers have come to the rather uninspired conclusion that both nature (generally associated with genes) and nurture (typically representing environmental factor, learning, and culture) will obviously be of importance" (p. 11).

Brain-Culture Connections: The Perspective of the 'Social Brain'

The 20,000 to 25,000 genes that control the human body and the mind do not directly connect with the cultural and human behavioral traits. The information stored in the genes is translated into protein molecules by another genetic property called the RNA. This process, termed "genetic expression"—the expression of heritable traits in protein molecules—is again mediated and controlled by the brain. Thus, in understanding the process of socialization, the understanding of brain-culture connections also has a high import.

In recent years, there has been growing within the science of neurology a new perspective described as the "social brain" (Goldberg, 2001; Graziano, 2013; Lieberman, 2013; Dehaene, 2014; Gazzaniga, 2018). A human brain that weighs about a pound is probably one of the most complex and unique creations of nature. A brain is composed of 100 billion nerve cells and 10 trillion connections between and among the nerve cells (synapses). About 5,000 to 6,000 genes control these billions of nerve cells and synapses of the brain. A human brain is also composed of different structures and regions. The critical brain regions include the frontal lobe, parietal lobe, temporal lobe, and occipital lobe. These and other areas of the brain control and perform various functions. One of the core assumptions of the perspective of the social brain is that different parts of the brain and even the structuration of other brain regions are mediated and controlled not just by genetic expressions but also by social and cultural factors and forces.

Brain, Consciousness, and Socialization

A human becomes a human when the individual has a sense of consciousness, or a human mind. Consciousness is the ability of the brain to navigate the lives and activities of an individual socially. It is a knowledge, for example, about time and space—where we live and when we live. It is knowledge about what it means to have a mother or a father or not have a mother or a father. Consciousness is the knowledge about our social locations within the frameworks of gender, race, class, occupation, or a nation. Consciousness is the awareness about our love, sex, emotions, and social boundaries within which the expression of love, sex, and emotions is desirable and acceptable. Consciousness is our ability for self-reflection, self-pride, and self-evaluation.

The proponents of the social brain perspective examine how human consciousness is socially and culturally constructed. Matthew D. Lieberman (2013), a Harvard-trained psychologist, in his *Social: Why Our Brains are Wired to Connect*, made an argument that humans are essentially social animals: "Human sociality can be traced back at least as far as the first mammals more than 250 million years ago. Our sociality is woven into a series of bets that evolution has laid down again and again throughout mammalian history" (p. 9). Lieberman argues that humans' struggle for survival and human adaptive strategies for natural selection made sociality—an inner necessity to connect to other human beings—an essential part of human nature. The human adaptive systems "intensify the bond we feel with those around us and increase our capacity to predict what is going on in the minds of others so that we can better coordinate and cooperate with them. To the extent that we can characterize evolution as designing our modern brains, this is what our brains were wired for: reaching out to and interacting with others" (Lieberman, 2013, p. 9). Human brains, thus Lieberman (2013) argues, are wired to build social connectivity, to develop a sense of mindreading—a capacity for intersubjective communication—and to develop an understanding of harmonizing—meaning that neural ability and "neural adaptations that allow group beliefs and values to influence our own" (p. 12). Lieberman adds that in the process of socialization, either in childhood or in adulthood, the idea of the social brain—meaning humans' innate and insatiable urge to connect to others—can be used to enhance empathy, morality, productivity, leadership, and general well-being.

Michael Graziano (2013), a neuroscientist at Princeton University, in his book *Consciousness and the Social Brain*, defined consciousness as meaning that "something lovely buried inside us is aware of ourselves and our world" (p. 3). Without consciousness, we would have "no basis for curiosity, no realization that there is a world about which to be curious, no impetus to seek insight, whether emotional, artistic, religious, or scientific. Consciousness is the window through which we *understand*" (Graziano, 2013, p. 3). Graziano developed a theory of consciousness that is social. He described it as "attention schema theory." His theory states that consciousness is a social construction. Our consciousness grows as a result of our brain's ability to develop an "attentions scheme," or an attention model based on our existence within an interactive social world. The attention schema theory suggests that in response to social interactions, our brain constructs "a descriptive model of attention. Attention can be applied to a color, a sound, a touch, an emotion, a thought, a movement plan, and many other things external and internal. Attention is not limited to self-attention. It is a general operation that can be applied to almost any type of information" (Graziano, 2013, pp. 125–126). Human consciousness, in other words, is socially grown and constructed. Human consciousness "is a function of groups of people and not really a private matter. It is not a function of a single brain but is an interactive medium, a kind of social web of information within which humans are embedded as we relate to each other" (Graziano, 2013, p. 124).

The Birth of the Social Self: The Sociological Theories of Socialization

What human consciousness is to neurologists is what sociologists define as the birth of the social self. One of the core sociological discoveries is that society is both internal and external to individuals (Durkheim, 1933). We live in society, but society also lives in us. What does it mean to say that society is internal and lives in us? Where is the locus of society inside the human body? How is culture internalized?

Much as the discovery of neuroscience that human consciousness is socially constructed, the sociological discovery is that society is internalized through the development of the social self—through the development of "I" inside the human mind. Sociologists, in fact, describe the birth of human consciousness as the birth of the social self. Some sociologists even define "sociology" as the science of intersubjective understanding of relationships between "I" and "we"—individual and society (Berger & Luckman, 1966; Goffman, 1959). There are several theories and concepts in sociology that explore the mechanisms of the birth of the social self, such as Piaget's theory of the evolution of intelligence, Cooley's view of the "looking-glass self," Mead's theory of role-taking, and Kohlberg's theory of moral development. These theories have much informed many of the issues and complexities related to socialization.

Jean Piaget: Evolution of Intelligence

Morality and intelligence, Darwin said, are the dividing lines between humans and animals. Cognitive ability mainly was the driving force behind humans' struggle for survival and natural selection. Behavioral geneticists discovered that intelligence is about 50% to 60% heritable. The neurologists also found that human intelligence is predominantly genetic, and it is processed in different regions of the brain. Both behavioral geneticists and neurologists define "intelligence" as general cognitive ability. For them, intelligence is not just academic skills or skills for test-taking. Intelligence is the overall cognitive ability to reason, comprehend, synthesize, and learn from experience. This broad cognitive ability, the geneticists believe, is about 20% genetic during childhood. But as we age, the effect of genes on our cognitive ability increases. Therefore, geneticists would suggest that social environments, such as parenting, can play a significant role in shaping intelligence in the early years of a child's life.

Still, the role of parenting begins to be neutralized from the times of adolescence and throughout adulthood. Swiss zoologist-turned-psychologist Jean Piaget developed an evolutionary theory of childhood intelligence in the 1930s—a time long before the explosion of modern genetic and neurological research on intelligence in the 1980s and 1990s (Piaget, 1928, 1952). Based on observation of his children's intelligence development, Piaget theorized that childhood intelligence grows in four stages—sensorimotor development (birth of the self and the "I"), preoperational stage, concrete operational stage, and formal operational stage. Piaget's theory is based on assumptions closely related to those of the genetic and neurological theories of intelligence. Piaget found that a child begins to learn independent of any learning motivations. Learning for a child is natural and independent of any stimuli from adults or older children.

Similar to social neurologists, Piaget assumed that a child's brain begins to learn by developing internal models of representations—interior schemes or attention schemas (Graziano, 2013). A child also improves the cognitive ability for assimilation, adjustment, and harmonization of knowledge and experience. During the sensorimotor stage of cognitive development (birth to 18–24 months), a child learns through object recognition and symbolizations. During the preoperational stage (2–7 years), a child begins to learn a language, begins to be imaginative, learns to express emotions, and develops thinking in symbolic terms. The cognitive ability during the preoperational stage, however, is selfish. Children at this stage are not interested in the world beyond their immediate environment. In the concrete operational stage (7–11 years), children begin to develop logic and reason and the ability for problem-solving. They begin to recognize the generalized others—the world beyond their immediate environment. The formal operational stage (adolescence to adulthood) is one of growing what neurologists call general cognitive ability, including reasoning, comprehending, and developing abstract thinking. Piaget theorized that these four cognitive development stages are universal to all cultures and civilizations and are socially and culturally invariant.

Charles H. Cooley: Social Consciousness and the 'Looking-Glass Self'

Charles H. Cooley is one of the most celebrated American sociologists of the early 20th century. As many classical sociologists, his aim was to grapple with the puzzle of how society is internalized in the mind of an individual. Cooley elaborated his theory of social consciousness in his three works, published before the 1920s: *Human Nature and the Social Order* (1902/2012), *Social Organization* (1909), and *Social Processes* (1918/2013). Cooley theorized, based on observation of his children, that the human mind and human consciousness are social constructions. A human mind is not a mere biophysical or biogenetic entity. For an individual, to be human means to be conscious of their society. Individuals and society are inseparable. There is no existence of an individual apart from society, and there is no existence of society unless it is meaningfully created and recreated by individuals.

From about age 2, Cooley observed that a child begins to develop a sense of social self—or a sense of "I"—based on interactions and communications with significant others. This birth of the self is the birth of imagination about the social world within which the individual is born and begins to grow. "Very soon," Cooley (1909/2012) contended, "the mind begins to discriminate personal impressions, and to become naively self-conscious and naively conscious of society" (p. 8). From early childhood, the social self begins to evolve because a child begins to become aware, "in a reflective way, of the group and his social relation to it. He does not say 'I,' nor does he name his mother, his sister, his nurse, but he has images and feelings out of which these ideas will grow" (Cooley, 1909/2012, p. 8).

When a child begins to grow, their human mind or self-reflective capacity also begins to be widened. "Later comes the more reflective consciousness," Cooley (1909/2012) said, "which names both himself and other people and brings a fuller perception of the relations which constitute the unity of this small world. And so on to the most elaborate phases of self-consciousness and social consciousness. Self and society go together as phases of a common whole" (pp. 8–9). The human mind of an individual or the social consciousness of an individual, according to Cooley (1909/2012), has three interconnected dimensions. The first is that an individual has a sense of self-consciousness—meaning "what I think of myself" (p. 12). Second, an individual has a sense of social consciousness—meaning "what I think of other people" (Cooley, 1909/2012, p. 12). Third, an individual has a sense of public consciousness—meaning a collective view of the social milieu. Cooley (1902) said, "I conclude, therefore, that the imagination which people have of one another are the *solid facts of society* and that to observe and interpret these must be a chief aim of sociology" (p. 121).

What is more particularly significant for socialization theories is Cooley's idea that an individual is self-conscious about how they are perceived, defined, described, and evaluated by their significant and generalized others. The social consciousness that exists in an individual's mind is like a mirror—a looking-glass self—in which the individual perceives the way they are defined and profiled by others. The self-consciousness of "I" is significantly shaped and molded by the nature of its image in the mirror society. In other words, according to Cooley, if an individual is negatively perceived and demonized by others, that person will develop a negative personal perception inside their social mind. If an individual is positively perceived and praised by others, that person will develop a positive personal perception inside their social mind.

The positive shaping of the social mind, for Cooley, is particularly significant during childhood socialization. Cooley (1909/2012) coined the term "primary group" as characterized by "face-to-face association and cooperation" (p. 23), such as family, parents, peers, neighborhoods, communities, schools, and churches—groups that are mostly present during the childhood socialization of an individual. Cooley (1909/2012) said "they are primary in several sense, but chiefly in that, they are fundamental in forming the social nature and ideals of the individual" (p. 23). Within the primary groups, Cooley (1909/2012) said, "human nature comes into existence. Man does not have it at birth; he cannot acquire it except through fellowship, and it decays in isolation" (p. 30). Added Cooley (1909/2012): "What else can human nature be than a trait of the primary group?" (p. 30). He believed that most social ideals of love and emotions, friendship and cooperation, care and compassion, tolerance and empathy, justice and injustice, right and wrong, good and evil, and desirable and undesirable spring from the primary groups.

George H. Mead: Role-Taking and Birth of the Social Mind

George H. Mead, like Cooley, was a brilliant American sociologist who made some enduring contributions toward understanding the birth of the human mind, human self, and socialization. Mead elaborated his theory of the mind and human self in his book *Mind, Self, and Society* (1934). For Mead, the human mind and self are social constructions. A human is not born with a mind. The mind grows and evolves as the individual begins to interact with the social world. Mead theorized that the mind is not a passive physical entity inside the human brain. The mind is not like a blank slate that passively stores external information. The human mind, for Mead, is an active, living, and dynamic entity. It grows and evolves by actively participating in the social world—the world of human acts and interactions. The mind becomes an active and dynamic entity by participating in the social world of ceaseless interactions and creating and understanding the meaning of the social world expressed in terms of language, symbols, and gestures. The external social world does not enter the mind with some preconceived meanings and significance of social facts and events. The mind instead creates a meaning of the social world by its active and continuous engagement with that social world.

A human mind is a meaning-creating entity. The mind, for Mead, "is the presence in the behavior of significant symbols. It is the internalization within the individual of the social process of communication in which meaning emerges" (Morris, 1934, p. xxii). The social world that is mediated inside the mind is not a physical thing but a set of symbols and meanings. The core theoretical argument of Mead is that the mind does not create society; society creates the mind. By actively participating with the social world and developing a unique reflexive capacity, the mind internalizes the values, meanings, and significance of the social world. Mead (1934) said the "reflexiveness, then, is the essential condition within the social process, for development of the mind" (p. 134). It is through reflexiveness that an individual learns the attitudes of others toward oneself and adjusts and orients their opinions toward others. "It is by means of reflexiveness—the turning back of the experience of the individual upon himself—the whole social process is thus brought into the experience of the individuals involved in it; it is by such means, which enable the individual to take the attitudes of others toward himself, that the individual is able consciously to adjust himself to that process" (Mead, 1934, p. 134).

For Mead, mind, self, and consciousness are interconnected, and all of them are socially created and evolved. "The self is something," Mead (1934) argued, "which has a development; it is not initially there at birth, but arises in the process of social experience and activity" (p. 135). "It is impossible," Mead (1934) continued, "to conceive of a self-arising outside of social experience" (p. 140). The self grows and evolves, much as the growth and evolution of the mind, by developing a reflexive capacity to understand the gestures, language, and communications of the interactive social world within which it evolves. Mead discovered that in the evolution of the mind and the self, the core is the notion of role-taking. It is primarily by taking and learning the role of others that the self internalizes the objectivity and reality of the social world. "Man is essentially the role-taking animal" (Morris, 1937, p. xxi).

For Mead, society was not just a consciousness of belonging or solidarity, as Durkheim described. A society is an objective boundary within which people play different roles—such as mother, father, sister, brother, student, teacher, doctor, judge, or boss. These roles form many competing social structures, and they are shaped by relevant norms, values, beliefs, and expectations. A child, according to Mead, begins to take the role of others in the form of playing and imitation. "A child plays at being a mother, at being a teacher, at being policeman, that is, it is taking different roles as we say" (Mead, 1934, p. 150). By way of playing and assuming the roles of others, a child slowly begins to develop a sense of the social process. During childhood, a child only learns to take the role of significant others who are the actors in the primary groups, such as a mother, father, or friend. The second stage is maturation and the time of game playing. The idea of a game for Mead was a metaphor. The idea of the game is a stage of adult role-playing when a child, in reality, begins to take the role of generalized others, such as the child becoming a student, teacher, mother, doctor, or judge. "If we contrast to play with the situation of the organized game, we note the essential difference that the child who plays in the game must be ready to take the attitude of everyone else involved in that game, and that these different roles must have a definite relationship to each other" (Mead, 1934, p. 151).

The self is born within a child through the beginning of imaginary role-playing based on imitation. Mead described this phase of the self as "the 'I.'" It is the impulsive phase of the self (Wilson, 1983, p. 128). In this stage, the self of a child "is constituted simply by an organization of the particular attitudes of other individuals toward himself [attitudes of the significant others] and the specific acts in which [the child] participates with them" (Mead, 1934, p. 158). In the second stage, the self goes through maturation through game playing when a child begins to participate in the larger society. Mead described this phase as the birth of "me" within the self. "The 'me' phase of the self is the product of the generalized other" (Wilson, 1983, p. 129). In this phase of the maturation of the self, the "I" becomes aware of the larger normative structure of society and what the society expects of the individual. With the birth of "me" within the self, "the self-conscious human individual, then, takes or assumes the organized social attitudes of the given social group or community" (Mead, 1934, p. 156).

Lawrence Kohlberg: Mind, Cognition, and the Evolution of Morality

Many behavioral geneticists, evolutionary anthropologists, and psychologists, as discussed earlier, believe that morality is an integral part of the evolution of humanity. The moral knowledge of what is right and wrong and the ethical traits of reciprocity, gregariousness, empathy, selflessness, and compassion were indispensable in the human struggle for survival and natural selection. From its classical time in the 19th century, sociologists believed that society is not just a legal or a cultural community; it is a moral community as well.

Durkheim (1933) particularly theorized that a collective sense of morality and a collective sense of bonding are the glues that keep us within the boundaries of socially desirable actions and behavior. For Durkheim, collective conscience was the soul of morality. Durkheim predicted that modern societies would be more vulnerable to crime, violence, anomie, suicide, divorce, and depression with the birth of individualism. For Durkheim, morality is primarily a social construction. "Morality," he said, "in all its forms is never met with except in society" (Durkheim, 1933, p. 399). The moral responsibilities of an individual are, in reality, responsibilities toward society. It is through the development of morality that an "individual becomes cognizant of his dependence upon society; from it comes forces which keep him in check and restrain him" (Durkheim, 1933, p. 401).

During recent decades, morality has been a subject of intensive research in sociology (Gibbs, 2019; Hitlin & Vaisey, 2010). Following the idea of collective morality theorized by Durkheim, many contemporary sociologists believe that understanding morality is the key to understanding crimes, violence, racism, sexism, hate, bigotry, abuse, exploitation, discrimination, xenophobia, and a variety of other social issues and problems. Understanding morality is needed to make sense of the rise of different socially marginalized groups and social movements. "We cannot understand deviance, scapegoating, and group hierarchies without factoring in the cultural and often moral meanings on which they are predicated. The study of social movements generally requires a consideration of the moral causes to which they are committed" (Lamont, 2010, p. vi). Through socialization, we develop a social mind, a social self, and social consciousness. But how does morality grow? If morality is a social construction, how does it enter into the mind, self, and consciousness of a child? If morality is innate and genetic, how does it socially and culturally evolve, and how is it expressed?

Harvard psychologist Lawrence Kohlberg's (1981, 1984) theory of moral development is one of the dominant perspectives on morality's evolution. As did Jean Piaget, Kohlberg also theorized that the growth of intelligence and morality's growth are inseparable. Piaget theorized that a child's mind is an active and dynamic agent, and intellect within a child evolves without many interventions of ideas and thoughts from the external world. Quite akin to the argument of social neurology, Piaget argued that intelligence within a child evolves by "constructing a complex system of action-schemes and organizing reality in terms of Spatio-temporal and causal structures ... these constructions are made with the sole support of perceptions and movements ... without the intervention of representation or thought" (Piaget & Inhelder, 2000, p. 4).

Kohlberg similarly maintained that the mind of a child is actively engaged in the construction of a moral sense in terms of some universal categories of morality. "Like Piaget," Kohlberg (1984) said, "I assumed that the child's active moral constructions, as distinct from passively learned assertions of adult moral cliches, would center on the child's sense of justice ... I assumed that the developing child was a philosopher, constructing meanings around universal categories or questions such as the question of fairness" (p. xvii). Morality evolves out of a child's active engagement with the social world. Kohlberg (1984) defined "moral development" as the exercise of moral reasoning, and "moral reasoning" is defined "in reference to objective and universal standards as well as to the individual's own moral judgment" (p. 519). Moral development is not simply an understanding of different ethical issues. Moral development is the development of moral reasoning.

Based on an experiment known as the "Heinz dilemma," Kohlberg (1981, 1984) developed a three-stage model of moral development. In the experiment, he asked a group of 72 boys ages 10–16 years whether it is ethical for a man in abject poverty to steal a drug from a chemist's office to save his (Heinz's) wife from dying of cancer. Kohlberg interviewed the students once every 3 years for 20 years. Each of the three stages of moral development again goes through two phases.

Kohlberg describes the first stage as preconventional morality, which involves two phases. In the first phase, a child's moral reasoning is dominated by a sense of punishment avoidance. In this stage, a child believes there is one single authority (i.e., father) to make moral rules and hence, moral rules are obeyed by a child for the avoidance of punishment. In the second phase, the child develops the reasoning that ethical standards have meanings for those who make ethical standards. In this phase, a child develops a sense that if they obey the rules, they will be rewarded. The child grows a self-interest orientation.

The second stage of moral development is conventional morality, and it also evolves through two phases. In the first phase, an adolescent internalizes reasoning that moral conformity is positively evaluated by society (good boy–nice girl orientations). The second phase is the development of reasoning to comply with a society's law-and-order orientations. The third stage—postconventional morality—involves a higher sense of morality. In the first phase of postconventional morality, an individual develops reasoning to critically evaluate society's competing moral issues, such as poverty, racism, sexism, and discrimination. The second phase involves universal moral orientations. In this phase, many develop reasoning about the values of upholding universal human rights and widespread social movements for reducing global poverty, improving global health, eliminating global discriminations and violence against women, criminalizing global child abuse, protecting global climate, and protecting endangered global species.

Very few individuals, however, Kohlberg believed, can reach this phase of a higher sense of universal morality. These different stages and phases of morality, according to Kohlberg, are qualitatively different from one another, and they evolve in an unvarying sequence.

Genes, Brain, and Society: Theories and Research on Socialization

Genes, brains, and the social environment affect socialization. There are three predicaments in the process of socialization related to these three domains. These three predicaments at birth are entirely uncertain. There is no clue at birth whether a child will be moderately smart or brilliant, whether the child will be a doctor or deviant, or whether they will be virtuous or violent. Socialization, therefore, is a crucial process for the making of a social being. Among infants of all species, human babies at birth, irrespective of their genetic compositions and heritable traits, are most vulnerable. A human baby cannot talk and walk, cannot eat on their own, or clean themselves. Their security and survival at birth are entirely in the hands of the parents and family (Table 4.1). Very few parents have a complete understanding of how the structures and functions of the brains of their babies begin to grow from the beginning of conception.

Few parents have a complete understanding of how the brain chemicals of babies work, what specific hormonal balance exists between dopamine and serotonin, and how the brains of babies begin to form synapses and neural networks from the beginning of birth. So far as genetic heritability and the structuration of babies' brains are concerned, socialization at all times and in all cultures begins mostly with common sense.

TABLE 4.1 The Sociological Theories of Socialization

Piaget's Theory of Cognitive Evolution	Cooley's Theory of Looking-Glass Self	Mead's Theory of Role-Taking	Kohlberg's Theory of Moral Development
A child's brain begins to learn in terms of some "schemes of thoughts"—some internal models of representations.	The self of a human evolves out of the individual's social interactions, particularly with primary groups. It is within the primary groups that "human nature comes into existence."	A human is not born with a mind. The mind grows and evolves as the individual begins to interact with the social world. The mind is not a passive physical entity inside the human brain. The human mind is an active, living, and dynamic entity.	The growth of intelligence and the growth of morality are inseparable. The mind is an active and dynamic agent within a child, and it evolves without many interventions of ideas and thoughts from the external world.
The internal models of representation naturally evolve in children's minds, and the social environment does not externally form them.	A self evolves through three stages: first, by developing an imagination about others; second, by creating an imagination on how others see the individual; and third, by developing an imagination to behave with reference to others.	The mind becomes an active and dynamic social entity by creating a meaning of the social world expressed in language, symbols, and gestures. A human mind is a meaning-making entity.	Moral development means the development of moral reasoning. Moral reasoning evolves in terms of some universal categories of morality and an individual's righteous judgment.
Intelligence evolves from lower to higher levels of reasoning and abstraction. The four stages of evolution intelligence are the sensorimotor stage, preoperational stage, concrete operational stage, and formal operational stage.	The mind of an individual is like a mirror—looking-glass self—in which the individual perceives the way they are defined and profiled by others.	In explaining the evolution of the mind and the self, the core is the notion of role-taking. It is primarily by taking and learning the role of others that the self internalizes the objectivity and reality of the social world.	There are three stages of moral development: preconventional morality, conventional morality, and postconventional morality. Through these different stages, moral reasoning develops from self, societal, to universal orientations.

In addition to the uncertainty of knowledge about heritability and the natural growth of the brain and consciousness, there is also much diversity in the social contexts within which human babies are born. When a baby comes into the world, that child does not enter a socially homogeneous world. About 353,000 babies are born each day worldwide, and about 11,000 are born in America each day. About four million babies were born in America in 2020. Some of these were babies born in families with middle- and higher-middle-class status who probably earn more than $150,000 a year. Some were born in families with extreme poverty who most likely do not earn more than $25,000 a year and are on welfare. Some were born in families with two college-educated parents, and many were born in families with a single parent who probably has less than a high school education. Some are born in stable families and some in dysfunctional and violent families. Many babies are born in families affected by drug addiction, parental incarceration, and alcoholism. The task of socialization—to transform a human baby into a social and moral individual—is intrinsically challenging. The socialization process, which is mostly governed by common sense, is still a puzzle for sociology. More understanding and an exploration of the theories and research on different facets of socialization—genetic, neurological, and social—are vital.

Poverty, Brain, and Socialization

Poverty is commonly defined as the absence of income, money, and wealth. But poverty also has many social and psychological dimensions. Poverty limits access to income, wealth, good education, good health care, and higher socioeconomic status. Poverty limits access not only to higher education and high-quality jobs but also destroys self-esteem and self-pride. Poverty reduces access to social capital—high-quality social connections and social networks. Poverty negatively affects lifestyles and life opportunities and increases the chances of criminality, violence, and victimization. From the perspective of socialization, poverty is a considerable challenge.

In recent years, much behavioral neurological research based on brain imaging has shown that poverty deeply affects the structures and functions of the brain (Plomin, 2018; Mitchell, 2018; Haft & Hoeft, 2017; Katsnelson, 2015; Babcock, 2014; Lipina & Posner, 2012). It is not surprising that children from impoverished families, even with good parenting, perform lower in standardized tests and have lower educational attainments. Research shows that higher scores in SAT and ACT are typically received by students from higher socioeconomic status. It is to address this differential performance that the U.S. College Board, a nonprofit organization that administers the SAT, recently introduced a new measure described as an "adversary score." This score "uses 15 factors, including crime rates, high school quality, and neighborhood poverty, to determine the hardships test-takers have overcome to achieve their score. The score will not include race as one of its factors. The average student would receive a 50 with scores ranging from 1 to 100" (Gage, 2019, p. 1).

From the point of view of socialization, the problem of poverty, however, is more fundamental. Poverty affects the very essence of our survival and socialization by negatively affecting our brain, mind, and consciousness. In this process of negatively affecting our brain, mind, and consciousness, poverty also neutralizes the positive dimensions of the heritability of intelligence. Most geneticists believe that about 60% of our intelligence is genetic. "Environmental difference account for the remaining 40 percent of the variance" (Plomin, 2018, p. 95). Many geneticists also believe that during early childhood, the social environment can play a more significant role. Therefore, children who live in poverty during the early childhood period are more likely to be negatively affected—meaning that many of the positive genetic traits of intelligence may remain dormant because of adverse brain development affected by poverty. A positive social environment for the intellectual growth of children is more crucial during the early childhood period. Many studies contend that "the first five years of life to be the most sensitive period for the damaging influence of economic deprivation" (Sleek, 2015, p. 3).

Social and behavioral neurological research has found that poverty leads to the secretion of stress response hormones, which negatively affect children's brain functions related to academic achievement, language development, and reading skills. The stress hormones negatively affect the frontal lobe—the brain's region described by one neurologist as the "organ of a civilization" (as quoted in Goldberg, 2001, p. 2). In his book *The Executive Brain: Frontal Lobes and the Civilized Mind*, neurologist Goldberg (2001) describes the frontal lobe as "one part of your brain that makes who you are and define your identity, that encapsulates your drives, your ambitions, your personality, your essence. The frontal lobes are the most uniquely human of all the brain structures, and they played a crucial role in the success and failure of any human endeavor" (pp.1–2). Goldberg (2001) further added that "the frontal lobes perform the most advanced and complex functions in all of the brain, the so-called executive functions. They are linked to intentionality, purposefulness, and complex decision making. The frontal lobes are the brain's command post" (p. 2).

Neurological research has shown that the growth and functions of the frontal lobes are damaged mainly by stress hormones related to poverty. "As a result of neuroendocrine changes related to stress, children in poverty may experience damaging structural changes" (Haft & Hoeft, 2017, p. 7) in the frontal lobes. Damage to the frontal lobe mainly affects the specific brain circuits that regulate language learning, memory, reading skills, and "the ability to control thoughts and emotions" (as quoted in Katsnelson, 2015, p. 3).

The hippocampus, located within the brain's medial temporal lobe, the neurologists have discovered, is the crucial region for long-term memory. It is the brain's region that controls the functions of the mind related to deliberately recalling prior knowledge, experience, and facts and events. Research by neurologists based on brain imaging has found that children raised in poverty have a relatively smaller hippocampus. "Much of the work over the past few years, though, has highlighted structural differences ... which plays a role in processing fear and other emotions, and in the prefrontal cortex, involved in decision-making and self-control. The most consistent finding has been that a smaller hippocampus in low-SES children" (Katsnelson, 2015, p. 4).

According to 2020 federal guidelines, a family of four earning less than $26,000 annually is under the poverty threshold. Data from the 2019 census show that about 12 million U.S. children live in families under the threshold of poverty. "During the most critical stage for brain development, 3.5 million children under 5 [in America] were poor in 2018, with 1.6 million of those children living in extreme poverty" (Children's Defense Fund, 2019, p. 1). Globally, "of the world's 2.3 billion children (those less than 18 years of age), 301 million live on less than $1.90/day in 2011 PPP [Purchasing Power Parity]. This means that 13 percent of the world's children are very poor" (Fens & Hammel, 2019, p. 1). Parenting and socialization for this enormous number of children are hugely challenging. But understanding the connectivity between poverty and brain development is crucial.

Parenting and Socialization: Parenting Matters

Genes and genetic expressions, heritable behavioral traits, and brain structures and functions that impinge on human growth and socialization are natural phenomena. But most behavioral geneticists, social neurologists, and sociologists contend that the effect of the social on innate human traits and the growth of the brain is vital. The fields of behavioral genetics and social neurology are based on the assumption of the centrality of the social in the shaping of human growth and socialization.

From the beginning of human social life, parenting has been the central focus of socialization. This is true of all times and all cultures and civilizations. Despite all forces of change and modernization, the significance of parenting in all modern societies has mostly remained the same. When geneticists talk about their discovery that 60% of intelligence is heritable, they indicate the significance of parenting in nurturing the rest of the 40% of intelligence. When social neurologists talk about the birth of the social brain and socially mediated consciousness, they attribute the significance of parenting. When Piaget and Kohlberg theorized about the evolution of intelligence and morality, they did not ignore the role of parenting.

Sociologists, since classical time in the 19th century, remained concerned about the fragility of family and parenting and the weakness of collective bonding because of the advent of modernity. Almost all great sociologists asserted that the fragility of the structure of the family is bound to be widened in modern societies because of the rise of urbanity, individualism, privacy, and materiality. They made predictions about the crisis of socialization in modern societies and increased anomie, crime, violence, divorce, loneliness, depression, and suicide (Durkheim, 1951; Berger et al., 1973; Etzioni, 1993,1999). American sociologist Robert Nisbet (1951) lamented that modernity has led to the decline and crisis of the community. The recent decades have seen the growth of a large amount of research on family, parenting, and socialization. Much sociological research has shown that family structures, parental education, parental socioeconomic status, parental cultural capital, and familial attachments are intimately connected to children's socialization.

Sociological research on the family structure has shown that a two-parent biological family structure has positive connections to children's educational attainment, educational aspirations, self-esteem, health, labor market employability, marital and family status, and moral development. It is observed that "elementary school children from intact biological families earn higher reading and math test scores than children in cohabiting and divorced single and always-single parent families" (Fagan et al., 2011, p. 1). It was further observed that "high school students who live in intact married families have a higher average combined GPA in English and math (2.9) than those in married stepfamilies, divorced families, or intact cohabiting families (2.6) and those in always-single-parent families or cohabiting stepfamilies (2.5)" (Fagan et al., 2011, p. 1). Research has shown that children raised in two-parent biological families are more likely to attend college: "Over 57 percent of children who live in intact biological families enter college, compared to 32.5 percent of children in stepfamilies, 47.5 percent of children in single-parent families, and 31.8 percent of children who live in families without either parent present" (Fagan et al., 2011, p. 1). Two-parent biological family structure also has a positive effect on children's behavior. Children "in single-parent families, married stepfamilies, or cohabiting stepfamilies are more likely than children in intact married families to have ever been suspended or expelled from school, to have participated in delinquent activities, and to have problems getting along with teachers, doing homework, and paying attention in school" (Fagan et al., 2011, p. 2). Research has also found that "students from stepfamilies and single-parent families are three times as likely to drop out of school as students from intact biological families, even when controlling for socioeconomic status" (Fagan et al., 2011, p. 2).

A report from the U.S. Department of Health and Human Services, Centers for Disease Control and Prevention, and the National Center for Health Statistics (Blackwell, 2010) on relations between family structure and children's health, based on data from the National Health Interview Survey, had also observed that the two-parent biological family is positively connected to children's mental and emotional growth. The report found that "children living in nuclear families (3%) were less likely than children in single-parent (4.6%), blended (3.8%), cohabiting (4.5%) families to have mental retardation or any developmental delay. Children in other families had the highest prevalence rates of mental retardation or any developmental delay" (Blackwell, 2010, p. 14). Data from six years of health survey also show that "less than 1% of children living in nuclear families received special education or EIS for an emotional or behavioral problem compared with 3.3% of children in single-parent families, 2.3% of children in blended families, 3.3% of children in cohabiting families" (Blackwell, 2010, p. 14). Children in the two-parent biological family or nuclear families are also less likely to have ADHD or learning disabilities: "Children aged 3–17 living in nuclear families (8.1%) were less likely than children in single-parent (14.9%), blended (16.1%), cohabiting (15.6%), extended (12.1%), or other (19%) families to have a learning disability or ADHD" (Blackwell, 2010, p. 15).

There is also a considerable amount of research on the relations between socialization and parental care and attachment. The Minnesota longitudinal study on parental care and child development is one of the more widely known studies, and one that has been conducted for more than 3 decades. The study was based on the tracking of the lives of 180 children from childhood to adulthood. The study observed that "(1) nothing is more important in the development of the child than the care received, including that in the early years; [and] (2) that the entire history of cumulative experience always impacts individuals ... early experience is not erased" (Stroufe et al., 2005, p. 19). The study further found that "parenting, not just the genes that parents provide, is an important influence on children" (Stroufe et al., 2005, p. 21).

We began this chapter on socialization with the puzzle of what it means to be social and how we become social. The core theme of this chapter is that for a better understanding of this puzzle, we need a new model—a model that can integrate the theories and research on human nature, human genetics, development of the human mind and consciousness, psychological studies on the development of intelligence and morality, and the sociological studies on the role of family and parenting.

Geneticist Plomin (2018) rightly said, "Nature and Nurture suggests a new way of thinking about the experience" (p. 51). The mind in us is not an empty slate, and the mind is not the passive receptor of what comes from the social environment. Social environments—the facts and events of the social—are "not 'out there,' imposed on us passively. They are 'in here,' experienced by us as we actively perceive, interpret, select, modify and even create environments correlated with our genetic propensities" (Plomin, 2018, p. 51). In the pursuit of deeper understanding of socialization, "this is a general model for thinking about how we use the environment to get what our DNA blueprint whispers that it wants. This is the essence of the nature of nurture" (Plomin, 2018, p. 51).

Suggested Questions, Essays, Assignments, and Quizzes

1. One of the critical areas of theorizing in contemporary sociology is the nature versus nurture debate. Sociologists assume we are not born social. We become social through a process of socialization. But recent discoveries about human DNA have shown that our genes control a significant part of our intelligence. Based on your review of this chapter, related class lectures, and your internet research, write an essay (two or three single-spaced pages, 12-point font) about the recent scientific findings on relations between human genetics and intelligence.

2. About two million Americans are within the criminal justice system, and many of them present symptoms of different kinds of antisocial personality disorders. We associate antisocial personality disorders with many social factors, such as dysfunctional families, broken neighborhoods, low-quality schools, and deviant peers, from our common-sense knowledge. Modern genetic discoveries, however, have shown that many of the antisocial personality disorders are genetic. Based on your reading of this chapter, related class lectures, and your internet research, write an essay (two or three single-spaced pages, 12-point font) describing some of the findings from

behavioral genetics on the relationship between genes and antisocial personality disorders.

3. Many behavioral geneticists, neurologists, and sociologists argue that the brain mediates our genes' effects on social behavior and that culture and brain development are connected. Based on your review of this chapter and your internet research, examine this statement by describing some of the significant research findings on brain-culture connections. Please provide examples.

4. The sociological theories of socialization focus on the development of intelligence, self, and morality. Based on your reading of this chapter and your internet research, write an essay (three or four single-spaced pages, 12-point font) describing Piaget's theory of different stages of the growth of human intelligence (you can make a chart showing Piaget's model of hierarchical order for the development of human intelligence).

5. The theory of the "looking-glass self" developed by Charles H. Cooley has made some enduring contributions to socialization literature. Based on your reading of this chapter and your internet research, write an essay (three or four single-spaced pages, 12-point font) explaining the looking-glass self. At the end of your paper, comment on the role of positive reinforcement by parents, teachers, and peers on childhood personality development.

6. The development of a moral sense of what is right and wrong and ethical and unethical is intimately connected to socialization. There is a considerable amount of sociological literature on moral development. Based on your reading of this chapter, related class lectures, and your internet research, write an essay (three or four single-spaced pages, 12-point font) describing Lawrence Kohlberg's theory of moral development. Make a critical comment on whether moral development will vary from one culture to another or if the stages of moral development are universal, as Kohlberg theorized.

7. A considerable amount of research by behavioral geneticists and neurologists show that poverty negatively affects brain development. Based on your reading of this chapter, related class lectures, and your internet research, write an essay (three or four single-spaced pages, 12-point font) summarizing some pertaining research on connections between poverty and brain development. In the context of your understanding of this research trend, suggest five police strategies for the learning enhancement of students in schools in economically disadvantaged communities.

8. Sociologists define socialization as a lifelong process, with two types of socialization: primary and secondary. What do sociologists mean by "primary socialization," and who are the crucial agents of primary socialization? Describe and provide examples.

9. Secondary socialization is related mainly to work, law, school, and public places. Based on your reading of this chapter, related class lectures, and your internet research, write an essay (three or four single-spaced pages, 12-point font) summarizing some of the norms, rites, and rituals we are compelled to observe in the formal workplace (you can add your own experience on how you were trained or told to behave in the workplace).

10. One of the crucial questions in the sociological literature on socialization is the role of parenting. In the world of common sense, parents are praised or blamed for everything that children do. Based on your reading of this chapter, related class lectures, and your internet research, write an essay (three or four single-spaced pages, 12-point font) describing the parenting role in socialization. In the context of the recent discoveries in genetic science on the heritability of

intelligence, antisocial behavior, and brain functions, comment on "Does parenting matter?"

References

Ayala, F. J. (1987). The biological roots of morality. *Biology and Philosophy*, *2*, 235–252. Retrieved from https://doi.org/10.1007/BF00128831 on December 20, 2020.

Ayala, F. J. (2010). The difference of being human. *Proceedings of the National Academy of Sciences*, *10*(2), 1–32. Retrieved from https://doi.org/10.1073/pnas.0914616107 on December 20, 2020.

Babcock, E. D. (2014). *Using brain science to design new pathways out of poverty*. Crittenton Women's Union.

Berger, P. L. (1963). *Invitation to sociology: A humanistic perspective*. Anchor Books–Doubleday.

Berger, P. L., Berger, B., & Kellner, H. (1973). *The Homeless Mind: Modernization and consciousness*. Random House.

Berger, P. L., & Luckman, T. (1966). *The social construction of reality: A treatise in sociology of knowledge*. Random House.

Blackwell, D. L. (2010). *Family structure and children's health in the United States: Findings from the National Health Interview Survey, 2001–2007. Vital Health Stat 10*, 246, 1–166. Retrieved from https://pubmed.ncbi.nlm.nih.gov/21388047/ December 20, 2020.

Blair, C., & Raver, C. C. (2016). Poverty, stress, and brain development: New directions for prevention and intervention. *Academic Pediatrics*, *16*(3 Suppl), S30–S36. Retrieved from https://doi.org/10.1016/j.acap.2016.01.010 on December 20, 2020.

Boehm, C. (2012). *Moral origins: The evolution of virtue, altruism, and shame*. Basic Books.

Boyd, R., & Richerson, P. J. (1985). *Culture and the evolutionary process*. University of Chicago Press.

Children's Defense Fund. (2019). *New census data reveals continued child poverty crisis in America*. Retrieved from https://www.childrensdefense.org/2019/new-census-data-reveals-continued-child-poverty-crisis-in-america/ on December 20, 2020.

Cooley, C. H. (1909). *Social organization: A study of the larger mind*. Schocket Books.

Cooley, C. H. (2012). *Human nature and the social order*. Hard Press Publishing. (Original work published 1902)

Cooley, C. H. (2013). *Social process*. Hard Press Publishing. (Original work published 1918)

Darwin, C. (2008). *The origin of species by means of natural selection*. Bantam Classics. (Original work published 1859)

Decety, J., & Cowell, J. M. (2016). Our brains are wired for morality: Evolution, development, and neuroscience. *Frontiers for Young Minds*, *4*(3), 1–16. Retrieved from https://doi.org/10.3389/frym.2016.00003 on December 20, 2020.

Decety, J., & Wheatley, T. (2015). *The moral brain: A multidisciplinary perspective*. MIT Press.

Dehaene, S. (2014). *Consciousness and the brain: Deciphering how the brain codes our thoughts*. Penguin Group.

Durham, W. H. (1991). *Co-evolution: Genes, culture, and human diversity*. Stanford University Press.

Durkheim, E. (1933). *The division of labor in society* (G. Simpson, Trans.). Free Press.

Durkheim, E. (1951). *Suicide: A study in sociology* (J. A. Spaulding & G. Simpson, Trans.). Free Press.

Ehrlich, P. R. (2000). *Human natures: Genes, culture, and the human prospect*. Island Press.

Etzioni, A. (1993). *The spirit of community: A reinvention of American society*. Simon and Schuster.

Etzioni, A. (1999). *The Limits to privacy*. Basic Books.

Fagan, P. F., Have, L. T., & Chen, W. (2011). *Marriage, family structure, and children's educational attainment*. Marriage and Religion Research Institute.

Fenz, K., & Hammel, K. (2019). *More than half of the world's poor are children*. Brookings Institution. Retrieved from https://www.brookings.edu/blog/future-development/2019/06/20/more-than-half-of-the-worlds-poor-are-children/ on December 30, 2020.

Gage, J. (2019, May). New SAT "adversary score" includes crime, poverty of test-taker neighborhoods. *Washington Examiner*. Retrieved from https://www.washingtonexaminer.com/news/new-sat-adversity-score-includes-crime-poverty-of-test-taker-neighborhoods on December 30, 2020.

Gambino, M. (2012). How humans become moral beings. *Smithsonian Magazine*. Retrieved from https://www.smithsonianmag.com/science-nature/how-humans-became-moral-beings-80976434/ on December 30, 2020.

Gazzaniga, M. S. (2009). *The ethical brain*. Dana Publishing.

Gazzaniga, M. S. (2015). *Tales from both sides of the brain: A life in neuroscience*. HarperCollins.

Gazzaniga, M. S. (2018). *The consciousness instinct: Unraveling the mystery of how the brain makes the mind*. Farrar, Straus, and Giroux.

Gibbs, J. C. (2019). *Moral development and reality: Beyond the theories of Kohlberg, Hoffman, and Haidt*. Oxford University Press.

Goffman, E. (1959). *The presentation of self in everyday life*. Doubleday Publishing.

Goldberg, E. (2001). *The executive brain: Frontal lobes and the civilized mind*. Oxford University Press.

Graziano, M. S. A. (2013). *Consciousness and the social brain*. Oxford University Press.

Haft, S. L., & Hoeft, F. (2017). Poverty's impact on executive functions: Global considerations. *New Directions on Child Adolescent Development*, *158*, 69–79. Retrieved from https://doi.org/10.1002/cad.20220 on December 30, 2020.

Haier, R. J. (2016). *The neuroscience of intelligence*. Cambridge University Press.

Hitlin, S., & Vaisey, S. (Eds.). (2010). *Handbook of the sociology of morality*. Springer.

Hoffman, M. L. (2000). *Empathy and moral development: Implications for care and justice*. Cambridge University Press.

Johanson, M., Vaurio, O., Tiihonen, J., & Lähteenvuo, M. (2019). A systematic literature review of neuroimaging of psychopathic traits. *Frontier in Psychiatry*, *10*, 1–39. Retrieved from https://doi.org/10.3389/fpsyt.2019.01027 on December 30, 2020.

Joyce, R. (2007). *The evolution of morality*. MIT Press.

Katsnelson, A. (2015). New feature: The neuroscience of poverty. *Proceedings of National Academy of Sciences of the United States of America, 112*(51), 1–15. Retrieved from https://doi.org/10.1073/pnas.1522683112 on December 30, 2020.

Kohlberg, L. (1981). *The philosophy of moral development, moral stages, and the idea of justice.* Harper & Row.

Kohlberg, L. (1984). *The psychology of moral development: The nature and validity of moral stages.* Harper & Row.

Laland, K. N. (2010). How culture shaped the human genome: Bringing genetics and human sciences together. *Nature Review Genetics, 11*(2), 137–148. Retrieved from https://doi.org/10.1038/nrg2734 on December 30, 2020.

Laland, K. N. (2017). *Darwin's unfinished symphony: How culture made the human mind.* Princeton University Press.

Laland, K. N., & Brown, G. (2011). *Sense and nonsense: Evolutionary perspective on human behavior.* Oxford University Press.

Lamont, M. (2010). Introduction: The return of the moral. In S. Hitlin & S. Vaisey (Eds.), *Handbook of the sociology of morality* (pp. v–vii). Springer.

Lieberman, D. Z., & Long, M. E. (2019). *The molecule of more: How a single chemical in your brain drives love, sex, and creativity—and will determine the fate of the human race.* Ben Bella Books.

Lieberman, M. D. (2013). *Social: Why our brains are wired to connect.* Crown Publishers.

Lipina, S., & Posner, M. (2012). The impact of poverty on the development of brain networks. *Frontiers in Human Neuroscience, 6*(238), 1–21. Retrieved from https://doi.org/10.3389/fnhum.2012.00238 on December 30, 2020.

Ma, G., Fan, H., Shen, C., & Wang, W. (2016). Genetic and neuroimaging features of personality disorder: State of the art. *Neuroscience Bulletin, 32*(3), 286–306. Retrieved from https://doi.org/10.1007/s12264-016-0027-8 on December 30, 2020.

Mead, G. H. (1934). *Mind, self, and society: From the standpoint of social behaviorist.* University of Chicago Press.

Mitchell, K. J. (2018). *Innate: How the writing of our brains shapes who we are.* Princeton University Press.

Morris, C. W. (1934). Introduction: George Herbert Mead as a social psychologist and social philosopher. In G. H. Mead (Ed.), *Mind, self, and society: From the standpoint of social behaviorist* (pp. ix–xxxv). University of Chicago Press.

Narvaez, D. (2014). *Neurobiology and the development of human morality: Evolution, culture, and wisdom.* W. W. Norton.

National Institute of Neurological Disorders and Stroke. (2010). *Brain basics: Genes at work in the brain* (NIH Publication No. 10-5475. National Institutes of Health, U.S. Department of Health and Human Services. Retrieved from https://www.ninds.nih.gov/Disorders/Patient-Caregiver-Education/Genes-Work-Brain on December 30, 2020.

Nisbet, R. (1951). *The quest for community: A study in ethics of order and freedom.* Oxford University Press.

Parsons, T., & Shils, E. (2001). *Toward a general theory of action.* Routledge and Kegan Paul.

Piaget, J. (1928). *The judgment and reasoning of the child.* Routledge and Kegan Paul.

Piaget, J. (1952). *Origins of intelligence in children.* International Universities Press.

Piaget, J. (2001). *The language of thought of the child.* Routledge and Kegan Paul. (Original work published 1923)

Piaget, J., & Inhelder, B. (2000). *The psychology of the child.* Basic Books.

Pinker, S. (1997). *How the mind works.* W. W. Norton.

Pinker, S. (2003). *The blank slate: The modern denial of human nature.* Penguin Books.

Plomin, R. (2020). *Blueprint: How DNA makes us who we are.* MIT Press.

Plomin, R., & Deary, I. J. (2015). Genetics and intelligence differences: Five special findings. *Molecular Psychiatry, 20* (1), pp. 98–108.

Polderman, T. J. C., Benjamin, B., de Leeuw, C. A., Sullivan, P. R., van Boochoven, A., Visscher, P. M., & Posthuma, D. (2015). Meta-analysis of the heritability of human traits based on fifty years of twin studies. *Nature Genetics, 47*, pp. 702–709.

Reichborn-Kjennerud, T. (2010). The genetic epidemiology of personality disorders. *Dialogues in Clinical Neuroscience, 12* (1), pp. 13–114.

Richerson, P. J., & Boyd, R. (2005). *Not by genes alone: How culture transformed human evolution.* University of Chicago Press.

Seo, D., & Patrick, J. C. (2008). Role of serotonin and dopamine system interactions in the neurobiology of impulsive aggression and its comorbidity with other clinical disorders. *Aggressive Violent Behavior, 13* (5), pp. 383–395.

Sleek, S. (2015). *How poverty affects the brain and behavior.* Association for Psychological Science. Retrieved from https://www.psychologicalscience.org/observer/how-poverty-affects-the-brain-and-behavior on December 30, 2020.

Sroufe, L. A., Egeland, B., Carlson, E. A., & Collins, W. A. (2005). *The development of the person: The Minnesota study of risk and adaptation from birth to adulthood.* Guilford Press.

Tomasello, M. (2016). *A natural history of human morality.* Harvard University Press.

Tomasello, M., & Vaish, A. (2013). Origins of human cooperation and morality. *Annual Review of Psychology, 64*, pp. 23–255.

Watson, J. D. (1968). *The double helix: A personal account of the discovery of the structure of DNA.* Simon and Schuster.

Werner, K. B., Few, L. R., & Buchotz, K. K. (2015). Epidemiology, comorbidity, and behavioral genetics of antisocial personality disorder. *Psychiatric Annals, 45*(4), pp. 195–199.

Watson, E. O. (1975). *Sociobiology* (Abridged ed.). Belknap Press of Harvard University Press.

Wilson, J. (1983). *Social theory.* Prentice-Hall.

Figure Credits

CHAPTER 5

The Structural-Functional Paradigm

Society as Structures and Systems

CHAPTER THEME

The goal of science is to discover new knowledge by developing new models, concepts, and theories. Theorizing, and not the collection of data or designing an experiment, is the core and the essence of science. Scientific progress implies progress in scientific theories that advance through conjectures and refutations. It is now widely accepted in science that scientific theories move through change and transformations in scientific paradigms. A scientific paradigm is a set of assumptions about a particular scientific problem or a puzzle shared and presumed as valid by a sizeable community of scientists of that specific scientific domain at a particular time. There are multiple paradigms in all scientific fields, from physics and biology to psychology, economics, and sociology. There are three major paradigms in sociology: structural functionalism, conflict sociology, and symbolic interactionism. Chapter 5 explains and examines the key assumptions and the analytical strategies of structural functionalism. The core idea in structural functionalism is that different structures and systems characterize the human social world, and they have different forms and patterns. These structural and systemic forms and patterns shape and mold human acts, actions, and behaviors. One of the puzzles in structural functionalism is what holds a structure together and how structure and agency (individuals) are connected. The structural functionalists assume that cultural consensus about a system's core values is the glue that keeps a structure together. Structural or systemic continuity is both a matter of control and socialization.

Introduction

The core learning goals in the previous four chapters included the understanding of different types of knowledge, the nature and characteristics of science, differences between science and philosophy and science and religion, the nature of sociology as a science, differences between sociology and other branches of social science, and the genetic and social dimensions of the nature versus nurture debate. After the completion of those chapters, students are expected to locate sociology within the broader domain of different types of knowledge and sociology's specific location within the field of social sciences. The core learning objectives in this chapter include the understanding of competing models and paradigms of sociology. After completing the chapter, students are expected to understand the role of theorizing in science and the core assumptions and analytical strategies of different models and paradigms of sociology. Chapter 5 aims to instill among students of the digital tribe an understanding and curiosity about how sociological analysis is done, how sociological analysis is unique, and how sociological eyes are different.

Role of Theorizing in Science

A world-renowned philosopher of science, Donald T. Campbell, once said that science is like a black cat in a dark room. The "black cat" is the "truth" that scientists seek to discover (Holzner, Campbell, and Shahidullah, 1985). But the truth is never wholly attainable. Newton's theory of gravity, Einstein's theory of special and general relativity, and Creek and Watson's theory of human genetic structures, for example, are still evolving. Theorizing is at the core of science. Scientific theories, however, are falsifiable, progressive, and changeable. There is always uncertainty and skepticism in the search for the metaphorical black cat. Scientific advances mean advances in scientific theories, models, and paradigms. The goal of science is not just collecting data, developing a new experiment, or innovating a unique methodology. The pursuit of science is discovering the truth—the black cat—through the development of theories, models, and paradigms.

Humans in no society do the things they do in the way sciences tell them to do. Human societies are like streaming videos that are unfolding vastly diverse and complex stories since the beginning of human stories. Sociology as a science seeks to capture these vastly complex nature and diversities in the unfolding of human stories. These stories are the stories of human actions and organizations, human ideas and intelligence, human politics and problems, human faith and religion, human achievements and failures, human love and emotions, human comedies and tragedies, human deviance and deficiencies, and human war, conflict, and violence. Humans developed religion and philosophy to make their stories known and intelligible. Sociology has the same pursuit of making human stories understandable, but does so following the rules and canons of science, and theorizing and modeling are at the core of the scientific rules and canons.

It is now a widely accepted notion within the scientific community that science is primarily deductive. A scientific understanding germinates in two major stages: first, by developing theories and hypotheses about the nature of a given problem or a reality and, second, by analyzing and testing the empirical data and evidence in terms of the proposed theories and hypotheses. Karl Popper (1959), a world-renowned British philosopher of science, described this process of generating scientific knowledge in the following way: "A scientist, whether a theorist or experimenter, puts forward statements, or system of statements, and test them step by step. In the field of empirical sciences, more particularly, he constructs hypotheses, or systems of theories, and test them against experience by observation and experiment" (p. 3). Popper (1963) further said, "The way in which knowledge progresses, and especially our scientific knowledge, is by unjustified (and unjustifiable) anticipations, by guesses, by tentative solutions to our problems, by conjectures. The conjectures are controlled by criticism, that is by attempted refutations" (p. xi).

The Scope of Sociological Theorizing

A theory can be defined in multiple ways. A theory sometimes is just an idea or an imagination or a conjecture to explain a particular reality; as Einstein said, "Imagination is more important than knowledge. Knowledge is limited. Imagination encircles the world" (as quoted in Viereck, 1929, p. 117) More precisely, a theory is a set of interrelated and logically connected set of verifiable or verified statements based on empirical data and experiments. In this sense, a theory is a set of high validity statements or generalizations. There are four specific domains of science: nature, life, mind, and society. These four domains make up the four specific fields of science: natural or physical sciences, life sciences, psychological sciences, and social sciences. There are hundreds of theories related to each of these science domains, and none of these domains is dominated by a single theoretical system. There is no single grand and unified theoretical system that explains the mysteries and complexities of nature in totality—the heart of the galaxies, the movement of the planets, the nature of gravity, the nature of light, and the relationships between space and time. Similarly, there is no single theory of nature and the realities of the human body, brain, and mind. Similarly, no single theoretical system can explain the realities and complexities in the human social and behavioral systems.

During the birth of sociology in the 19th century, some sociologists sought to develop grand theoretical systems to explain the nature and evolution of human societies. Auguste Comte, who fathered the name of sociology, sought to explain the development of human societies and behavior in terms of the ideas of knowledge and intelligence. He theorized that human societies evolved from theological, through militaristic, to the industrial phase of evolution because of human knowledge and intelligence. The role of knowledge and intelligence in human social development is beyond controversy, but human social stories are more complex and multifaceted. In the middle of the 19th century, German sociologist Karl Marx developed a grand scheme of analysis of human social events and stories in terms of economics—the ownership of the critical means of economic production and economic wealth. According to Marx's grand theoretical scheme, the economy forms the basic structure of society. Politics, knowledge, culture, literature, philosophy, and all other facets of society are built in the economic structure's image.

For Marx, human societies advanced from one stage to another. Human social institutions and culture evolved from one form to another because of conflicts between those who owned and those who did not possess the necessary means of economic production (i.e., land, capital, companies, corporations). Thus, class conflict is the propeller of human history (Marx, 1867/2011; Marx & Engels, 1848/2002). Modern sociology recognizes that economics is one of the crucial determinants of human actions and behavior, but Marx's grand theorizing of the whole of human historical evolution in terms of economic production alone remained highly controversial. Inspired by Marx's grant theorizing of human social evolution in terms of economics, American sociologist Immanuel Wallerstein in the 1960s and 1970s proposed a revised grand scheme that the modern world needs to be seen as an all-engulfing world capitalist system that has been evolving since the 16th century (Wallerstein, 2011, 2004). Within the modern capitalist system, some countries are at the core, and some are at the peripheries of advanced capitalism.

The countries at the core are economically, politically, and socially dominant. The countries at the peripheries are economically, politically, and socially dominated. Many sociologists have argued that both Marx's theory of the mode of production and class conflict and Wallerstein's model of the world capitalist system present a dynamic analysis of the nature and the logic of the capitalist economy and its role in shaping politics, power, technology, war, and violence. But these grand theoretical systems left many crucial issues of a human culture untouched and unexplained (Robertson, 1992). In the 1950s and 1960s, American sociologist Talcott Parsons presented another grand theory, titled general theory action, to explain human societies' evolution in terms of culture. Parsons theorized that it is culture and not economics that is at the core of the constitution and evolution of human social systems (Parsons & Shils, 1951/2001). Cultural analysis remains one of the major perspectives of modern sociology. Still, culture alone as the core determinant of all human actions and social behavior and the sole propeller of human social evolution is again believed to be limited.

Modern sociology does not give much credence to the idea of grand theorizing and the analysis of all of human actions and behavior and the whole of human evolution in terms of one single factor or linearity (Merton, 1967). Modern science, in general, believes in multilinear and multidimensional explanations. It is true of physics, real of biology, fundamental of psychology, and right of sociology. The nature and scope of modern sociological theories are middle range, multifactorial, and multilinear.

The bulk of contemporary sociological theories are concerned with theorizing on such middle-range issues as the role of parental income on children's educational attainment, the role of family structure on children's self-esteem, relationships between race and poverty, linkages between crime and poverty, connections between culture and obesity, connections between faith and healing, links between gender and voting behavior, or associations between work environment and depression and hypertension. The middle-range theories seek to explore the nature of such social factors as work, economy, politics, power, race, gender, family, marriage, divorce, education, and religion and the way they shape and mold our actions, believes, attitudes, perceptions, behavior, and even our body, brain, mind, and genetic properties. The significance of generating high-validity, middle-range theories in sociology was forcefully argued by American sociologist Robert Merton (1967). "Middle-range theories," Merton (1967) defined, "consist of a limited set of assumptions from which specific hypotheses are logically derived and confirmed by empirical investigation" (p. 68). The middle-range theories do not discard the idea of grand theoretical systems but use them as broader theoretical and philosophical orientations to develop more specific and empirically grounded middle-range theoretical concepts and hypotheses.

Theories, Models, and Paradigms

There are hundreds of middle-range theories in sociology related to almost all facets of human stories. The growth of middle-range theories, however, is not random and without some core theoretical and conceptual directions. As Merton (1967) himself conceptualized, middle-range theories "do not remain separate but are consolidated into wider networks of theory" (p. 68). These theory networks are not merely descriptive. They are "sufficiently abstract to deal with different spheres of social behavior and social structure" (Merton, 1967,

p. 68). Sociologists define these networks of middle-range theories as models and paradigms. Therefore, the study of theorizing in sociology begins with the study of different models and paradigms of sociological analysis. The words "models" and "paradigms" are used interchangeably even though they carry somewhat different meanings. The concept of "model" presents an ideal manifestation of a reality that may or may not be empirically valid. A model describes a given reality from which empirically relevant hypotheses can be drawn and tested.

German sociologist Max Weber (1949/2011) was the first to discover the significance of developing an ideal model or an "ideal type" as a stepping-stone for sociological theorizing. Weber theorized about capitalism, bureaucracy, cities, leadership, and many other social issues by first developing their ideal types of descriptions. Weber argued that an ideal model of capitalism is based on the ideas of materiality, science, and rationality. Capitalism, according to Weber, is not just an economy; it is a particular form of social action dedicated to material advancement in this world. Capitalism is a definite form of culture for the accumulation of wealth based on science and rationality. By developing this ideal model of capitalism, which, he believed, developed only in the West, Weber (1963) conducted a historical study of the birth of capitalism in different world regions. Weber theorized that the West approximated the development of an ideal model of rational capitalism because of its peculiar culture of materiality divinely sanctified by the Calvinist ethics of Protestantism. Weber (1963, 2013) argued that the regions dominated by Hinduism, Buddhism, Islam, and Judaism did not develop scientific and rational capitalism because those religions divinely sanctify among their believers a culture of "other-worldliness" instead of a culture "this-worldliness." Weber's ideal bureaucracy, science, cities, and leadership models are still widely used in organizational sociology, sociology of science, and urban sociology.

American sociologist Talcott Parsons (1971) and several modernization theorists in the 1960s viewed America as a model for a modern nation (Eisenstadt, 1966; Etzioni, 1968; Inkles, 1983; Lipset, 1979; Nelson, 1981). Their assertion was based on America's enduring values of democracy, equality, individualism, church and state separation, materiality, and urbanism. Thomas Jefferson was proud to surmise that America was born as an "Empire of Liberty" model for the world. In his inaugural address in 1801, Jefferson boasted that the American experiment of modernity was "advancing rapidly to destinies beyond the reach of mortal eye" (para. 1). Throughout the 4 decades of the Cold War with Russia, from the 1950s to the 1980s, this perception of America as a model for liberal democracy remained, in fact, as the driving force behind America's internationalism and foreign aid in the developing world. But from the beginning of the 2nd decade of the 21st century, many began to become skeptical over whether America does indeed represent an ideal model for democracy and liberalism. The rise and realities of a new culture of anti-intellectualism, racism, sexism, nativism, and isolationism in America from the middle of the 2nd decade of the 21st century do not fit into its model of a nation of modernity. America's new culture war has raised many new sociological puzzles (Shahidullah, 2019).

Much as with the concept of a model, the idea of a paradigm is also widely used in understanding progress in sociological theorizing. A model represents an ideal picture of a given social reality. On the other hand, a paradigm means a set of assumptions about reality or a group of middle-range theories about a fact widely shared by a community of scientists. The scientific core is a set of common assumptions about a problem that seems logical, consistent, and empirically relevant. As a model, a paradigm is an overarching frame of mind or a broader frame of thought, or a larger frame of reference that can generate new theories, new concepts, and new hypotheses. Harvard physicist and historian of science Thomas Kuhn has been primarily responsible for advancing the idea of paradigm in understanding the nature of scientific progress and scientific theorizing. In his book *The Structure of Scientific Revolutions*, Kuhn (1971) examined how scientific theories—not in any particular scientific specialty but science as a whole—grow, change, and advance. He theorized that scientific theories change from one stage of advancement to another because of changes in scientific paradigms—changes in core assumptions and views shared by a community of scientists. At a given stage of development in a particular field of science, or a specific area of the scientific puzzle, described by Kuhn as a stage of normal science, few theoretical ideas and assumptions become dominant and are shared uncritically by the adherents of that science or scientific field. As time advances, however, new ideas grow, and new puzzles develop that cannot be explained by the existing paradigm of normal science. In this stage, questions, concerns, and anomalies become widespread, and the old paradigm is challenged and even discarded. A new paradigm—a new explanatory model—then slowly begins to take shape and begins to be shared by scientists. The new paradigm dominates, Kuhn argues, for some time and then goes through the same process of falsification and refutations. Therefore, advancement in science is a paradigm shift process—a method of advancement in scientific theorizing and scientific perspectives.

This chapter and the two that follow examine three major paradigms dominant in contemporary sociology—structural functionalism, conflict perspective, and symbolic interactionism. These are not specific middle-range theories, nor are they examples of grand theoretical systems in sociology. These are somewhat different ways of explaining and theorizing the social world through sociological eyes. They have different assumptions about the nature of the social world. They have different analytical strategies. They have different ways of conceptualizing the relations between the individual and society—the problem of relations between "I" and "we." In fact, modern sociology can be described as a scientific field dominated by these three paradigmatic communities. Theorizing in sociology has been growing since the birth of sociology in the middle of the 19th century. Throughout the past 150 years, there has been a considerable synergy of theories, ideas, and imaginations about making the social world more intelligible and telling human stories in more mundane, objective, and scientific ways. The science of sociology, presently, is a huge body of old and new models, concepts, and paradigms. Out of these vast and complex bodies of sociological ideasevolving from the days of August Comte, Karl Marx, Max Weber, and Emile Durkheim in the 19th and early 20th centuries—the three ways of looking at the social world and the three frames of sociological theorizing have remained dominant: structural functionalism, conflict perspective, and symbolic interactionism.

The Sociological Paradigm of Structural Functionalism

The Concept of Structure: The Key Sociological Discovery

One of the key discoveries of sociology is that the facts and events of human social life and human actions and behavior are not random, unaimed, and chaotic. They are mainly structured, systemic, deliberate, and culturally regulated. From the beginning of the birth of sociology in the middle of the 19th century, sociologists have been theorizing about how social structures and systems are born; how they shape the way we think, act, and behave; and how they change and evolve over time. This particular sociological eye of structuralism began to grow in two directions from the early days of sociology—to theorize about the meaning and the constitutions of social forms, patterns, structures, and systems and the way they shape and mold human social behavior.

FIGURE 5.1   Émile Durkheim

Classical sociologists Durkheim and Simmel were the early pioneers of structuralism. Émile Durkheim theorized that every form of society, whether a family or a clan, a tribe or a nation, is governed by a structure of collective mentality, or "collective consciousness." This structure of collective consciousness is the shaper of human actions and behavior. Through his research on suicide, Durkheim showed that individuals who are far apart from the structure of collective consciousness or group solidary are more vulnerable to committing suicide. The system of collective consciousness is born out of individual choices, preferences, values, and beliefs. It is held within a group over a long period based on shared customs, habits, rituals, language, mythology, history, and traditions. Once a collective consciousness is born and crystallized in a group, Durkheim theorized, it takes a life of its own. It becomes the prime shaper and mover of individual actions, behavior, hopes, dreams, and destinies.

In his book *Elementary Forms of Religious Life*, Durkheim (1912/2015) described that "collective representations are the result of an immense cooperation, which stretched out not only into space but into time as well; to make them, a multitude of minds have associated, united, and combined their ideas and sentiments" (p. 16). Durkheim contended that the concept of society or collective representations is both internal and external. An individual is "social" only when that person lives within a group with other humans and shares and builds the collective order. Internally, within an individual's mind, the structure shapes and molds that person's actions and behavior. The collective representations, for Durkheim, more importantly, are "exterior" to an individual. They exist out there as an objective and inviolable constraining force. An individual, Durkheim said, is under structural constraints to conform to the social collectivity. The structural paradigm in modern sociology has evolved during the last century based primarily on this notion of the structure of collective consciousness discovered by Durkheim.

Another significant tradition of structuralism in modern sociology came from the writings of German sociologist Georg Simmel in the late 19th century. Human social relationships, Simmel (1972) theorized, are divided into different forms and structures. Understanding the nature, meaning, and content of these social forms and systems and how they shape and mold individual actions and behavior, Simmel argued, is the prime task of sociology. For Simmel, a society is a complex web of human social interactions characterized by different structures or forms, such as family, community, city, or nation. The role of sociology is to explore how individuals subjectively think, act, and behave within these objectified structures and cultures and what collective norms, rules, and expectations govern their actions. Simmel theorized that space, time, numbers, and distance, among other social forces, shape and mold human interaction forms and patterns. His research has shown how we behave with strangers, how people think and behave in a metropolis, and how we changed after transitioning from a barter economy to a money economy under capitalism.

The second direction of sociological theorizing about structuralism—one that also began from the beginning of the birth of sociology—was concerned with understanding the new social structures of modernity and industrialization emerging in the wake of the disintegration of the old forms of monarchy and medievalism. About this particular direction of structuralism, the significant contribution came from Marx's theory of historical materialism and the Marxian explanation of capitalism's structure (Marx, 1867/2011; Marx & Engels, 1848/2002). Marx theorized that the economic system of production, particularly the form of ownership of the strategic means of production in all phases of the evolution of human civilization, was the key shaper and molder of politics, power, class, education, culture, philosophy, and ideology. Marx explained how under capitalism, the bourgeoisie—the capitalist class—and the proletariat—the working class—are locked in an eternal struggle for power and control. In a capitalist society, he believed, all facets of social life are dominated by the capitalist class and the culture and ideology of the bourgeoisie. Marx envisioned that humanity would not be able to escape the structure of class exploitation until the class society, the capitalist system, is forceable broken by a proletarian revolution and a socialist structure power is created.

Marx's prediction remained highly controversial, but his theory of historical materialism made considerable inroads on the sociological understanding of the structuralist paradigm. Along with Marx, almost all classical sociologists theorized about the directionality of human social life in the wake of the transition from the old structures of feudalism and medievalism to the new forms of capitalism and modernity. The classical sociologists were much concerned about how the new systems of industrialization, capitalism, urbanism, consumerism, and the unique cultural values of individualism, secularism, and privacy would shape and mold the modern mind. Throughout the whole of the 20th century, one of the core theoretical directions of sociology was to expand, refine, and redefine these two streams of structuralism that came from the classical sociology of the 19th century: the structural analysis of society, in general, and the structural analysis of modern industrial capitalism, in particular.

Social Structure: The Concept, Meaning, and Assumptions

The Historicity of the Concept of Social Structure

Sociologists argue that the social institutions of politics, economy, family, religion, and culture are universal. Human societies have been organized through and around these social structures since the beginning of human civilization. The concept of a structure, therefore, is not a modern innovation. Primitive societies, most anthropologists argue, were highly organized and structured. The science of anthropology is an expansive body of knowledge about the structures and patterns of primitive government, economy, family, marriage, kinship, and faith and beliefs. Anthropologist Edward Westermarck (1862–1939) conducted a series of research on primitive societies in the late 19th century, particularly in Morocco. His major works were *The History of Human Marriage*, published in 1894, and *The Origin and the Development of The Moral Ideas*, published in 1906. Westermarck theorized that our primitive ancestors were concerned, highly organized, and structured in contrast to a common perception in the 19th century. Based on his research, he found that the structure of monogamy and the pattern of monogamy marriage emerged in primitive societies much before the birth of modern civilization. In her celebrated work *Sex and Temperament in Three Primitive Societies*, published in 1935, American anthropologist Margaret Mead also showed how in three tribes in New Guinea, the attitudes toward sex and gender roles significantly varied depending on their different patterns of culture and ecology.

Long before modern sociologists began to explore the meaning and the constitution of social structure or the idea of structural functionalism, many anthropologists, in fact, explored the ideas of "structure" and "function" as conceptual tools for understanding primitive societies. British anthropologist Radcliff-Brown (1952), based on his research on Andaman Island, Australia, Africa, and China, theorized that the idea of social structure is a kind of a general law for making sense of the primitive world. For him, a social structure is invisible, but it has a life or a force of its own. A primitive social structure, such as kinship, was highly structured and functional. He theorized that an elementary task is performed in the science of social anthropology when we observe, describe, classify, and compare a concrete reality—a social process—and the way it unveils and unfolds in a particular space in a specific time.

But a more scientific approach is developed when we discover the structures and forms that are the general principles of an evolving social reality. Radcliff-Brown (1952) theorized that "when we use the term structure, we are referring to some sort of ordered arrangement of parts or components. Musical composition has a structure, and so does a sentence. The components of the of social structure are persons, and a person is a human being considered not as an organism, but as occupying position in social structure" (p. 10). He further expands that "the social relationships on which the continuing network constitute social structure, are not haphazard conjunctions of individuals, but are determined by the social process, and any relationship is one in which the conduct of persons in their interrelationship with each other is controlled by the norms, rules, and patterns" (Radcliff-Brown, 1952, p. 10). For Radcliff-Brown (1952), "the three concepts of process, structure and function are thus the components of a single theory as a scheme of interpretation of human social systems" (p. 12).

One of the most forceful expositions of the structural-functional paradigm came in the 1960s from the writings of French anthropologist Claude Levi-Strauss (1962). In his book *The Savage Mind*, Levi-

Strauss maintained that vital to understanding primitive cultures and social structures is the way the primitive mind worked. Levi-Strauss examined how the primitive mind named different plants and animals, described various rites and rituals, conceptualized various myths and mythologies, categorized space and time, and classified other social groups and their functional roles and behavior. Modern science, he said, means conceptualization, ordering, classification, abstraction, and generalization. In his extensive analysis of different facets of primitive cultures, Levi-Strauss observed that this was exactly how the primitive mind functioned and the way the primitive mind created different social structures, forms, and patterns.

The notion of structure is also embedded in different philosophies on the rise and formation of human societies. Aristotle's famous dictum was that humans are political animals. They have natural propensities to build groups, communities, cities, and states. Men are naturally driven to live within stable political structures because men are logical, rational, and moral. They have the ability to think in terms of moral categories. Plato said that justice is the glue that binds a polity together. The crucial need for a political structure for civilization was the central theme in the political philosophies of Hobbes, Locke, and Rousseau's social contract theories. All argued, albeit in different ways, that humans were born with the natural rights to life, liberty, equality, property, and the pursuit of happiness. But without a civil political structure and without the structures of law, justice, and democracy, human lives will be precarious and full of crimes and violence.

Many historical studies have shown that with the birth of the structure of the state, human violence has significantly declined. Historian Norbert Elias (1939/1994) theorized in his book *The Civilizing Process: Sociogenetic and Psychogenetic Investigations* that the rise of modern states after the decline of feudal absolutist monarchies is the reason why crime and violence declined in most areas of Western civilization. The birth of the social structure of the state led to a series of behavioral transformations in the lives of the people. The modern states emerged, Elias theorized, as a result of the evolution of civilizing processes—evolution in the manners and behaviors of people. He argued that with the progress of civilizing processes in the West, people internalized a sense of self-control. People learned to control impulsivity and to restrain what Freud called the blind forces of instinctual gratification. Social control became more of a matter of self-control from within. In Elias's word, they had a "psychogenetic" evolution in manners and behaviors, which affected the rate of violence in the whole civilization. Harvard psychologist Steven Pinker (2011), in his book *The Better Angels of Our Nature: Why Violence Has Declined*, made almost a similar argument. Pinker argued that the birth of the modern state, and within the modern state the growth of the social structure of gender equality and the respect for women, the invention of the media, expansion of the system of education, and the acceleration in trade and commerce, led to the decline of human violence in modern civilization.

Science and the Concept of Structure

The concept of structure, of course, is not the discovery of the sociologists. In fact, sociologists borrowed this concept from science, particularly the science of biology and its contribution to discovering the human body as a system or a structure. British sociologist Herbert Spencer was the first to theorize that a society is like a human organism. The concept of structure is central to almost all branches of science. The science of astronomy is based on understanding the galaxy as a natural system of interconnected stars and planets. Polish scientist Nicolas Copernicus discovered in 1542 that all the planets revolve around the sun. It is this discovery that marked the beginning of modern science in the 17th century.

Modern physics has discovered that the smallest unit of matter is an atom, and there is an atomic structure. British scientist Ernest Rutherford, described as the father of modern physics, discovered in 1911 that the atomic structure is composed of a massive space—a nucleus—populated by the particles of protons (positively charged) and neutrons (negatively charged), and the behavior of these particles are shaped by the action of the structure of the atom. It is this discovery that led to the invention of the atomic bomb, whose creation has permanently changed the nature of relations between and among the different nations within the global political system. The concept of structure is also very central to the whole science of biology. Biology has discovered that it is not just the human body that is made up of a system of interconnected and interdependent parts and organs; the trillions of human cells also are structural. One of the crucial discoveries in biology came with discovery of the structure of DNA by the British scientists Francis Creek and James Watson in 1953. Creek and Watson found that DNA is the smallest molecule in the human body that resides within each of the trillions of human cells. Their discovery of DNA's double helix structure brought fundamental changes to our understanding of how the human body, brain, and mind work and how the structure of DNA shapes and molds even the human social stories of success, faults, and frailties.

The concept of structure generally presents a vision of a physical entity that is visible, observable, and touchable. But a social structure is not a physical entity; it is not visible and observable through human eyes. It is not made of stones, bricks, or sticks. A social structure is a set of laws, rules, regulations, norms, rites, rituals, and institutions. A social structure is also a set of goals, visions, missions, and expectations. A social structure is a social construction, and it is not biological or genetic in origin. A social structure is a conceptual whole within which different parts and elements are interconnected and interdependent. Each component of a social structure has some roles and functions. The survival and the continuity of a structure depend on the proper functioning of the parts and components that make up the structure. A social structure is like a human body in that included in it is different interrelated and interdependent organs. The growth and survival of a human body are crucially dependent on the proper functioning of its constituent organs. That is why this particular paradigm is also described as the paradigm of structuralism functionalism.

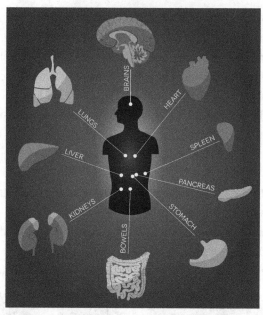

FIGURE 5.3   Structure of Human Anatomy

One of the crucial meanings of a social structure, however, is that its goals, visions, and expectations may not necessarily be the goals, visions, and expectations of its various parts and components. The essence and the significance of the "whole" may be different from those of its various components. Structural sociologists contend that a social structure has a life of its own, a direction of its own, and a destiny of its own. It is external, and it grows and evolves in terms of its logic, reason, and rationality. Therefore, the crucial responsibility of individuals, according to the structuralists, is the internalization of the social structure. The whole of social life for an individual can be described as a process of internalizing the social structures within which the individual lives.

An example can be provided by a modern corporation. Each corporation, such as Apple, Google, or Amazon, is a massive structure with its own set of laws, rules, regulations, norms, rites, and rituals and its own set of goals, visions, missions, and expectations. The people working for these corporations are functional in so far as knowledge and expertise are concerned. But their goals, ideas, hopes, and dreams may not necessarily be exactly those of the companies. The internalization of the structural imperatives and proceeding through socialization are, therefore, the crucial responsibilities of the individuals who are a part of different social structures. The structuralists assume that a social structure may not be like stones and bricks, but in essence, they are more rigid than stones and bricks. A social structure is a social force. Much as the force of wind and gravity, a social structure shapes our actions and behavior and controls the narratives of our life stories. A social structure is a facilitating factor in our social life, and it makes our social life more functional, productive, and predictive. Equally, a social structure is also a constraining factor. It forces us, such as laws, to conform and to behave in socially desirable manners.

The structuralists also assume that a social structure is imperative, legitimate, and consequential. A structure is essential because social life centers around different social structures. Using the metaphor of Thomas Hobbes, the structuralists would argue that human social life would be precarious and nasty, brutish, and short without humans creating and living within social structures of different kinds. Social order is predicated on the birth of different social structures, such as family, economy, polity, and religion. The essentiality of social structures for creating social order makes it legally and culturally legitimate (Table 5.1). Family as a social structure, for example, is universally legitimate. From the beginning of human civilization, the family emerged as a legitimate social structure to govern human relationships involving sex and reproduction. The social structure of polity emerged and became legitimate from the beginning of civilizations to govern the distribution of power, property, and privilege and to command and control the human passions of crimes and violence. The structuralists also argue that a structure is highly significant and consequential. A social structure not only shapes our roles, class, status, power, and privilege but also shapes our body, brain, mind, and genes. The effect of social structures is both external and internal. Our class location, for example, not only shapes our income, power, and privilege but also, in multifaceted ways, affects our mind, hopes, dreams, and destinies. Social structures are the prime creators and shapers of human social stories.

TABLE 5.1 The Hierarchy of Human Action Systems: Talcott Parsons

Cultural system	Values, beliefs, faiths, symbols, attitudes, perceptions, law, and technology
Social system	Economy, politics, family, education, social hierarchy, religion
Personality system	Mind, consciousness, and personality
Biological system	Human body composed of trillions of cells
Biogenetic system	The structure of DNA

Structuralists use the words "structure" and "system" interchangeably. But there are some conceptual differences. The concept of structure primarily implies forms, shapes, and patterns. It means authority, command, and control for the preservation and the continuity of the whole structure. The concept of a system, on the other hand, implies connectivity and interdependence between and among the different parts and elements of a system. The idea of a system also means that a system must always remain in balance and harmony, much as a human body. When a part of the human body malfunctions, the whole body is not thrown out of existence. A human body is a self-regulating mechanism, and it is always supposed to remain in a state of homeostasis through self-regulation. Sociologists analyzing a society or a part of a society as a system, therefore, primarily examine how and whether it functions or can function as a self-regulating mechanism. The self-regulating mechanism of a social system goes through stress and strains and even breaks up when social connectivity within a system is disrupted if interdependence becomes fragile and the cultural consensus is violated. In many modern families, stress and strains are growing because of the lack of internal systemic cohesion resulting from divergent values, norms, choices, and preferences.

One of the major assumptions of the structuralists is that each structure has a pattern, a shape, and a form. A structure, therefore, is not just a concept of a whole; it is also a particular form of a whole or a totality. The structuralists argue that the relationship between a structure and its various components is primarily shaped by its specific forms and patterns, which, in turn, shape its specific rules, roles, norms, goals, powers, and commands. How individuals within a structure will act, behave, and function depends on their particular forms and patterns. For example, in a democratic political structure, the laws and regulations of the command and distribution of power are qualitatively different from those of monarchy and authoritarian power structures. In a two-parent family structure, patterns and rituals of parental control and command are different from those of a single-parent family, a stepfamily, or a blended family. The functions of various structural components depend primarily on structural forms, patterns, and visions. For example, within military organizations, social relationships are relatively more formal, legalistic, and hierarchical based on the structures of command and control. On the other hand, in a school, social relationships are relatively less formalistic and less hierarchical and based more on expertise and experience. Similarly, in a family, social relationships are shaped more by love, feelings, and emotions. Understanding the nature and diversity in the forms and patterns of different social structures, such as differences between preindustrial and industrial social systems, is one of the significant theoretical interests in structuralism (Table 5.2).

What Holds a Structure Together?

Structuralism's other central issue involves what holds a structure together. The stability and continuity of social order, whether it is a family or a polity, has been central to human growth and survival since the beginning of human civilizations. One of the most common assertions is the need for undisputable command and control. This position was philosophically advocated and justified by political philosophers Niccolò Machiavelli in his book *The Prince*, published in 1513, and Thomas Hobbes in his book *Leviathan*, published in 1651. In his book, Machiavelli said "it is much safer to be feared than loved because ... love is preserved by the link of obligation which, owing to the baseness of men, is broken at every opportunity for their advantage; but fear preserves you by a dread of punishment which never fails" (Chapter XVII). Hobbes, in his book, surmised that the sovereign of a polity or a political commonwealth must have the absolute power to control, decide, and dominate. These sermons of Machiavelli and Hobbes provide the core of what is commonly described today as authoritarian control, authoritarian attitudes, and authoritarian personalities. A huge number of modern social structures, ranging from family to corporations to governments, are guided by this philosophy of control and domination.

Many structuralists, however, assume that mere control, coercion, and dominations cannot keep a structure together for a long time. Those structures that are based on mere control and dominations are more likely to be weak and fragile. They are more vulnerable to crimes, corruption, and violence. The competing assumption among many structuralists is that value consensus is the glue that binds a structure together. The idea of value consensus means that the overarching structural goals and values must be shared by individuals who form the structure. There must be a continuing process of learning, socialization, and integration. Sociologist Talcott Parsons theorized that each structure needs to perform at least four different but interconnected sets of functions to keep a structure together: adaptation, goal attainment, integration, and pattern maintenance (AGIL). Adaption means that a social structure and its members will have to dance with the tune of time. With the change of time, knowledge, technology, and culture, the larger contexts of social structures are always changing. The people who are in command of a social structure, such as the board of a company and the people who comprise that company as employees, will have to accept the larger forces of social change and transformations. In the face of social change in the larger environment, the rigidity of a structure can lead to its dysfunctions and even dissolution.

Structural Forms/ Institutions	Preindustrial (1500–1900)	Industrial/High Tech (1900–2000)
Economy	Agricultural/farm-based	Industrial/factory/service
Technology	Craft/cottage industries	Science-based/digital
Nature of production	Domestic consumption	Global market–oriented
Place of work	Farm/lands	Factory/office/virtual
Labor	Bonded/serf/legally defined	Free labor
Major classes	Aristocrats/nobility	Upper/middle/lower
Division of labor	Men at work/women at home	Men and women at work
Major wealth	Land	Capital/knowledge
Politics	Monarchy/aristocracy	Democracy
Legitimacy of power	Based on birth/divine sanctions	Representations/expertise
Bureaucracy	Patrimonial/patronage	Rational/legal/professional
Sources of law	Monarchy/canonical law	Legislatures/court/executive
Education	Elitist/closed	Open/mass education
Family	Extended/joint family	Nuclear/alternative types
Marriage	Primarily for reproduction	Love and romanticism
Cohabitation	Socially/legally unacceptable	High level of acceptance
Control of sex	Highly regulated	Loosely regulated
Divorce	Socially stigmatized	No-fault divorce
Religion	No church-state separation	Church-state separation
Religiosity	High	Low
Sources of knowledge	Religion/sacred texts	Science and philosophy
Philosophy	Primarily God-centered	Primarily human-centered
Ideology/worldview	Conservative	Liberal/global
Social orientation	Hierarchical/ascribed status	Equality/achieved status
Cultural orientation	Collectivistic	Individualistic

In America today, many new social forces, such as digitalization, the #MeToo movement, and Black Lives Matter, are gathering significant ground. The American corporations that are more sensitive to the emerging issues and challenges are more likely to be creative and productive. This is primarily the political function of a structure. Goal attainment, on the other hand, is the economic function of a structure. A structure that is economically productive and innovative is more likely to be strong and sustainable.

Another crucial function of a structure is integration, which means the cultivation of collective solidarity and a collective sense of bonding. It is described primarily as a sociological function. No social structure is completely homogeneous; most are composed of diverse genders, races, and religions. Google, for example, has about 130,000 employees (as of 2020), and they come from different races, genders, countries, and cultures. They have different levels of education and expertise, and they have divergent political beliefs. As a company, for Google to survive and thrive, it has a significant function of cultivating a sense of collective bonding among its divergent actors and agencies.

Finally, according to Parson's AGIL model, a social structure has also a cultural function to continuously produce and reproduce its core goals, visions, and missions through a process of symbolization, such as the notion of corporate culture, the description of a company as a "family," or such political slogans as "Make America Great Again" or "Build Back Better." The central idea about what holds a structure together, for most structuralists, is the notion of value consensus through the performance of a series of crucial political, economic, social, and cultural functions.

The concept of functional analysis is based on three significant assumptions (Merton, 1967). First, functions are imperative for the maintenance of the whole system and to ensure systemic unity, integration, and continuity. Second, functions are universal and facilitating. From the beginning of human social life, for example, rape, incest, murder, and adultery were punishable. Punishment serves the universal function of maintaining social peace and security. From the beginning of human social life, hierarchy became a central notion in organizing human roles, rules, and organizations. Therefore, structuralists assume that social hierarchy and social stratification serve the universal function of maintaining social order (Davis & Moore, 1945). Third, structuralists believe that systemic functions are indispensable and vital. For a nuclear family with children, for example, the role of socialization is essential.

In a modern democratic polity, the functions of distribution and allocation of power based on representations are vital; however, the roles and the efficacy of all systemic and structural processes are not equally visible. Social structures have both manifest and latent roles and functions (Merton, 1967). The manifest functions of a religion, for example, are the observance of religious prayers and worships, reading the holy texts and Scriptures, and performing the religious rites and rituals. The latent and unseen functions of religion are creating a sense of collective bonding among its believers or cultivating a sense of individual spirituality. The manifest function of modern education is to create a current workforce. One of the latent functions of contemporary education is developing an understanding of self-confidence and enhancing social status.

Structure-Individual or Structure-Agency Connections

One of the enduring theoretical issues in structural functionalism is structure and individual connections, or the structure and culture connections. There is a strong sense among many structuralists who follow the Durkheim perspective that a structure is an objective reality. Individuals living within a structure must conform to the structural rules of the game. In an extreme sense, the structure is like a prison. An individual living within a political system, for example, must conform to its values and visions and must not rebel and revolt. The strains of a system will be self-regulating and does not need rebellions or violence from the individuals who make up the structure. The structural authority, command, control, and hierarchy must not be challenged and disputed for the sake of structural unity, preservation, and continuity (Table 5.3).

Talcott Parsons argued that a structure and individuals are connected through the mediation of culture. Parson's central thesis was that personality and society are two different human action systems and are hierarchically organized. At the top of the personality and social systems is the cultural system—a shared system of values, symbols, and beliefs—that works as a cybernetic control mechanism on other systems, including the biogenic and biophysical systems. Thus, Parsons (1970) argued that "a social system is a function of a common culture, which not only form the basis of intercommunication of its members, but which defines, and so in one sense determines, the relative status of its members" (p. 22). A social system or a social structure can function only if its human agencies internalize the common culture. "The inescapable conclusion," Parsons (1970) said, "is that not only moral standards but all the components of the *common culture* are internalized ... as part of the personality structure" (p. 23).

TABLE 5.3 What Keeps a Social System Together?

What Keeps a System Functional?	What Makes a System Dysfunctional?
Compliance to authority Compliance to power and command Compliance to legitimate laws Respect for social hierarchy Building stable social relationships Following socially defined social roles Compliance to common goals and expectations Internalization of the social control mechanisms Shared values, faith, and beliefs	Failure to exercise authority (i.e., parental, school, organizational, legal) Failure to enforce command and control Failure to maintain the hierarchy Violation of rules, roles, and functions Violation of cultural consensus Lack of socialization and internalization

British sociologist Anthony Giddens in the mid-1970s provided a more refined analysis of structure and agency connections. Giddens's basic notion was that a structure must be seen as dual in nature. A structure is a shaper and molder of individual actions and behavior. A structure, however, is also shaped and molded by individual actions and behavior: A structure or a social system shapes people's symbolic world and practices. The symbolic world of the people—the culture—also reproduces a social structure and a social system. Structures and cultures are not opposed to each other; they rather presuppose each other. Giddens (1979) said that "every social actor knows a great deal about the conditions of the reproduction of the society of which he or she is a member. Failure to acknowledge this is a basic insufficiency of functionalism and structuralism alike" (p. 5). Giddens (1979) also said, "The proposition that all social agents are knowledgeable about the social systems which they constitute and reproduce in their actions is a logically necessary feature of the conception of the duality of structure" (p. 5). Giddens described his theory as the theory of structuration, which means that structure is not a steady state but rather a process that is continuously created and recreated by human agencies. The notion that transpires from Giddens's theory of structuration is the relative autonomy of individuals who comprise a structure. A social structure, for Giddens, is not like a prison or an inviolable objective reality (Table 5.4). For example, the individuals who live within a structure, a government, a company, or a family have the autonomy to shape and mold its nature and articulations through knowledge, participation, discourses, and reflexivity (Giddens, 1991).

TABLE 5.4 Structural-Functionalist Paradigm: Key Assumptions

Characteristics	Examples
The structure is a social force.	We are forced to conform to laws; we are forced to share the values of a company or an institution within which we work.
The structure is a collective social actor.	A company, a school, or a city, for example, can be taken to court for litigations.
The structure is legitimate, and it has its logic and rationalities. Structure is syntactic	The goals, visions, and missions of the U.S. Department of Defense, for example, are driven by the logic and rationalities of U.S. national security. Legitimacy is based on the Constitution.
The structure is objective, external, and constraining.	Parental control in a family is objective and external; legal control of behavior is objective, exterior, and constraining.
The structure is subjective and internal.	Children in a family are expected to understand the shared family values and expectations.
The structure is more significant than an individual.	The goals, visions, and demands of a workplace are much higher and more significant than those of the employees.
The structure is functional and a facilitating agent.	The family contributes to the development of children in socially productive and desirable manners.
The structure is relatively permanent, and structural change is evolutionary.	In most societies, family, economy, politics, religion, and educational systems are relatively permanent. Structural change is incremental.

THE PROFILE OF SYSTEMIC ANALYSIS

Sociology's first discovery was that society is amenable to scientific analysis. Sociology can theorize, generalize, and make predictions about the nature and the evolution of social institutions, actions, behavior, and predicaments. Sociology's other important discovery was that society is characterized by different systems, forms, and patterns. The concept of a system is one of the central notions in science. In a sense, science is a search for systems, structures, and patterns in different realms of realities—nature, body, mind, and society.

For example, physicists seek to understand the quality of the planetary system, the solar system, and atomic and molecular structures. In biology, the core of scientific research is to understand how the human body comprises different systems and structures (e.g., circulatory system, nervous system, digestive system, cellular system, and DNA construction) and how they are interconnected and interdependent. One of the tremendous scientific curiosities in biology is the study of brain structure, and many discoveries have shown that different configurations of the brain have different roles and functions. Sigmund Freud fathered the science of psychology by creating the theory of the mind's id, ego, and superego structure. Sociology borrowed the system's concept primarily from biology in the formative years of classical sociology in the 19th century.

The notion of "system" implies a structure within which different parts have different functions and are interconnected and interdependent. The system's idea means that it is characterized by a form, a style, and a pattern. The shape, style, and pattern of a system will grow and evolve if its parts and components usually function and are interconnected. A system will become dysfunctional or can disintegrate if its different elements are not performing their expected roles and functions.

Sociology has discovered that most societies are made up of at least five major social systems: economy, politics, family, education, and religion. These systems have different forms and patterns and different shapes and styles. A capitalist system of economy, for example, is different from a socialist economic system. A monarchical form of government is different from a democratic form of government. A two-parent nuclear family system is different from a single-parent family system, and Christianity as a form of religion is different from Hinduism and Islam. Structural sociologists theorize that social structures, much as physical entities, are objective—they are out there; they are external to us. Individuals within a system will have to conform to its norms, values, laws, and expectations. Social structures have control and a constraining role on the behavior of individuals. Social systems and structures, in fact, shape the way we are.

Structural Functionalism: The Key Analytical Strategies

The structural-functional paradigm is not the description or an analysis of any particular society or a specific social structure. It is a perspective—a unique sociological eye—to describe and analyze an institution or a social system. The standpoint of structural functionalism includes some key analytical directions or strategies. One of the crucial things to know in the beginning is the form of a structural pattern. Suppose the structure of the political system of a country, for example, is under consideration. In that case, the first thing to explore is whether it is a liberal democratic political system, an authoritarian political system, a monarchical political system, a theocracy, or a tribal political system. These shapes and patterns will suggest how it is internally organized, its essential components and institutions, and what values, visions, and missions serve as the glue to keep the structure together.

Iran, for example, is a theocratic form of government. The Iranian constitution is based on the Qur'an. America, on the other hand, is a form of the liberal political system. It is based on the values of constitutionalism, democracy, federalism, separation of power, checks and balances, the rule of law, church and state separation, equality, individualism, and the Lockean philosophy of natural rights to life, liberty, and the pursuit of happiness. No one will have a genuine understanding of the American political system unless these institutional features and cultural values are examined and explored. Power, authority, command, functions, and cultural consensus are key ingredients of a social structure or a social system. The understanding of the forms and patterns of a structure will suggest how its power and commands are exercised, how its different functions are performed, and how cultural and symbolic consensus is achieved and sustained (Table 5.5). In analyzing a particular system, one also needs to explore its various regions of stress and tensions and the way systemic stress and tensions are resolved to keep the system in a state of self-regulation.

TABLE 5.5 Structural-Functionalist Paradigm: Key Analytical Strategies

<u>Explore</u> the structural and systemic forms and patterns (e.g., two-parent family vs. single-parent family; rural vs. urban; agricultural economy vs. global digital economy).
<u>See</u> the way a structure is internally organized (extremely hierarchical vs. team building management).
<u>Probe</u> the nature of connectivity between and among different structural parts and components (i.e., routinized vs. innovative; top-down vs. feedback loop).
<u>Investigate</u> the extent to which systemic functions are performed (AGIL framework).
<u>Describe</u> the nature of structural authority, power, command, hierarchy, and control (e.g., liberal vs. conservative; democratic vs. authoritarian political structures).
<u>Examine</u> how structural power and commands are exercised (e.g., democratic vs. authoritarian parenting; top-down vs. bottom-up approaches to management).
<u>Study</u> the value framework of a structure and the ideology that holds a system together (e.g., traditional vs. modernism; liberalism vs. conservatism vs. theocratic; localism vs. globalism).
<u>Analyze</u> the regions of structural stress and dysfunctions (e.g., extent of intimate partner violence in a family or the extent of diversity in family values; the nature of political or religious violence within a political system; or equal opportunities vs. discriminations within an economic system).

Structural Functionalism in Action

The American Political System

One of the unique examples of a social structure that has been working for about 245 years and a social structure that has created one of the most modern nations in the world is America's political system.

America's political system was formally created after the Declaration of Independence in 1776. At an age when the whole of Europe was experiencing turbulent social, economic, and intellectual transformations in the wake of the disintegration of the feudal and aristocratic social order, and at an age when most of the world was under colonial domination by the European powers, America led the beginning of the birth of a new social and political order based on the core values of democracy, equality, individualism, church and state separation, and the inalienable human rights to life, liberty, and the pursuit of happiness.

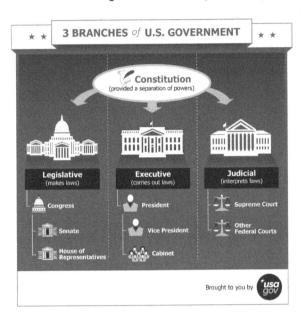

FIGURE 5.4   Structure of the American Government

What is remarkable is not just the creation of a unique political system but also its continuity for 245 years as a model for a modern political system. During the past 245 years, America has gone through much political stress, strains, turmoil, and turbulence, from the Civil War to World War I, to World War II, to the Great Depression, and the Cold War, but the basic structural properties and the cultural consensus that binds those properties together remained largely unchanged. The American Constitution that was born in 1776 and crystallized in its modern form in 1790 has undergone many amendments, but the Constitution itself was never thrown away (Table 5.6).

The core of the American political system is a written constitution that has created a unique structure based on three separate but interdependent branches: executive, legislative, and judicial. It has also created a federal or dual system of government with a defined set of powers of governance. The executive branch is the American presidency, and it governs the functioning of the principal executive departments and agencies. The president is elected for 4 years by the electoral college. The legislative branch does not elect the American president as is the norm in parliamentary political systems of Canada, England, India, and many other countries. In a parliamentary political system, the Prime Minister can be removed by a vote of no confidence by the parliament. In the American Presidential system, the President can only be impeached for high crimes and misdemeanor by a two-thirds majority of the Senate.

In America, the president nominates the heads of the executive departments, but they are subject to review by the Senate. America's legislative branch is composed of two houses—the Senate and the House of Representatives. Every 6 years, two senators are elected from the 50 states. Every 2 years, the House of Representatives is elected from the states, and the number of representatives depends on the size of the population. Congress makes legislation, but the legislation must be signed by the president to confer the status of federal statutes. To become law, all legislation made by Congress must be approved by a majority vote from both houses of Congress.

The American judicial branch is composed of three tiers of courts: The Supreme Court, appellate courts, and district courts. The president nominates the federal judges, but they are subject to confirmation by the Senate. There are nine justices on the Supreme Court, and they are appointed for life. The Supreme Court has the ultimate authority to examine the constitutionality of laws made by Congress. No federal or state laws can be made in America in violation of the federal Constitution. Four of the major features of the American political system include constitutionalism, federalism, separation of powers, and checks and balances.

TABLE 5.6 The Profile of the American Political System

The Constitution of the United States		
Major Systemic Components	**Major Systemic Forms and Patterns**	**Major Systemic Values: Sources of Systemic Consensus**
Executive Branch President Departments Agencies **Legislative Branch** Senate House of Representatives **Judicial Branch** Supreme Court Appellate courts District courts	Constitutionalism Federalism Presidential form of government Representative government Bicameral legislature Separation of powers Checks and balances Two-party system Liberal vs. conservative ideology Electoral college Presidential term limit Divided government: federal vs. state Universal suffrage	Democracy Equality Individualism Church-state separation Privacy Capitalism Modernism Urbanism Materialism Pragmatism Globalism Knowledge society/digital society Credentialism Open society Cultural diversity/multiculturalism Voluntarism Natural rights Universal human rights

The structural sociologists (e.g., Talcott Parsons) theorized that cultural consensus is the glue that binds a structure together, assures structural unity, and builds the connectivity between structure and agency (individuals). During the past 245 years, America's political system history can be described as the history of building and strengthening the cultural consensus. One way of creating and recreating the cultural consensus within the polity was the widening of the core values of democracy, equality, individualism, and church-state separation for inclusive politics. Amendment 13 to the Constitution, passed after the Civil War, in 1865, abolished slavery. Amendment 15, in 1879, prohibits states from denying the right to vote based on race, color, or previous conditions of servitude. Amendment 19, passed in 1920, prohibits denying the right to vote based on gender. These amendments widened the door for inclusive politics and the boundary of democracy and equality within the American polity.

The culture of inclusive politics became further widened over the past 70 years following enactment of a series of laws by Congress, including the Civil Rights Act of 1964, the Americans with Disability Act of 1991, and the Matthew Shepard and James Byrd Jr. Hate Crimes Prevention Act of 2009. During the past 70 years, the U.S. Supreme Court has also made a series of rulings that significantly widened the culture of the open society, democracy, equality, individualism, religious tolerance, and church-state separation. Some of these significant rulings include *Engel v. Vitale* of 1962, *Lemon v. Kurtzman* of 1971, *Griswold v. Connecticut* of 1965, *Roe v. Wade* of 1973, *Brown v. Board of Education of Topeka* of 1954; *Lawrence v. Texas* of 2003, and *Obergefell v. Hodges* of 2015. There is, however, no denying that the widening boundary of inclusive politics in America has also generated huge structural stress and strains. Some of these stress and strains are becoming increasingly visible with the emergence and the strengthening of the far-right and extremely conservative ideology in American politics during the 2nd decade of the 21st century.

The concept of structuration developed by Giddens—the idea that a structure is not just an abstraction but a process of continuous creation and recreation of a social system by the individuals who comprise it—can also be examined in the context of the evolving nature of the American political system. Giddens's primary thesis states that the individuals within a system, through their critical knowledge and discursive thoughts, work as agents of change and transformation. They do not only and uncritically take the system as it unfolds in front of them, and they are not always acting under the control and domination of systemic rules and hierarchy.

Within the American political system, the different constitutional amendments, congressional acts and statutes, and Supreme Court decisions that widened the boundary of inclusive politics and open society did not always come from the top hierarchy of command and control of the political system. The plan of inclusive politics had to be formed and advanced by real-world people by organizing social movements of different kinds at different times of history. Amendment 19 gave women the right to vote in 1920, but the women's movement for voting rights began in 1848. Amendment 13 abolished slavery in 1865, but the abolitionist movement began in the 1830s. In the 1960s and 1970s, Congress enacted much civil rights legislation, and the U.S. Supreme Court made many rulings for inclusive culture and politics, but those laws were made in the context of a series of popular movements and upheavals, including the civil rights movement of the 1960s and the sexual revolution and gay rights movements of the 1970s. A social system needs a cultural consensus for its survival and continuity, but cultural consensus grows and evolves through a process of many historical changes and transformations.

Rural-Urban Continuum and Voting Behavior in America

Sociologists spend a great deal of time exploring how our actions, choices, preferences, attitudes, perceptions, and behavior vary depending on whether we live in rural or urban areas. Rural and urban social systems are structurally and culturally different, and this is true of almost all countries and regions of the world. The forms and patterns of the rural economy, politics, family, education, culture, and technology are qualitatively different from those of predominantly urban areas (Table 5.7). The industrial and urban civilization that began to evolve from the middle of the 19th century has given birth to a new culture of urbanism as a way of life (Wirth, 1938). Sociologists examine how urbanism, instead of ruralism, shapes and molds the way we act, think, and behave.

We can study, for example, how rural and urban people in America are different in their political beliefs and attitudes, particularly in their voting behavior. According to the U.S. census of 2010, about 71.2% of the U.S. population in 2010 (total U.S. population in 2010 was about 308 million) lived in urban areas (Ratcliff et al., 2016). About 19.3% of Americans lived in rural areas. This means that about 60 million Americans in 2010 lived in rural areas. The U.S. census defines rural and urban differences primarily in terms of population density, land use, and distance. The 2010 census defined two types of urban areas in terms of the density of population: urban areas (with a population of 50,000 or more) and urban clusters (with a population of about 2,500 but less than 50,000). According to the Ratcliff et al. (2016), "Rural is defined as all population, housing, and territory not included within an urbanized area or urban cluster.

As a result, the rural portion of the United States encompasses a wide variety of settlements, from densely settled small towns and 'large-lot' housing sub-divisions on the fringes of urban areas, to more sparsely populated and remote areas" (p. 2). The 2010 census also defined two categories of rural people in America: mostly rural, and completely rural. In 2010, there were about 704 counties that were "100 percent or completely rural. These counties have no areas that are identified as urban and are home to less than 2.0 percent of the total U.S. population" (Ratcliff et al., 2016, p. 6). Data from the U.S. Department of Agriculture also showed that America's rural population is currently growing after a steady decline in the past decade (Cromartie & Vilorio, 2019). "The decline in rural population, which began in 2010 and reached its lowest level in 2011–12 with a loss of nearly 62,000 residents, has since begun to reverse. In 2016–17, rural counties added population for the first time this decade" (Cromartie & Vilorio, 2019, p. 1).

Rural and urban America are different in terms of many structural factors, forms, and patterns (Table 5.7). Racially and ethnically, rural areas are less diverse than urban areas. "In 2017, Whites accounted for nearly 80 percent of the rural population (compared to 58 percent in urban areas). While Hispanics were the fastest-growing segment of the rural population, they account for only 9 percent of the rural population (20 percent in urban areas). Blacks made up 8 percent of the rural population (13 percent in urban areas)" (U.S. Department of Agriculture, 2018, p. 3). Rural America is aging faster than urban America. Data from the U.S. Department of Agriculture (2018) show that America's "rural population has grown older as the baby boomer generation ages into retirement. As a result, the labor force participation rate has dropped considerably, corresponding to a reduction in rural employment of roughly 277,000 between 2013 and 2017 (holding the other factors constant)" (p. 4).

The aging population and a variety of other factors affect rural employment growth. "Rural employment has grown at about 0.5 percent per year, with periods of stagnation (2012–13, 2016). Estimated rural employment in the second quarter of 2018 was still 1.8% below its prerecession level. Rural America includes 14% of the nation's population but has accounted for only 4% of employment growth since 2013" (U.S. Department of Agriculture, 2018, p. 3). The poverty rate in rural America is higher than that of urban America, and this has existed since the 1960s. The poverty gap between rural and urban areas is currently increasing.

Although the poverty rate is higher among Black people in rural America, most of the rural poor are White people: "Despite the much lower poverty rate among Whites, the majority of the rural poor are White. They accounted for 80 percent of the general rural population and 65 percent of the rural population in poverty in 2017" (U.S. Department of Agriculture, 2018, p. 4).

The rural social system and its social and economic forms and patterns in America are relatively more in favor of the ideology of the Republican Party, particularly the right-wing Republican Party and its nativistic political ideology of "Make America Great Again." A 2016 study on the pattern of rural voting observed that "rural voters vote more Republican, while urban voters vote more Democratic, and that divide grew this year from where it was in 2012 and 2008. It's a nuanced divide, too; strikingly, as counties get progressively more rural, they more or less steadily grow more Republican" (Kurtzleben, 2016, p. 1).

A similar observation was made in a 2018 study by the Pew Research Center. The study observed that America's rural and urban areas "are also becoming more polarized politically. Americans in urban and rural communities have widely different views when it comes to social and political issues. From feelings about President Donald Trump to views on immigration and same-sex marriage, there are wide gaps between urban and rural adults" (Parker et al., 2018, p. 1). The study noted that 44% of rural voters in 1998 voted for Republicans. In 2017, it increased to 58%. Involving immigration, for instance, 57% of rural voters, compared with 35% of urban voters, believe that migrated people from other countries threaten American values and creeds.

TABLE 5.7 Comparative Patterns of Rural and Urban Social Systems in America

Forms and Patterns	Rural Systems	Urban Systems
Economic dimension	Predominantly agricultural; traditional manufacturing industries; moderately high rate of unemployment; relatively high level of poverty-aging workforce	Predominantly high-tech industrial; expanding digital economy; low level of unemployment; middle to upper socioeconomic class; relatively young workforce
Political dimension	High support for conservative values and ideology; low level of political consciousness and participation	High support for liberal values and ideology; high level of political consciousness and participation
Social dimension	Collectivistic in social orientation; high level of religiosity; racially less diverse; not college educated; relatively strong family values	Individualist in social orientation; college educated; moderate to the low level of religiosity; racially diverse; privatized family values
Cultural dimension	Localization; nativistic; closed society orientation, more sedentary; ruralism as a way of life	Global in orientation; values the open society approach; culturally diverse; more mobile; urbanism as a way of life
Internet penetration	Low level of internet penetration; digital divide	High level of internet penetration; digitalization as a way of urbanism

With respect to same-sex marriage, 52% of rural voters, compared with 35% of urban voters, believe such marriages are a very bad thing (Parker et al., 2018, p. 2). The Pew Research Center study also found that

"Trump's ratings are particularly warm in rural areas, where four-in-ten rate him warmly. By contrast, 19% of people in urban areas give Trump a warm rating" (Parker et al., 2018, p. 3). This rural-urban variation in voting behavior in America shows how social structures and social systems shape and mold our actions, attitudes, beliefs, and perceptions.

Suggested Questions, Essays, Assignments, and Quizzes

1. What is the role of theorizing in science in general? How are theories different from models and paradigms? Describe and explain with examples.

2. What are the three different paradigms in sociology? What are some of the core assumptions of the systemic or the structural-functional paradigm? Briefly describe these assumptions, developing a chart as presented in the chapter.

3. The concept of a system is fundamental to modern science. Sociology borrowed the concept of the system from biology. How is the concept of system defined and conceptualized in the scientific analysis? Based on class lectures, your review of the chapter, and your internet research, describe how the system's concept is central to the science of astronomy, physics, and biology (copy and paste relevant images from the internet.

4. One of the puzzles in structural sociology is what holds a structure together, or how is social order possible? What holds, for example, a family together or a government together? Based on your reading of this chapter, describe and explain why the structures of millions of families in America are breaking up and becoming dysfunctional. Use some relevant data from studies conducted by the Pew Research Center or the U.S. Census Bureau to back up your analysis.

5. What are some of the structural-functional paradigm's analytical strategies, or how to understand a social structure or a system? Use some of these strategies and develop an essay (three or four single-spaced pages, 12-point font) in explaining some of the recent change and transformations in the American economy (e.g., the rise of the digital economy) and the way they are affecting work, family, and politics (e.g., voting behavior).

6. Copy and paste a chart on the American political system from the internet, such as the chart presented in this chapter. Based on lectures and your reading of this chapter, write an essay (four or five single-spaced pages, 12-point font) describing: (a) the core values of the American political system, (b) the issues of separation of powers, and (c) the problem of checks and balances. Comment in this context, at the end of your essay, on the structural constraints within Congress that impeded the process of the impeachment of President Donald Trump in 2019.

7. Function is one of the core concepts used in explaining a society from the structural-functional paradigm. What do sociologists mean by manifest and latent functions of a social system? Describe the American political system's manifest and latent functions in a chart (functional descriptions in terms of bullets are acceptable).

8. In recent years, America became highly politically polarized, particularly the divide between urban and rural America, which is noticeably growing in the context of voting behavior. During 2016 and 2020, rural White America overwhelmingly voted for the Republican Party. In the context of this emerging political landscape, describe the fundamental structural differences between rural and

urban America and their effects on the future of American politics and democracy.

9. Quiz: A sociological paradigm is a set of assumptions about a given social reality. One of the core functions of a paradigm is to make us able to develop theories and hypotheses. Develop five hypotheses from the perspective of structural functionalism concerning the nature and functions of the contemporary American family, and briefly explain those hypotheses. (Hint: High rate of male incarceration among African Americans is positively connected to the fragility of the two-parent family structure.)

10. One of the core assumptions of the structural-functional paradigm is that structures matter. Structures shape, constrain, and facilitate our acts and behavior. The number of single-parent family structures is growing in America. Data show that a single parent heads about 25% of American households, and about 86% of single-parent families are headed by mothers. In this context, write an essay (three to four single-spaced pages, 12-point font) describing and explaining the structural impediments and constraints of single-parent families headed by mothers. (Hint: The structural-functional paradigm emphasizes such concepts as roles, order, functions, control, and command.)

References

Cromartie, J., & Vilorio, D. (2019). *Rural population trends*. U.S. Department of Agriculture. Retrieved from https://www.ers.usda.gov/amber-waves/2019/february/rural-population-trends/on December 30, 2020.

Davis, K., & Moore, W. E. (1945). Some principles of stratification. *American Sociological Review, 10* (2), 242–249. Retrieved from https://doi.org/10.2307/2085643 on December 30, 2020.

Durkheim, E. (2015). *The elementary forms of religious life*. Free Press. (Original work published 1912)

Eisenstadt, S. N. (1966). *Modernization: Protest and change*. Prentice-Hall.

Elias, N. (1994). *The civilizing process: Sociogenetic and psychogenetic investigations*. Blackwell Publishers. (Original work published 1939)

Etzioni, A. (1968). *The active society*. Free Press.

Giddens, A. (1979). *Central problems in social theory: Action, structure, and contradiction in social analysis*. Stanford University Press.

Giddens, A. (1991). *Modernity and self-identity: Self and society in the late modern age*. Stanford University Press.

Holzner, B., Campbell, D. T., & Shahidullah, S. M. (1985). Introduction: The comparative study of science and the sociology of scientific validity. *Science Communication, 6*(4), 307–328.

Jefferson, T. (1801). *First Inaugural Address*. The Avalon Project at Yale Law School. Retrieved from https://avalon.law.yale.edu/19th_century/jefinau1.asp on December 20, 2020

Inkles, A. (1983). *Exploring individual modernity*. Columbia University Press.

Kuhn, T. S. (1971). *The structure of scientific revolutions*. University of Chicago Press.

Kurtzleben, D. (2016). *Rural voters played a big part in helping Trump defeat Clinton*. NPR. Retrieved from https://www.npr.org/2016/11/14/501737150/rural-voters-played-a-big-part-in-helping-trump-defeat-clinton on December 2020.

Levi-Strauss, C. (1962). *Savage mind*. University of Chicago Press.

Lipset, S. M. (1979). *The first new nation: The United States in historical and comparative perspectives*. W. W. Norton.

Marx, K. (2011). *Das kapital (capital): A critique of political economy* (S. Moore, Trans.). Create Space Independent Publishing Platforms. (Original work published 1867)

Marx, K., & Engels, F. (2002). *The communist manifesto*. Penguin Classics. (Original work published 1848)

Mead, M. (1935). *Sex and temperament in three primitive societies*. Dell Publishing.

Merton, R. K. (1967). *On theoretical sociology: Five essays, old and new*. Free Press.

Nelson, B. (1981). *On the roads to modernity: Conscience, science, and civilizations*. Rowman and Littlefield.

Parker, K., Mesasce Horowitz, J., Brown, A., Fry, R., Cohn, D., & Igielnik, R. (2018). *Urban, suburban, and rural residents' views on key social and political issues*. Pew Research Center. Retrieved from https://www.pewresearch.org/social-trends/2018/05/22/urban-suburban-and-rural-residents-views-on-key-social-and-political-issues/

Parsons, T. (1970). *The social systems (with new Forward by Neil J. Smelser)*. Free Press.

Parsons, T. (1971). *The system of modern societies*. Prentice-Hall.

Parsons, T., & Shils, E. A. (2001). *Toward a general theory of action* (Abridged ed.). Routledge. (Originally published 1951)

Pinker, S. (2011). *The better angels of our nature: Why violence has declined*. Penguin Books.

Popper, K. (1959). *The logic of scientific discovery*. Routledge-Taylor.

Popper, K. (1963). *Conjectures and refutations: The growth of scientific knowledge*. Routledge.

Radcliff-Brown, A. R. (1952). *Structure and function in primitive society: Essays and addresses.* Free Press.

Ratcliff, M., Burd, C., Holder, K., & Fields, A. (2016). *Defining rural at the U.S. census bureau: American community survey and geography brief.* U.S. Census Bureau. Retrieved from https://www2.census.gov/geo/pdfs/reference/ua/Defining_Rural.pdf on December 30, 2020.

Robertson, R. (1992). *Globalization: Social theory and global culture.* Sage Publications.

Shahidullah, S. M. (2019). America's global project on modernity: Continuity, change, and challenges in the 21st century. In S. M. Shahidullah (Ed.), *Modernity, modernization, and globalization: Issues and challenges of the 21st century* (pp. 45–80). NOVA Science Publications.

Simmel, G. (1972). *Individuality and social forms* (D. N. Levine, Ed. and Intro.). University of Chicago Press.

U.S. Department of Agriculture. (2018). *Rural America at a glance, 2018 edition.* Retrieved from https://www.ers.usda.gov/webdocs/publications/90556/eib-200.pdf?v=9610.5 on December 30, 2020.

Viereck, G. (1929). What life means to Einstein. *Saturday Evening Post.* Retrieved from https://www.saturdayeveningpost.com/wp-content/uploads/satevepost/what_life_means_to_einstein.pdf on December 30, 2020.

Wallerstein, I. (2004). *World-system analysis: An introduction.* Duke University Press.

Wallerstein, I. (2011). *Modern world system: The second era of the great expansion of the capitalist world economy.* University of California Press.

Weber, M. (1963). *Sociology of religion.* Beacon Press.

Weber, M. (2011). *The methodology of social sciences* (E. Shils & H. A. Finch, Trans. and Ed.). Routledge. (Original work published 1949)

Weber, M. (2013). *The Protestant ethic and the spirit of capitalism.* Penguin Twentieth-Century Classics. (Original work published 1905)

Wirth, L. (1938). Urbanism as a way of life. *American Journal of Sociology, 44*(1), 1–24. Retrieved from http://www.jstor.org/stable/2768119 on December 30, 2020.

Figure Credits

Fig. 5.1: Source: https://commons.wikimedia.org/wiki/File:Emile_Durkheim.jpg.
Fig. 5.2: Copyright © 2020 by HaticeEROL. Reprinted with permission.
Fig. 5.3: Copyright © 2013 Depositphotos/megija.
Fig. 5.4: Source: https://www.usa.gov/branches-of-government.

CHAPTER 6

The Conflict Paradigm in Sociology

Society as an Arena of Social Conflicts

CHAPTER THEME

The conflict paradigm is another unique perspective or a unique sociological eye through which to make sense of the social world. The structural paradigm begins with the assumption that consensus is the key to create a social order. The conflict paradigm begins with the assumption that a human social order is universally and inherently fragile because of divergent and conflicting roles, values, beliefs, attitudes, and perceptions among different groups based on such factors as race, gender, class, ethnicity, nationality, sexual orientations, religion, culture, and ideology. The proponents of the conflict paradigm suggest that sociology's core is to understand and examine how different groups conflict with one another and how conflicts are generated, expressed, and mitigated by power and authority. The conflict paradigm also begins with the questions, "How is social change possible?" and "What social factors and forces drive a social system to change from one form to another and one age to another?" The conflict paradigm is based on the idea that different kinds of social conflicts are the driver of all historical records of social change and transformations. The role of social conflicts in shaping social forms and patterns is universal across all societies, cultures, and civilizations. The phenomenon of human strife led to the birth of the great world religions, the development of world philosophy, the growth of modern science, and the emergence of a modern civilization based on reason, humanism, science, individualism, and democracy. The more recent intellectual legacy of the development of the conflict paradigm in sociology goes back to the theory of class conflict developed by German sociologist Karl Marx in the middle of the 19th century. In more recent times, particularly in American sociology, the Marxian notion of class as an ownership category has been substantially revised. The contemporary conflict sociologists study class conflict more as a political or a power phenomenon. The phenomenon of power, they assume, is at the root of all forms of social conflicts. Understanding the nature of power, particularly political power, and how it creates, sustains, and mitigates social conflicts of different shapes and dimensions is vital for conflict sociology. The recent literature on conflict sociology has generated a large number of high-validity theories and generalizations about the nature of America's power elite, governing class, systemic racism, struggle with poverty and discrimination, and modernity regarding sex, women, and feminism.

Introduction

A scientific paradigm changes from one set of assumptions to another when an existing paradigm fails to explain many emerging scientific concerns and puzzles related to a particular scientific domain or a specific scientific field. The structural-functional paradigm provides many valid and relevant explanations of social systems, forms, and patterns and the way they shape and mold our acts, actions, and behavior. The structural paradigm, however, is limited in explaining how social structures and systems change from one form to another and from one pattern to another. One of sociology's fundamental discoveries is that society is a social process. Social structures and systems change from age to age and from generation to generation. With social change and transformations, human acts, actions, and behavior also experience change and transformations. With its many modernist values, such as democracy, equality, and individualism, modern society is vastly different from the societies of medieval times. The Americans of the 2nd decade of the 21st century are vastly different in their values, beliefs, and preferences from those of the 19th and early 20th centuries. The digital tribe of the 21st century lives in a vastly different social and cultural world than the baby boom generation of the 1950s and 1960s. Structuralists fail to explain what social factors and forces drive large-scale social change and transformations. They assume that a structure may experience stress and strains, but it is primarily self-regulating.

The structuralists take a snapshot approach. They stop the motion of a social system at a given point in time and then seek to understand how it functions and what holds it together. The structural-functional perspective is relevant for social mapping—a mental image or a description of the interconnected and intersecting social roles, institutions, organizations, hierarchies, power, command, and control. It can describe the key points of social power, authority, and symbolic attractions. But it is limited to examine why a social map changes from time to time. Structural functionalism is a "consensus" approach to the understanding of society. Its core mission is the discovery of how social order is possible. The conflict paradigm in sociology has come to discover how social change is possible and what social factors and forces propel a social system, large or small, to change from one form to another, and from one age to another. The conflict paradigm discovered that social conflict of different kinds is the driver of all historical records of social change and transformations. Social conflict's role in shaping social forms and patterns is universal across all societies, cultures, and civilizations. This chapter will examine the historicity of the concept of social conflict, explore the birth of the idea of conflict in classical sociology, describe the key assumptions and analytical strategies of the conflict paradigm, and explain different forms of social conflicts and their roles in shaping multifaceted social change and transformations in American society.

The Historicity of the Concept of Social Conflict

The history of all great religions and all great civilizations of the world is inseparable from social conflict and violence. The religion of Judaism was born because Moses challenged the existing social arrangements of slavery of the Egyptian civilization and escaped with slaves who resided at the lowest rung of social hierarchy. Jesus died on the cross because he challenged the prevailing assumptions of social arrangements made by the Jews. The existing Quraysh ruling class castigated prophet Muhammed in Mecca for his challenge of their polytheistic beliefs and the preaching of the monotheistic religion of Islam. Prophet Muhammed eventually migrated to Medina to spread his new faith. Hinduism was born in India about 4,000 years ago, brought by the Aryans who invaded India and destroyed Mohenjo-Daro's and Harappa's existing civilizations. Buddhism was born about 2,500 years ago because Buddha challenged the prevailing polytheistic belief systems of Hinduism.

In ancient Athens, Socrates, the father of modern philosophy, was poisoned to death because he came in conflict with the Athenian ruling class for his ideas of applying reason, justice, and morality in political governance. Socrates said, "The unexamined life is not worth living." Aristotle said that humans have an intrinsic desire to engage in politics, and conflict is inevitable within a polity because different people have a different sense of justice and morality. Democracy and the rule of law, Aristotle argued, can lead to harmony and consensus in a polity. The notion of conflict is also central to the political philosophies of Hobbes, Locke, and Rousseau. They all believed that humans have the natural right to life, liberty, property, and the pursuit of happiness. But the realization of natural human rights remained limited before the birth of political society because humans are essentially selfish, greedy, and competitive. The conflict was endemic in the state of nature because of the absence of law and justice. Rousseau (2020) said humans are nearly reasonable, but modern civilization—the birth of the bourgeoisie man and mentality—has made them nasty, unequal, and competitive. Rousseau imagined that "MAN is born free; and everywhere he is in chains" (Book 1, p. 1). Rousseau (2020) contended that "the first man who, having fenced in a piece of land, said 'This is mine,' and found people naïve enough to believe him, that man was the true founder of civil society" (The Second part, p. 1).

The birth of modern science also created a massive conflict of ideas between naturalistic philosophy and the Catholic Church in the Middle Ages. The discovery of the heliocentric theory by Nicolaus Copernicus—the discovery that heralded the beginning of modern science—created a massive conflict with the Catholic Church. The heliocentric view brought not just the birth of modern science but also a new form of human knowledge based on natural philosophy and not divine providence. This was expressed in a letter written by Copernicus to Pope Paul III in 1543 in which he defended his discovery and said, "There will be those fools ... who will venture a refutation based on some passage of scripture ... I shall not waste my time on them" (as quoted in King, 2014, p. 247). In the preface of his *Revolutions of Celestial Spheres* written to Pope Paul III, Copernicus wrote, "Perhaps your Holiness will not be surprised so much that I have dared to publish these theories of mine ... not hesitating even to commit in print my thoughts on the motion of the earth. ... I have chosen to dedicate these theories of mine to your Holiness, rather than to any other person" (as quoted in King, 2014, pp. 245–247). Galileo, in his dialogue on the *Two Chief World Systems, Ptolemaic and Copernican*, published in 1632, more forcefully defended the Copernican discovery and confirmed the validity of the naturalistic explanation. In a letter to Grand Duchess Christina in 1615, Galileo said that "in disputes about natural phenomena, one must not turn immediately to Scripture, but rather utilize the evidence of sense experience and demonstration based on them" (as quoted in King, 2014, p. 253). In 1633, the Catholic Church accused Galileo of heresy (i.e., the denial of divine truth). Charles Darwin's *On the Origin of Species*, published in 1859, which found that humans evolved from lower species through millions of years of evolution, was discorded by the Catholic Church, and the conflict between evolutionism and creationism is still prevalent today.

Social conflict has been the reason for changes and transformations in most of the world's civilizations. Human civilizations were born, grown, and destroyed primarily because of human invasions, violence, and conflicts. The birth of modern society in the 18th and 19th centuries would not have been possible without forcibly destroying the foundations of medieval monarchies and aristocracies. During the French Revolution of 1789, which destroyed the French monarchy and built the foundation of modern democracy in France, thousands of people were guillotined. Italian sociologist Vilfredo Pareto probably rightly surmised that "history is the graveyard of aristocracies" (as quoted in Finer, 1966, p. 249). The birth of the Protestant Reformation in the middle of the 15th century and the division between Catholicism and Protestantism have remained an eternal source of conflict within Christianity. The Reformation led by German theologians Martin Luther (1483–1546) and John Calvin (1509–1564) brought inner doctrinal transformations to rearticulating the relationship between God and individuals. Luther said that "others ... have attacked the life. I attack the doctrine" (as quoted in Bainton, 1977, p. 24). Luther attacked "not the abuses of medieval Catholicism, but Catholicism itself as an abuse of Gospel [which] was the object of his onslaught" (Bainton, 1977, p. 24). It is estimated that Europe's Thirty Years' War (1618–1648) erupted primarily because the Protestant Reformation and resulted in the deaths of about eight million people.

European colonialism is primarily a history of conflict, exploitation, and domination of one country by another or one race by another race for centuries. From the 15th to the middle of the 19th century, for about 400 years, most of Asia, Africa, and Latin America were under the colonial domination of Europe's major powers, including Spain, England, the Netherlands, Germany, and France. The societies and cultures of the colonized countries were deliberately and forcibly shaped and changed to primarily serve the colonial powers' interests. Some historians have shown that with the progress of civilization, particularly the birth of the modern state with the sole monopoly on the instruments of power, human conflict and violence have significantly declined. The 20th century, however, has shown that conflict is still an endemic feature in modern societies. World War I, World War II, and the Cold War were three of the major conflicts of the 20th century. The social, political, and economic events of most world societies were shaped and affected by these three global conflicts. World War I and World War II, by destroying the political institutions of fascism and Nazism and some of the remnants of old European monarchies and aristocracies, signaled the triumph of liberal democracy. World War II also led to decolonization and the beginning of modernization in the developing world. The present international system—composed of a series of multilateral institutions, such as the United Nations, North Atlantic Treaty Organization (NATO), the World Trade Organization, the World Bank, and the International Monetary Fund—came in the wake of World War II's end and the beginning of a new era of the globalization of liberal democracy. But the world soon plunged into a new ideological conflict between liberal democracy and the world socialist system. In the late 1940s, China became a communist country, and in the 1950s and 1960s, the then USSR (Union of Soviet Socialist Republics) embarked on a global political agenda of spreading socialism not just in Eastern Europe but also in many countries of Asia, Africa, and Latin America. This led to the birth of the Cold War with America's military engagement for the control and containment of Soviet socialist expansionism. In the second half of the 20th century, the ideological conflict of the Cold War dominated world events, including the world of social sciences. The 20th century concluded with the end of the Cold War. But the 21st century began with the birth of another global conflict—the global war on terror, which created in the world a new era of nativism, localism, racism, and religious conflicts and violence. Human history is a history of human conflict, and that this conflict is one of the main drivers of human history probably cannot be overstated. The conflict paradigm in sociology hardly deals with intersocietal or intercivilizational conflicts. It is primarily a perspective for understanding intrasocietal conflicts of different forms and their role in social progress, change, and transformation. The just cited excursion into the history of human conflict and its role in forming the great world religions, shaping world science and philosophy, creating a modern liberal civilization, and charting modernity dynamics, has a great import.

The Intellectual Legacy of the Conflict Paradigm in Sociology: The Marxian Perspective of Class Conflict

Karl Marx is a significant historical figure in sociology and social science in general. Marx developed a theory of class conflict as the driver of all of human history and civilizations. The mainstream conflict paradigm in sociology is not the Marxian theory of class conflict. Instead, it is a paradigm of understanding social realities in the context of a broader set of conflicts based on race, gender, power, status, culture, ethnicity, and ideology. The mainstream conflict paradigm studies class conflict, but it defines class primarily in terms of wealth and income and not just in terms of the Marxian idea of the mode of economic production. The theory of class conflict developed by Marx in the middle of the 19th century cannot be ignored in any serious sociological analysis of the role of conflict in society. Marx began with a philosophy of human conflict, examined the evolution of human conflict in sociological terms, and then again became a philosopher and a political advocate of socialism and communism. Some of the great works of Marx that contained his philosophy of human nature, his sociology of conflict in a capitalist society, and his utopian notion of socialism and communism include *The German Ideology* (written with Frederick Engels in 1846 but not published until 1932), *The Manifesto of the Communist Party* (written with Frederick Engels, 1848), and *Capital: A Critique of Political Economy, Vol. 1* (1867).

Marxian Philosophy of Humans as Producing Animals

Aristotle said that humans are passionately, or almost biologically, a political animal. Marx said that humans are intrinsically producing animals. They are passionate about the things they make, which could be a simple hammer, a GM truck, or just a pair of Nike sneakers. They are deeply emotional about the things they produce from nature through their labor and energy. They are at peace with their soul when the products they make belong to them. They are sad, depressed, and alienated when the things they produce belong to others. This notion is the core of Marx's materialistic interpretation of human history. As Marx (1867/2013a) said in his *Capital: A Critique of Political Economy*, "To begin with, the question under discussion is material production. Individuals, producing in a society, and socially determined production of individuals is, of course, the point of departure" (p. 70).

Before the birth of civilizations and civil societies, Marx believed that humans lived in a state of primitive communism. In this state, there was no private property. There was no class, and hence, there was no class conflict. Under primitive communism, humans owned their labor, they held their products, and therefore lived in harmony with themselves and the soul. There was no inequality, no domination, and no conflict. With the growth of material production, particularly with the transition from hunting and food gathering to agricultural methods of production, primitive communism, however, disintegrated and gave birth to class-based civilization. The advent of agriculture led to the birth of private property, and private property led to class conflict. Since the dawn of private property and class conflict, the history of human society is a history of class struggle. As Marx and Engels (1848/2013) described in *The Manifesto of the Communist Party*, "The history of all hitherto existing society is the history of class struggles. Freeman and slaves, patrician and plebeian, lord and serf, guild-master and journeyman, in a word, oppressor and oppressed, stood in constant opposition to one another, carried on an uninterrupted, now hidden, now open fight, a fight that ended in the common ruin of contending classes" (p. 44).

FIGURE 6.1   Karl Marx

Marxian Sociology and the Theory of the Mode of Production

Marx's sociology begins with his theorizing that class is primarily an economic category related to the mode of production of society and not just income and wealth. Marx argued that each epoch of history, after the birth of class society, is characterized by a mode of production—the social structure within which people work. Thus, work, for Marx, was essentially social in nature. Man, according to Marx (1867/2013a), "is not only a social animal but an animal that can individualize himself only within society. Production by an isolated individual outside society—a rare event" (p. 70). A mode of production includes the techniques or the means of production, such as lands, capital, and technology. A mode of production also consists of a social relationship between those who own and control the means of production and those who do not own and control the means of production but only work to produce the material goods and services. Marx defined class not in terms of income and wealth but more fundamentally in terms of the ownership of the strategic means of production. In terms of ownership, each historical mode of production was characterized, according to Marx, by two classes: the owners and nonowners of the means of production.

Based on his philosophy of humans as producing animals, production as a social arrangement, and class as a social category defined by ownership, Marx came to describe that there were three significant modes of production in human history: the slave-owning mode of production, the feudal mode of production, and the capitalist mode of production. Marx further expanded his theorizing and argued that the mode of production is the basic structure or the foundation of a society. The mode of production defines each facet of the superstructure, including such things as power, state, laws, class, status, culture, and ideology. For Marx, what was most fundamental was that the sole mission of the superstructure of a society is to create, expand, and strengthen the basic structure of the mode of production. But within a class-based mode of production, class conflict between those who own and those who do not own the means of production, Marx argued, is inevitable, indisputable, and universal. The working class in each mode of production will always be driven by their passions to regain the "lost paradise" of primitive communism. The class struggle, therefore, is the propeller of change from one mode of production to another mode of production. In *The Manifesto of the Communist Party*, Marx and Engels (1848/2013) argued that "in earlier epochs of history, we find almost everywhere a complicated arrangement of society into various orders, a manifold gradation of social rank. In ancient Rome, we have patricians, knights, plebeians, slaves; in the Middle Ages, feudal lords, vassals, guild-masters, journeymen, apprentices, serfs; in almost all of these classes, again, subordinate gradations" (p. 44).

Marxian Theory of Alienation

Marx argued that despite the capitalist bourgeois society that emerged in the modern time being a relatively more open society because it does not define classes in terms of the law, class conflict is much broader and more expansive in the bourgeois era. "The modern bourgeoisie society that has sprouted from the ruins of feudal society," Marx and Engel (1848/2013) contended, "has not done away with class antagonisms. It has but established new classes, new conditions of oppression, a new form of struggle in place of the old ones" (p. 44). He theorized that there are two classes in the capitalist society—the bourgeoisie and the proletariat. The bourgeoisie owns and controls the strategic means of production. The proletariat—the working class—does not own anything but their labor. In Marx's view, production relationships under capitalism are much more exploitative and much more dehumanizing than those of the slave and feudal modes of production. Since under capitalism, the scale and the volume of the output are more extensive, higher is the degree of exploitation of the working class. The mechanism through which the working class under capitalism is exploited is the usurpation of the surplus value by the capitalist class. For example, if a worker is producing goods and services worth $1,000 in 8 working hours, that worker is getting about $15 per hour (about $120) for 8 hours' labor. The higher the volume of production under capitalism, the higher is the degree of usurpation of the surplus value by the capitalists. This theorization goes back to the Marxian philosophy of humans as producing animals.

Marx further expanded his theory of exploitation by arguing that under capitalism, the product created by the working class is objectified. His product is his creation, but it belongs to others, and therefore, his product haunts him as an objectified and external force. Marx (1867/2013a) said, "The worker becomes the poorer, the more wealth he produces, the more his production increases in power and range. The worker becomes an ever-cheaper commodity the more commodities he creates" (p. 57). The working class under capitalism is in the process of alienation and dehumanization because they are completely separated from their own products. Marx (1867/2013a) contended that "*alienation* of the worker in his product means not only his labor becomes an object, an *external* existence, but that it exists outside him, independently, as something alien to him, and that it becomes a power on its own confronting him; it means that the life which he has conferred on the object confronts him as something hostile and alien" (p. 58). This Marxian construction of the working-class psychology under capitalism is an integral part of Marx's sociological theory of class conflict.

Marxian Philosophy of Socialism and Communism

It is from this theory of class conflict under capitalism that Marx turned to his philosophical prediction that social conflict cannot be avoided without the elimination of private property. Marx, therefore, visualized that the working class of the whole of the capitalist world one day will revolt, and the capitalist system will be disintegrated. With the advance of capitalism as a dominant world economic system, the world's working class will be increasingly pauperized, and this will eventually lead to the birth of a global revolt against the capitalist system. He foresaw a future in which "the weapons with which the bourgeoisie felled feudalism to the ground are now turned against the bourgeoisie itself" (Marx & Engels, 1848/2013, p. 47). The capitalist system was born from the ashes of feudalism. From the ashes of capitalism, there will emerge a new social order of socialism and communism. According to Marx & Engels (1848/2013), the "theory of the communist may be summed up in the single sentence: Abolition of private property" (p. 52).

The Marxian theory of class conflict made many remarkable and enduring sociological discoveries. The first is Marx's theory of the materialist interpretation of history. Marx theorized that economy—the material system of production—is the foundation of a society. The culture, knowledge, ideas, and ideology are mere reflections of a society's materialistic foundations—the mode of production. Secondly, Marx defined class mainly in terms of the ownership of the material means of production and not based on income or wealth. Third, Marx examined just one form of social conflict—the conflict between the owners and the nonowners of the means and forces of production. Fourth, Marx developed a grand theory of thousands of years of human history in terms of the notion of class conflict. Finally, Marx came to a sociological theory of class conflict by way of a philosophy of man as a producing animal. Eventually, Marx became a philosopher of a utopian world of socialism and communism. Karl Marx is one of the most intriguing intellectuals of the modern world. The whole body of social science in the 19th and 20th centuries, particularly sociology, can be described to have grown and maturated in response to Marx. Sociology was born in the middle of the 19th century by discovering that knowledge, ideas, and culture, and not just the economic mode of production, form the basic foundation of a society. Auguste Comte, who fathered the science of sociology, theorized that societies have evolved based on the evolution of human intelligence. Max Weber, who fathered the growth of academic sociology in Germany, theorized that the Calvinist theology of the Protestants was the clue for understanding the rise of rational capitalism in the West and not in other civilizations. Emile Durkheim, who fathered the rise of academic sociology in France, theorized that collective consciousness is the key to understanding society's structure. The Marxian theory of class conflict within the realm of sociology, indeed, went into eclipse for nearly 100 years after its formulation in the *Manifesto of the Communist Party* in 1848. The Marxian theory of class conflict, and indeed the whole of the materialist interpretation of history, was reincarnated in sociology during the 1960s and 1970s in the global political context of the rise of the Cold War. In the 1960s and 1970s, the vitality of sociology as a science began to be questioned. One camp began to describe sociology, particularly structural sociology, as a bourgeoise science. Another camp began to be called radical or Marxian sociologists. The contemporary conflict paradigm in sociology was born primarily in response to the reincarnation of the Marxian theory of class conflict and the birth of Marxian radical sociology in the 1960s and 1970s.

The Contemporary Conflict Paradigm in Sociology: The Key Assumption

The Philosophy of Human Nature

The Marxian theory of conflict left the issues of power, ideology, race, gender, religion, education, ethnicity, and culture mostly outside the boundary of its analytical scheme. The sociological paradigm of conflict has evolved in recent decades, primarily centering on these multifaceted sources of human inequality and human conflicts (Dahrendorf, 1959; Coser, 1964; Goldthorpe, 1987; Wolfe, 1998; Mills, 1956/2000; Domhoff, 1976/2013). In addition to the Marxian theory of class conflict, the legacy of the sociological paradigm of conflict can be traced back to two intellectual traditions. The first is Darwin's theory of the evolution of human nature. Charles Darwin, in his *On the Origin of Species*, published in 1859, theorized that human nature has some intrinsic features of competitiveness, aggressiveness, domination, subjugation, and control. These features are inherent to human nature because humans had to struggle for millions of years for survival. Many contemporary evolutionary psychologists, based on Darwin's theory of the evolution of human nature, also believe that competitiveness, deceitfulness, selfishness, boastfulness, jealousy, egocentrism, hate, anger, sex, greed, cruelty, wickedness, and many likewise traits prone to generate human conflicts are familiar to people of all historical times and all cultures and civilizations. Therefore, the proponents of the conflict paradigm assume that the human traits of control and domination are universal, inevitable, and permanent in human societies.

The Sociology of Power

The second intellectual tradition that has remained a central analytical direction in the sociological paradigm of conflict is the centrality of power as the driving source of human actions and human conflicts. From the days of Socrates, Plato, and Aristotle in ancient Greece, through the time of the Age of Enlightenment in the 18th century and the birth of the social contract theories of Hobbes, Locke, and Rousseau, and the days of the birth of social science in the 19th century, based particularly on the writings of Max Weber and Sigmund Freud, power has been a central concern on discourses on human nature and human social conflicts, change, and transformations. Darwin's theory of evolution and his notion of the survival of the fittest is also centered on the idea of the instinct of human power—a notion further refined by the concept of the "selfish gene" discovered by Richard Dawkins (1976/2010). Freud theorized that the human instinct of power is disruptive and nearly destructive. Therefore, he argued, culture and civilization are essential for taming and rechanneling the instinct of human control (Freud, 1930/2010). German sociologist Max Weber discovered that the instinct of human domination is universal and is an essential part of human nature. Among the proponents of the conflict paradigm, there is a consensus that power is the creator and shaper of most of the crucial dimensions of human social conflicts, such as race conflict, gender conflict, ethnic conflict, religious conflict, and ideological conflict. Social conflicts arise from various sources, including competing economic interests; historical wars, violence, and discriminations; differential access to resources; ethnic rivalries; religious intolerance; and ideological polarities. Power is the binding social force for creating, expanding, and sustaining these sources of social conflicts. Power is also the binding force for mitigating these social conflicts.

The concept of power in sociology is commonly understood in the context of social actions and social relationships. It is defined as the capacity of an individual or a group of individuals to get things done despite the will of others not to do so. Power is intimately connected to domination, legitimacy, and authority. Social conflicts emerge in different realms of life and different shapes and forms because of the dynamics of articulations in the nature of power, domination, legitimacy, and authority. Sociologically, when power is legitimized, it becomes an authority. Legitimate power can take different forms (e.g., political power, corporate power, professional power, parental power, and spousal power). The legitimacy of power is primarily based on law. But it is also based on customs and traditions. Parental control of children is not mainly based on law but on customs, cultures, and traditions. Spousal power is both legal and customary. The legitimacy of executive and professional power is based on expertise, leadership, and credentialism. But the legitimacy of political power is primarily based on law. The power of Congress, the president, governors, mayors, courts, and law enforcement, for example, is defined by law. Political power is mainly critical because it leads to the differential allocations and distributions of power, resources, rewards, status, and honors. Since these allocations are made by legitimate authorities, they are generally accepted and justified. But the allocations and distributions of power and resources, both material and nonmaterial, are also inherently conflicting.

The effects of political power are both external and internal. Externally, the social groups that are discriminated against and live at the periphery of political power have limited access to power and material and nonmaterial resources. Their lifestyles are different, and their life opportunities are blocked and restricted. They are deprived of wealth and social capital. Poverty is endemic to those who are victims of discrimination, domination, and exploitation. Externally, power can constrain access to material resources, such as income and wealth, and nonmaterial resources, such as freedom, rights, and liberty. A debate in America is currently growing, for example, over whether women's reproductive rights, granted and expanded in the 1960s and 1970s (i.e., *Roe v. Wade*), are going to be taken away if the power of balance within the Supreme Court is changed or whether same-sex marriage that was legalized by the Supreme Court in 2015 (i.e., *Obergefell v. Hodges*) is going to be overturned, and homosexuality will again be criminalized.

What is even more fundamental is that discriminatory and dominating political power can also be internally harmful and damaging for groups that are discriminated against and dominated. The power and the governing class both shape and form the psychology of the mind of those who do not have power and who are governed. Social conflict is not only materially but also psychologically destructive. Marx examined this aspect of conflict through his theory of alienation. There is also a whole tradition of thought that has theorized this notion as the "colonization of the mind," which means that the groups that are dominated and discriminated against begin to see themselves and define themselves in terms of the traits and the qualities of those who rule and govern. This leads to the justification and perpetuation of control and domination. In the literature on domestic violence, this is sometimes described as Stockholm syndrome. But its many forceful expositions are found in the literature on colonialism, feminism, and critical race theory (McWhorter, 2001; Fanon, 1961/2005; Feagin, 2006; Foucault, 1975/2012; Du Bois, 1903/2012). In his *The Wretched of the Earth*, Frantz Fanon (2005), one of the most widely known African political philosophers, showed how colonial domination in Africa created a distorted "Black consciousness" about the superiority of the colonial masters in terms of race, language, culture, and, in a sense, the whole of humanity. In his *The Souls of the Black Folk*, W. E. B. Du Bois (1903/2012), described as the first African American Harvard sociologist, theorized that centuries of White racial domination created a fractured soul—double-consciousness—among Black people in America. "After the Egyptian and Indian, the Greek and Roman, the Teuton and Mongolian," Du Bois (1903/2012) argued, "the Negro is a sort of seventeenth son, born with a veil, and gifted with a second sight in this American world—a world which yields him no true self-consciousness, but only let him see himself through the revelation of the other world" (p. 2). Du Bois (1903/2012) added, "It is a peculiar sensation, this double-consciousness, this sense of always looking at one's self through the eyes of others, of measuring one's soul by the type of a world that looks on in amused contempt and pity. One ever feels his twoness—an American, a Negro; two souls, two thoughts, two unreconciled strivings; two warring ideals in one dark body" (p. 2). French philosopher-turned-sociologist Michael Foucault defined power in a more generalized sense of a pervasive social force and argued that power and knowledge are the instruments of control and domination in all spheres of social life and relations. Power resides in the hands of a political sovereign and in the hands of experts and professionals, such as doctors and psychiatrists, who sometimes define what we are and our absolute subjectivity—our body, mind, and the soul (Foucault 1961/1988, 1975/2012). Therefore, at the core of the conflict perspective is the idea to examine and explore how domination and exploitation of one social group by another is enforced primarily by unequal and discriminatory allocations of power and how unequal and discriminatory allocations of power shape and form the nature and articulations of different facets of social conflicts and different dimensions of human social stories.

Social inequalities and social conflicts, conflict theorists assume, are universal and permanent in human societies, primarily because of humans' intrinsic nature of competitiveness and selfishness and, secondly, because of the human instinct of power and domination. These two facets of human nature are interconnected and interdependent. Hence, a social structure, large or small, the proponents of the conflict perspective argue, is inherently fragile and unstable. No society is in complete balance and harmony because of internal inequalities in class, race, gender, culture, religion, and ideology. Social conflicts create not just stress and strains but also revolts and rebellions. Social conflicts lead to strains and stress, and stress and strains lead to social change. When a particular form of conflict is minimized by creating new social structures, new forms of conflicts and discriminations emerge, and a social system again experiences stress and strains. Social conflict is the driving mechanism for social change, the formation of social structures, and the stability of social order (Table 6.1).

TABLE 6.1 The Conflict Paradigm: Key Assumptions

Inequality and discriminations of different kinds are universal, inevitable, and permanent in human societies. They, of course, take various forms and shapes at other times and in different ages.
A social system, large or small, is never in complete balance or harmony because of internal inequalities in race, gender, power, class, politics, ideology, and culture.
Power, authority, and ideology are the prime creators and shapers of social conflict. The effects of power are both external and internal. Externally, power can limit access to power, material resources, rewards, ranks, and honor. Internally, the exploitation and domination based on power can lead to alienation, a sense of powerlessness, and even the birth of a distorted sense of double consciousness.
Inequalities and social conflicts always threaten the balance of a system. Maintaining order and balance by the force of authority and power alone makes a system more fragile and dysfunctional.
Social inequalities cannot be permanently removed from society. Social inequalities, however, must be based on legitimate grounds. Inequalities in modern societies based on ascriptive qualities, such as gender, race, age, and religion, are not legitimate.
The removal of inequalities and discriminations that are not based on legitimate grounds reduces the sources of systemic stress and revolts and rebellions. Prejudices are removed when different groups are equally valued and empowered.
Social conflicts lead to stress and strains, and stress and tensions lead to social change and transformations. When a particular form of changed structure stabilizes, new forms of discrimination emerge, and a social system again experiences strains and stress or revolts and rebellions. Thus, the social conflict is the driving mechanism of social change and stability.

The Contemporary Conflict Paradigm in Sociology: The Key Analytical Strategies

Dimensions of Social Conflict

The sociological paradigm of social conflict has discovered that social conflict is multidimensional. Class is not the only dimension of the conflict in society. Conflict has various other dimensions, such as race, gender, age, ethnicity, religion, culture, and ideology. Modern conflict theorists have also widened the definition of class. They do not define a class in terms merely of the ownership of the means of production, as Marx did, but also in terms of income, status, and wealth. Marx left the role and the analysis of the middle class almost entirely out of his scheme of thought. This was probably because in the 19th century when Marx developed his theory of class conflict, there was scarcely a professional middle class.

In modern societies, the middle class is an important category. The relative size of the middle class in a country defines and describes its nature of class conflict and class polarization. The growth and expansion of the middle class in a country are generally seen as a strategy of conflict mitigation. Marx predicted there would be a high level of class consciousness within the pauperized working class under capitalism. Sociologists observe that in America, class consciousness is primarily a middle-class phenomenon. Most people in America would like to describe themselves as belonging to the middle class irrespective of their income and status. Social class is not a legal category. One is not defined by law about their class background. In all modern societies, social class is characterized by social mobility—legally and culturally accepted means of moving from one class to another, primarily through education and professional status attainment.

There is now a high degree of consensus among conflict sociologists that the Marxian notion of a class, defined in terms of the ownership of the means of production, is restricted and misleading in modern societies where knowledge and education are the critical wealth properties. In the 1970s, sociologist Daniel Bell (1973), in his *The Coming of Post-Industrial Society*, predicted how scientific knowledge and professionalism would be the central organizing forces of modern societies in the late 20th century. A similar prediction was made by economist Robert Reich (1992) through his idea of the coming age of the "symbolic analysts"—knowledge class—contained in his book *The Work of Nations: Preparing Ourselves for the 21st Century Capitalism*. The arrival of the global digital society in the 21st century has probably permanently shifted the Marxian notion of a class under capitalism as a production category to a new type of knowledge professionals.

Modern societies are also becoming culturally very different from that of 19th-century societies. In most modern societies, mere survival issues are being increasingly replaced by issues of equality, democracy, human rights, human dignity, cultural diversity, and self-expression (Inglehart, 2018). Therefore, the converging issues of social conflicts are now shifting from class to race, gender, ethnicity, culture, religion, and ideology (Dahrendorf, 1959; Coser, 1964). Conflict theorists of today are more inclined to explore how pathways to the critical property of knowledge and education—and access to the critical cultural trajectory of equality, human rights, and human dignity—depend on different social dimensions of race, gender, ethnicity, culture, and sexual orientations and how they are controlled, mediated, and mitigated by power, authority, and ideology.

Dynamics of Social Conflict

Social conflicts are not always about bloodshed. Social conflicts are not always expressed in terms of battles and violence and movements and crusades. Social movements are both overt and covert, or manifest and latent to use the metaphor of sociologist Robert Merton. Social conflicts are overt when people are openly discriminated against and victimized. Overt social conflicts emerge when different oppressed groups are mobilized and when organized social movements are created to send a message to power and authority. Social conflicts are covert when people feel the stress and strains of discrimination, but there is a high degree of social and psychological tolerance, and there is no political mobilization to express the griefs and grievances openly. The Black Lives Matter movement of 2020 in America, for example, has become an overt challenge to allegedly race-based police brutality. But the way Blacks are discriminated against in lending practice is a covert conflict. The #MeToo movement in 2020 has become an overt challenge to sexual harassment in the workplace. But Princeton University's discrimination against female professors by paying them compensation lower than Princeton's male professors in similar rank and status is covert discrimination and an invisible gender conflict. The National Coming Out Day on October 11, 2021 is an overt response to the discrimination against the LGBTQ+ community. The legalization of same-sex marriage by the U.S. Supreme Court in 2015 (i.e., *Obergefell v. Hodges*) is an overt response to mitigate the conflict concerning sexual orientations. But the issue of marriage equality perceived by some sections of evangelical Christians as a violation of biblical rules is an expression of covert conflict. In the general election of 2016, as a part of this perception, 81% of evangelical Christians voted for Donald Trump compared with 19% for Hilary Clinton, who openly expressed her support for marriage equality (Martínez & Smith, 2016).

FIGURE 6.2   Black Lives Matter

The overt and covert dimensions of social conflict, however, are not permanent. They change from time to time, depending on the nature and the intensity of the conflict and conflicting episodes. In the 1950s and 1960s, race conflict in America, for example, was overt, and the civil rights movement galvanized the whole country, from the Montgomery, Alabama, bus boycott in 1955 to Martin Luther King Jr.'s *I Have a Dream* speech in Washington, DC, in 1963. Then Malcolm X was assassinated in 1965, and King was assassinated in 1968. After the Civil Rights Act of 1964 that criminalized discrimination based on race and color, race conflict in America remained mostly covert. After the ascendency of Barack Obama to the presidency, many dreamed of a new era of racial harmony in America. But from the beginning of the presidency of Donald Trump in 2016, particularly after the brutal killing of George Floyd in Minneapolis in 2020 by police, race conflict in America again became overt, and the Black Lives Matter movement began to galvanize the country.

Similarly, after the U.S. Supreme Court criminalized sexual harassment in a series of decisions in the 1980s and 1990s (i.e., *Meritor Savings Bank v. Vinson* in 1986; *Faragher v. City of Boca Raton* in 1998; and *Burlington Industries v. Ellerth* in 1998) and after it came to the center of national discourses in the wake of the Anita Hill and Clarence Thomas episode in 1991, gender conflict concerning sexual harassment remained largely covert. But sexual harassment and gender conflict in America's workplace again became overt and moved to the center of national discourses in the wake of a series of allegations against several celebrities,

CEOs, and politicians that surfaced in 2019 and 2020. This led to the #MeToo movement's galvanization—an organization intended to help women who had survived sexual violence created by Black activist Tarana Burke in 2007. The dynamics of social conflicts and their overt and covert manifestations at different times are, therefore, of great import to conflict sociologists.

FIGURE 6.3   End of Systemic Racism

Nature and Expressions of Social Conflict

The conflict paradigm is primarily an approach to understanding intergroup conflicts within a society. Multiple groups characterize any society at any given time. Humans have an insatiable thirst to create and belong to groups. Humans have also had a peculiar sense of likeness and similarities. Historically, we have always gravitated toward forming groups with those who look like us, act like us, and talk like us, feeling a sense of oneness with those who belong to our race, gender, ethnicity, faith, culture, and ideology. Across world societies and cultures, the preference to marry, for example, is always within the same race and ethnicity, exact color and creeds, same language and nationality, and the same faith, sects, and religion.

In America, before *Loving v. Virginia* was decided by the Supreme Court in 1967, interracial marriage was a crime. In most of the Middle East, particularly in Saudi Arabia, Kuwait, and Abu Dhabi, native women are legally and culturally barred from marrying outside their tribes, nations, and monarchies. In India, known to be the world's largest democracy, interreligious marriage, particularly between Hindus and Muslims, are few and far between, and sometimes it may lead to violence. In Pakistan, marriage between Muslims and Christians are culturally unacceptable. Examples are not few and far between in Pakistan, where interreligious couples were the victims of honor killings.

This universal human preference for likeness and similarities tends to create, sociologists have observed, a divided world within the same society described as in-groups and out-groups. We all are culturally gravitated to belong to our in-groups, within which we develop a sense of bonding and oneness, a sense of collective solidarity, and genuine love and affinity. The people of the out-groups are largely alien and unknown to us. We do not belong to the world of the out-groups, and our relationships with them are artificial and transient. Sociologically, every society is, therefore, intrinsically fractured and divided. Social conflicts emerge primarily out of these fractured and divided group realities. As such, sociologists are keen to discover the nature, intensity, and expression of social conflict across the spectrum of in-groups and out-groups. The in-groups and out-groups can take different shapes and forms depending on class, race, gender, ethnicity, culture, and ideology.

The intensity and expression of social conflicts may take different forms and patterns. All forms of social conflicts involve domination and exploitation, which may be physical, sexual, economic, political, cultural, or emotional. In extreme forms and patterns of social conflict, domination and exploitation may lead to social exclusion, destruction, and extinction. Slavery in America, for example, was a form of power and exploitation that was physical, sexual, economic, political, and emotional. It was a complete denial of the humanity of the slaves. The Holocaust of Nazi Germany that took the lives of about six million Jews in the mid-1940s is an example of a pattern of destruction of a particular religious group. The Bosnian war of ethnic cleansing in the early 1990s is an example of a social conflict dedicated to the total extinction of the ethnic Muslims and Croats in Bosnia. Most social conflicts, however, are limited in scope and primarily take the form of intergroup and intrasocietal conflicts characterized by physical, sexual, economic, and emotional domination and exploitation. For example, intimate partner violence may involve domination that is physical, sexual, economic, and emotional. Discrimination against the LGBTQ+ community, on the other hand, is a form of domination that is mostly political and emotional. It is political because of their blocked opportunities for equal rights and privileges, and it is emotional because of social exclusion. Sociologists explore these and many other forms of expressions of social conflicts and examine how power and ideology lead to their formations, transformations, and mitigations (Table 6.2).

TABLE 6.2 Conflict Paradigm: Key Analytical Strategies

Explore the different domains and the converging regions of conflict, such as class, race, gender, ethnicity, culture, religion, and ideology.
Examine how power and ideology create, sustain, neutralize, and mitigate social conflicts by enacting new laws and creating new social structures and how the creation of new rules and social structures, in turn, creates new foci of conflicts (e.g., the effects of *Roe v. Wade* in 1973 and *Obergefell v. Hodges* in 2015 on subsequent political and ideological discourses on the nature of the U.S. Supreme Court).
Observe the nature of domination and exploitation in terms of various modes of expression, such as physical abuse, sexual abuse, economic abuse, emotional abuse, social exclusion, annihilation, and extermination (i.e., natural social exclusion between in-groups and out-groups).
Describe the covert and overt dynamics of social conflicts at different times and at different ages and how power and ideology are related to the dynamics of social conflicts (e.g., the U.S. Congress and Supreme Court on marriage equality).
Look beyond political debates and discourses that are on the surface (e.g., behind the political metaphor of "Make America Great Again" there is a long history of the culture war in America centering on issues of racial equality, gender equality, and marriage equality).
Explore how different conflicting issues are debated and discussed in the public sphere and how different conflicting problems are addressed in political and ideological terms, such as conservatism and liberalism or the "right" and the "left."

Think about how the foci of social conflicts in modern postindustrial digital societies shift from a demand for access to material resources to a more significant need for social equality, social justice, equal justice, freedom, universal human rights, and respect for cultural diversity.

The Conflict Paradigm in Sociology: Selected Theories and Schools of Thought

C. Wright Mills: The Power Elite

Sociologists assume that we should always look behind and through social realities because they are still not what we see and observe on the surface. There are layers and layers of social realities. Sociologist Peter L. Berger (1963) called it the "debunking role" of sociology. One of the prominent theories that has remained at the center of debates and discourses on social conflict in America is the theory of the power elite, coined by sociologist C. Wright Mills. America is historically known to the world to be a unique land of democracy and equality. French political philosopher Alex de Tocqueville, who came to visit America to see the functioning of American democracy in the 1830s, was surprised to see the American zeal for self-governance, voluntarism, and political participation. Sociologist Seymore Martin Lipset (1979) described America as the "first new nation" created based on the ideology of "Americanism"—a doctrine of liberty, equality, and democracy. Mills's idea of power elite presents a picture of another America—an America of the rich and the famous and an America of dubious democracy, particularly the structure of power that has been growing from the 2nd decade of the 20th century. "The classic commentaries of the American politics—those of Tocqueville, Bryce, and Ostrogorski—rest," Mills (1956/2000) argued, "upon the nineteenth-century experience. ... But during the twentieth century, and especially after the First World War, other forces have greatly modified the content and the importance in America of political institutions" (p. 227).

The power elite theory explains that power in America is controlled by a group of strategic elites who occupy the command posts in American politics, economy, and the military. Mills generalized, however, that it is probably one of the enduring features of power and politics in all modern societies. The power elites, Mills (1956/2000) described, "are in command of the major hierarchies and organizations of modern society. They rule the big corporations. They run the machinery of the state and claim its prerogatives. They occupy the strategic command posts of the social structure, in which are now centered the effective means of the power and the wealth and the celebrity which they enjoy" (p. 4). The power elites decide the political agenda for social change and reforms. They determine whether it will be a war on poverty, a war on drugs, or a war on crimes. They decide when to go to war and with which countries to go to war. They determine what military weapons to make, who will make them, and where and how to sell the weapons. The power elite, Mills (1956/2000) observed, "are the ones who determine their duty, as well as the duties of those beneath them. They are not merely following orders: they give orders. They are not merely 'bureaucrats': they command bureaucrats" (p. 286). Racially, the network of the power elite is made up predominantly of White and Protestant males. They have economic wealth and have "cultural capital"—access to the network of power, knowledge, and technology. The power elite is not a formal organization that is visible and observable. It is an informal network, and one not based on ideas of conspiracy or a form of dictatorial governance. The power elite is an in-group, and the power elite members intensely and deliberately socialize within the power elite. The power elites share a typical mindset. "In so far as the power elite is composed of men of similar origin and education, in so far as their careers and their styles of life are similar," Mills (1956/2000) said, "there is the psychological and social basis for their unity" (p. 19).

The power elites make the strategic political, economic, and social policy decisions, making them primarily to advance and protect their ideas, values, and interests. They do not even hesitate, Mills (1956/2000) argues, to make national policy decisions even though those decisions might work against the common good. "We must remember," Mills (1956/2000) argued, "that these men of the power elite now occupy the strategic places in the structure of American society; that they command the dominant institutions of a dominant nation; that, as a set of men they are in a position to make decisions with terrible consequences for the underlying populations of the world" (pp. 286–287). It is the shared ideas, values, and interests that bind the power elites together. In the view of Mills, the power elite is thus an invisible force of political domination, and it contributes to sustaining conflict as an endemic feature in America's social and political order.

G. William Domhoff: Who Rules America?

Among the proponents of the conflict paradigm, there are considerable debates and disputes over how a class is to be defined and described. The two strands of thought are the Marxian analysis of class and the Weberian analysis of class. The adherents of the Marxian view define a class as an ownership category. In a capitalist society, the bourgeoisie who own the strategic means of production form the dominant class—the capitalist class. For Marxian sociologists, power in a capitalist society is a part of the superstructure that serves and protects the economic interests and the ideology of the capitalist class. Conflict sociologists who follow the Weberian tradition, on the other hand, define a class as a power category—the people who occupy the dominant power form the dominant class.

Sociologist G. William Domhoff (1967/2005) developed a theory of who rules America by combining both the Marxian and the Weberian strategies of defining a class. He contended that a class is both an economic and political category. People belong to a class in terms of whether they have access to capital and power and whether they have a sense of belonging to a class. He said that power is not merely an economic category. "Class can also refer to a group of families with similar aspirations and values, to families who perceive each other as equals and freely intermarry" (Domhoff, 1967/2005, p. 3). Based on this assumption, Domhoff (1967/2005) theorized that there is an "identifiable," "observable," and "differentiated" upper class in America "with more or less definite boundaries" (p. 4). This upper class, Domhoff (1967/2005) argued, is America's "governing class" (p. 5). This governing class "is a social upper class which owns the disproportionate amount of a country's wealth, receives a disproportionate amount of a country's yearly income, and contributes a disproportionate number of its members to the controlling institutions and key decision-making groups of the country" (Domhoff, 1967/2005, p. 5).

America's governing class is made up of those who not merely influence but control the corporate economy, who command and hold the power of the federal government—the office of the presidency, Congress, and the institutions of the federal judiciary. He said that by "control," "we mean to imply dominance, the exercise of 'power' (ability to act) from a position of 'authority.' ... Synonym for power would rule, govern, guide, and direct" (Domhoff, 1967/2005, p. 11). For Domhoff, the governing class is more extensive and broader than what Mills defined as a power elite in America. He further expanded that the governing class is a closed group with a shared set of values and aspirations, but a group that is in a continuous process of change and mobility. "People are moving into (not to mention out of) this group all the time ... the co-optation of a bright young man into the upper class occurs through education at private schools, elite universities, and elite laws schools; through success as a corporate executive; through membership in exclusive gentleman's clubs; and participation in exclusive charities" (Domhoff, 1967/2005, p. 5).

Joe Richard Feagin: Systemic Racism: A Theory of Oppression

Richard Feagin, a Harvard-trained sociologist, has researched race and social conflict in America for nearly 4 decades. One of the most widely known and examined theories of Feagin's is termed "systemic racism: a theory of oppression." The theory of systemic racism was developed in the broader contexts of the expansion of European colonialism in the New World of America from the 16th century, the 400 years of the history of slavery and the expansion of capitalism in America, and the 244 years of the birth of the American nation in 1776. His theory is based on the assumption that the American nation was created by White European colonialists who brought and implanted in America the European colonial mentality of "White man's burden" of civilizing the world—a phrase coined by Rudyard Kipling in a poem in 1897. The birth of the American nation, for Feagin (2006), began with the birth of huge civilizational conflicts between the old and the new worlds. With the beginning of the institution of slavery in America—an institution the European colonialists deliberately created and expanded—a new dimension of the civilizational conflict between White people and Black people was born. Feagin theorized that systemic racism in America began at the beginning of slavery, and it is a historically created and embedded social and economic system. From the Civil War of 1861 to the Civil Rights Act of 1964, many significant social and policy advancements have been made; however, systemic racism, Feagin argues, has remained pervasive in American society.

Systemic racism, for Feagin (2006), "encompasses the racist ideology, attitudes, emotions, habits, actions, and institutions of whites" in America (p. 2). It is historical, structural, systemic, and cultural. Systemic racism was characterized until the formal abolition of slavery by extensive physical, sexual, economic, political, and social oppression. After the end of slavery and the promulgation of Amendment 13 in 1865, and the enactment of the Civil Rights Act of 1964, systemic racism and racist oppressions took a different shape. It became more economic, political, cultural, and psychological. Feagin (2006) said, "From a systemic racism perspective, U.S. society is an organized racist whole with complex, interconnected, and interdependent social networks, organizations, and institutions that routinely imbed racial oppression" (p. 17). At the core of systemic racism, Feagin theorized, there remains a White racial frame of mind. "Central to the persistence of systemic racism has been the development of a commonplace white racial frame—that is an organized set of racialized ideas, stereotypes, emotions, and inclinations to discriminate" (Feagin, 2006, p. 25).

The racial frame of mind, which is mostly unseen and invisible, leads to discriminatory actions, and discriminatory actions are expressed and articulated by the society's core institutions of the economy, politics, education, family, work, religion, and culture. This racial frame is a historical legacy of the European colonial mentality, and it is deeply ingrained in the minds and brains of White people. According to Feagin (2006), White people "imbed their racialized framing of the world deeply in their minds (brains) and thereby make such framing much harder to counter" (p. 26). The racialized frame "is more than cognitive, for it also includes racialized emotions that are linked to cognitive stereotypes and visual images" (Feagin, 2006, p. 27). The White racialized frame of mind is recreated in every generation through socialization, networks of friends and families, and cultural media. Feagin (2006) further elaborated that "negative stereotypes and images of African Americans and other Americans of color are used continuously, refurbished, played with, amended, and passed along in millions of white kinship and friendship networks, from one community to the next, and one generation to the next" (p. 44).

FIGURE 6.4   Joe Richard Feagin

MARTIN LUTHER KING JR.: DREAM SPEECH

"I have a dream that one day this nation will rise up and live out the true meaning of its creed: "We hold these truths to be self-evident, that all men are created equal." I have a dream that one day on the red hills of Georgia, the sons of former slaves and the sons of former slave owners will be able to sit down together at the table of brotherhood. I have a dream that one day even the state of Mississippi, a state sweltering with the heat of injustice sweltering with the heat of oppression, will be transformed into an oasis of freedom and justice. I have a dream that my four little children will one day live in a nation where they will not be judged by the color of their skin but by the content of their character. I have a dream today. And if America is to be a great nation (Yes), this must become true."

Source: MLKEC-INP, Martin Luther King, Jr. Estate Collection, in private hands

William J. Wilson: More Than Just Race

William J. Wilson is a Harvard-educated Black sociologist of significant national and international reputation. In his book *More Than Just Race: Being Black and the Inner City* (2009), Wilson presented a theory of racial conflict in America somewhat different from systemic racism developed by Joe Richard Feagin. Wilson (2009) agrees that "racism is historically one of the most prominent cultural frames and has played a major role in determining how whites perceive and act towards blacks" (p. 15). But the ideology of racism—"beliefs that one race is either biologically or culturally inferior to another"—Wilson (2009) argued, "has declined significantly" in America (p. 15). Wilson theorizes that racial conflict in America is not merely a matter of race as a biological phenomenon, but is intertwined with a series of structural and cultural factors. Wilson said any systematic and pragmatic understanding of racial conflict in America must consider the nature and the evolution of two sets of sociological factors: structural and cultural. The structural aspects are mostly of power, policy, and the development of objective economic forces. The cultural factors are the factors intrinsic and subjective to Blacks Americans' cultural milieu living in America's inner cities.

Wilson made two critical sociological observations. His first concerned the growth of Black ghettos and inner cities, particularly in the South. He argued that a series of social and economic changes and transformations of the past half century, particularly those evolving from the 1970s and 1980s, have contributed to creating a distinctively identifiable group of impoverished Black people in America's inner cities. Some of these economic and structural forces include expanding global capitalism, the rise of the information economy, globalization, the birth of a knowledge society, rapid improvements in transportation and communications, and suburbanization. These forces have led to the growth of the knowledge-based and high-tech service economy and the decline of America's low-tech manufacturing industries. Because of these twin forces, millions of non-college-educated and low-skilled Black workers in recent decades remained trapped in poverty and inner cities. "One of the combined effects of these factors," Wilson (2009) observed, "was the emergence of depopulated ghettos, especially in cities of the Midwest and Northeast" (p. 60). Poverty, particularly male poverty, contributed, in turn, to the growth of inner-city crimes, drugs, violence, incarceration, divorce, single parenting, and family disintegrations. Wilson (2009) said concentrated poverty is positively connected to "social isolation (from mainstream institutions), joblessness, drop out of school, lower educational achievement, involvement in crime, unsuccessful behavioral development and delinquency among adolescents, nonmarital childbirth, and unsuccessful family management" (p. 46).

Wilson's (2006) second sociological observation about the continuity of racial conflict and racial inequality involved the birth of a peculiar "culture of poverty" in Black ghettos and inner cities. This culture of poverty is a culture of distinctive "*meaning-making* (shared views on how the world works) and *decision making* (choices that reflect shared definitions of how the world works)" that define "issues of trust/street smarts and 'acting black' or 'acting white'" (Wilson, 2009, p. 17). In the view of Wilson, the culture of inner-city poverty is a culture of frustration, isolation, powerlessness, desperation, poor health, poor education, and negation of the mainstream perceptions about social mobility, law, and justice. The culture of inner-city poverty, a culture that is passed from one generation to another generation of Black people living in poverty through socialization, Wilson (2009) believes, is "dysfunctional," damaging to social mobility, and "contribute to the perpetuation of poverty" (p. 19). Wilson, however, confirms that, eventually, racial conflict in America is a structural phenomenon. It is perpetuated structurally by the birth of inner-city Black poverty that came as a result of the massive social and economic transformations of recent years—transformations that are unseen and unobservable through common eyes. Wilson (2009) concludes by saying, "Culture matters, but I would have to say it does not matter as much as social structure" (p. 152).

The Feminist Theory

At all ages and at all times, men loved, adored, courted, and even committed suicide for women. In many great civilizations of the past, queens and princes ruled and governed. The stories of Egyptian queen Cleopatra and of Romeo and Juliet have made permanent marks in the human chronicle of love and war. But still, one of the most invasive and universal forms of social conflict is between men and women. Since the beginning of organized religion some 5,000 years ago with the birth of Hinduism in India, and from the earliest days of the birth of human civilizations, differences between men and women remained one of the most protracted social and philosophical concerns. Women are given the role, rank, and status subordinate to men in all the great religions of the world—Hinduism, Judaism, Buddhism, Christianity, and Islam (Lapsley, 2005; Sharma & Young, 1999).

The ancient Hindu custom of burning alive a Hindu widow on her deceased husband's funeral pyre—a tradition, described as *sati*, that existed until 1832 when it was legally banned by then-Bengal British Governor-General Lord William Bentinck—is probably one of the more blatant examples of how women were perceived by one of the great religions of the world. Until the middle of the 19th century and the promulgation of the Widow Remarriage Act of 1856, Hindu widows were not legally and culturally allowed to remarry. The Law Code of Manu, which is a more than 2,000-year-old Hindu legal and religious text, does not recognize women as individuals. The Code described that women are to be dominated and protected by their fathers when they are young, by their husbands when they are married, and by their sons when they are widows. The Code strictly forbids Brahmins (the upper caste) from marrying a Sudra (lower caste) woman. When a Brahmin "foolishly marry low-caste wives," the Code said, "they quickly reduce even their families and children to the rank of Sudras" (Olivelle, 2004, p. 44).

The Jewish rabbis of the Talmud believe that different roles for men and women are divinely ordained (Sharma & Young, 1999). Pope Francis, who became a pope at the dawn of the 21st century, said that women's doors to become priests are permanently closed in Catholicism. He believes that Jesus wanted only men to be his evangelists. Until the advent of modernity and the birth of the ideas of reason, humanism, enlightenment, natural rights, and equality in the 19th century, and the birth of the principle of universal human rights in the middle of the 20th century, the patriarchy has been the dominant paradigm that defined the nature, role, status, and duties of women. Although women's consciousness about the domination of patriarchy goes back to the beginning of the Middle Ages (Lerner, 1990), it is from the beginning of modernity in the 19th century that the institution of patriarchy began to be widely challenged. From the middle of the 20th century, a new feminist theory began to take shape in debates and discourses on gender conflict in American sociology in particular and social science in general.

One of feminist theory's core assumptions is that gender hierarchy—the idea that some social roles and responsibilities are inherently "masculine" while others are naturally "feminine"—is a social construction. There are biological differences between men and women, but gender division in society is not genetic or ordained by God. It is a sociological phenomenon—a social construction defined and dictated by men of all ages (Gilligan & Snider, 2018; Eisenstein, 1998). The institution of patriarchy is also a cultural paradigm that defined, deified, and demeaned women of all ages and societies. As a culture, patriarchy is both external and internal. Externally, "patriarchy exists as a set of rules, values, codes, and scripts that specify how men and women should be in the world" (Gilligan & Snider, 2018, p. 6). Internally, patriarchy defines the mind and the whole trajectory of the psychology of women. "More insidiously, patriarchy also exists internally, shapes how we think and feel, how we perceive and judge ourselves, our desires, our relationships, and the world we live in" (Gilligan & Snider, 2018, p. 6).

The feminist theorists assume that men are, by nature, incapable of fully comprehending, understanding, and empathizing with the issues concerning women. By nature, women have different views and perceptions about almost all social and political issues, including power, love, sex, rape, incest, marriage, divorce, children, domination, oppression, and exploitation. Women have different logic and rationalities of defining and empathizing the principles of equality and inequality, justice and injustice, legal and illegal, and moral and immoral (Millet, 1970/2016). The feminist theorists argue that patriarchy's culture is antithetical to the culture of modernity—the culture of universal human rights, equality, democracy, humanism, individualism, reason, and enlightenment. A modern social order dedicated to reducing gender conflict, feminist theorists argue, must therefore recast and redefine the conceptions of patriarchy, power, law, knowledge, and epistemology (Smith, 2012).

Selected Questions, Essays, Assignments, and Quizzes

1. What are some of the central assumptions of the conflict paradigm? Sociologists assume that power, authority, and ideology are the prime shapers of social conflict, and the effects of power are both external and internal to individuals. Explain in this context W. E. B. Du Bois's concept of social conflict and double consciousness.

2. The contemporary sociological paradigm of conflict's intellectual legacy goes back to the theory of class conflict developed by Karl Marx in the middle of the 19th century. Describe and explain the Marxian theory of class conflict, focusing on the Marxian philosophy of humans as producing animals, his materialistic view of the mode of production and class conflict, and his alienation theory.

3. The paradigm of social conflict has discovered that social conflict is multidimensional. Class is not the only dimension of the conflict in society. The conflict has various dimensions, such as race, gender, age, ethnicity, religion, culture, and ideology. Discuss and explain the multidimensional nature of social conflict in America. Provide examples.

4. What are the major dimensions and dynamics of social conflict? What does it mean to say that social conflict is both overt and covert? Describe some of the social movements that became galvanized in America from the middle of the second decade of the 21st century (Hints: #MeToo and Black Lives Matter movements).

5. There are many conflicting issues in America, such as the legalization of abortion, legalization of marijuana, legalization of same-sex marriage, gun control, universal health care, global warming, and immigration. How do different races, genders, classes, and religious groups view and perceive these issues differently? On what grounds do they hold divergent views and opinions (develop a chart showing the different points and different groups' different perspectives)?

6. What are some of the vital analytical strategies of the conflict paradigm? What do sociologists mean when they say the foci of social conflicts in modern postindustrial digital societies shift from a demand for access to material resources to a more significant need for social equality, social justice, equal justice, freedom, universal human rights, and respect for cultural diversity? Describe and explain with examples.

7. Describe and explain the C. Wright Mills theory of the power elite. What are the different groups, according to Mills, who make up the power elite? Can we describe the power elite as a class in the Marxian sense of the term? To what extent does Mills' theory of power elite justify the sociological hypothesis that power is a significant driving source of human actions and human conflicts?

8. Joe Richard Feagin developed the theory of systematic racism in America. What did he mean when he theorized that America's systematic racism is historical, structural, systemic, and cultural? Describe in this context five major statutes enacted by Congress and five major U.S. Supreme Court decisions made in recent years to address or mitigate the issues of racial conflict and race discrimination in America.

9. Sociologist William J. Wilson theorized that racism in contemporary America is about more than just race. He alluded us to examine two sets of factors in understanding racism: economics and culture. Based on class lectures and your reading of the section on "More than Just Race" in this chapter, discuss and examine those two sets of factors responsible for discriminatory race relations in America (you can add a comment at the end of the essay on whether you agree or disagree with Wilson's theory of more than just race).

10. What are the core arguments of the feminist theory of social conflict? In this context, describe five major statutes enacted by Congress and five major U.S. Supreme Court decisions made in recent years that address or mitigate the issues of gender conflict and gender discrimination in America.

References

Bainton, R. (1977). *Here I stand: A life of Martin Luther*. Mentor Publishing.
Bell, D. (1973). *The coming of post-industrial society: A venture in social forecasting*. Basic Books.
Berger, P. L. (1963). *Invitation to sociology: A humanistic perspective*. Anchor Books–Doubleday.
Coser, L. (1964). *The functions of social conflict: An examination of the concept of social conflict and its use in empirical research*. Free Press.
Dahrendorf, R. (1959). *Class and class conflict in industrial society*. Stanford University Press.
Dawkins, R. (2010). *The selfish gene* (40th anniversary ed.). Basic Books. (Original work published 1976)
Domhoff, W. G. (2005). *Who rules America?* McGraw-Hill Education. (Original work published 1967)
Du Bios, W. E. B. (2012). *The souls of the Black folk*. CreateSpace Independent Publishing Platform. (Original work published 1903)
Eisenstein, Z. R. (1998). *The female body and the law*. University of California Press.
Fanon, F. (2005). *The wretched of the earth*. Grove Publishing. (Original work published 1961)
Farganis, J. (1991). *Readings in social theory: The classic tradition to post-modernism*. McGraw-Hill.
Feagin, J. R. (2006). *Systemic racism: A theory of oppression*. Routledge.
Finer, S. E. (Ed.). (1966). *Vilfredo Pareto: Sociological Writings* (trans. by D. Mirfin). Frederick A. Praeger.
Foucault, M. (1988). *Madness and civilization: A history of insanity in the age of reason*. Vintage. (Original work published 1961)
Foucault, M. (2012). *Discipline and punish: The birth of prison*. Vintage Publishing. (Original work published 1975)
Freud, S. (2010). *Civilization and its discontent* (Reprinted ed.). W. W. Norton. (Original work published 1930)
Gilligan, C., & Snider, N. (2018). *Why does patriarchy persist?* Polity Press.
Goldthorpe, J. H. (1987). *Social mobility and class structure in modern Britain*. Oxford University Press.
Healey, J. F., & O'Brien. E. (2014). *Race, ethnicity, gender, and class. The sociology of group conflict and change*. Sage Publications.
Inglehart, R. (2018). *Cultural evolution: People's motivations are changing and reshaping the world*. Cambridge University Press.
King, M. L. (Ed. and Trans.). (2014). *Renaissance humanism: An anthology of sources*. Hackett Publishing.
Lapsley, J. E. (2005). *Whispering the word: Hearing women stories in the Old Testament*. John Knox Press.
Lerner, G. (1994). *The creation of feminist consciousness: From the Middle Ages to eighteen-seventy*. Oxford University Press.

Lipset, S. M. (1979). *The first new nations: The United States in historical and comparative perspective*. W. W. Norton.

Martínez, J., & Smith, G. A. (2016, November 9). *How the faithful voted: A preliminary analysis*. Pew Research Center. Retrieved from https://www.pewresearch.org/fact-tank/2016/11/09/how-the-faithful-voted-a-preliminary-2016-analysis/ on December 20, 2020.

Marx, K. (2013a). Capital: A critique of political economy, Vol. 1. In J. Farganis (Ed.), *Readings in social theory* (pp. 70–72). McGraw-Hill. (Original work published 1867)

Marx, K. (2013b). Economic and philosophic manuscript. In J. Farganis (Ed.), *Readings in social theory* (pp. 56–63). McGraw-Hill. (Original work published 1844)

Marx, K., & Engels, F. (2013). The manifesto of the Communist Party. In J. Farganis (Ed.), *Readings in social theory* (pp. 44–55). McGraw-Hill. (Original work published 1848)

McWhorter, J. (2001). *Losing the race: Self-sabotage in Black America*. Free Press.

Millet, K. (2016). *Sexual politics*. Columbia University Press. (Original work published 1970)

Mills, C. W. (2000). *The power elite*. Oxford University Press. (Original work published 1956)

Olivelle, P. (2004). *The law code of Manu* (P. Olivelle, Trans.). Oxford University Press.

Reich, R. B. (1992). *The work of nations: Preparing ourselves for the 21st century capitalism*. Vintage.

Rousseau, J. J. (2020). *Discourse on the Origin of Inequality*. Independently Published. (Original work published 1754)

Rousseau. J. J. (2020). *The Social Contract (trans.by G.D.H. Cole)*. Independently Published (Original Work published in 1762)

Sharma, A., & Young, K. E. (1999). *Feminism and world religions*. State University of New York Press.

Smith, D. E. (2012). *The everyday world as problematic: A feminist sociology*. University of Northwestern Press.

Wilson, W. J. (2009). *More than just race: Being Black and poor in the inner city*. W. W. Norton.

Wolfe, A. (1998). *Marginalized in the middle*. University of Chicago Press.

Figure Credits

CHAPTER 7

The Symbolic Interactionist Paradigm

Society as Meanings and Symbols

CHAPTER THEME

Symbolic interactionism is another sociological paradigm that has generated a considerable volume of research in recent years. Drawing theoretical inspiration from the subjectivist traditions of philosophy, science, and sociology, Harvard sociologist Herbert Blumer coined the term "symbolic interactionism" in the 1960s. One of the questions that has been central to the theoretical tradition of subjectivism is the nature of social reality, or the relationship between individuals and society—the connections between "I" and "we." Are individuals the creation of society, and do they remain enslaved by the objective social world? Or do individuals create a social reality in terms of their interpretations, reasons, thoughts, feelings, and logic? The symbolic interactionist perspective is based on the assumption that the "I," or the self, creates the society in terms of its frames and logic of thought. Still, logic and ideas arise from human social life, human interactions, and human communications. The "I" and the "we" are, therefore, inseparable and indivisible. To see "I" as apart from the "we" is sociologically misleading. The connectivity between "I" and "we" is mediated and negotiated through the meaning of the "objects" that comprise the social reality. These objects may be physical, such as a tree, river, or stone. The objects may be social, such as race, class, gender, religion, work, law, and bureaucracy. The objects that comprise the social reality may also include knowledge, ideas, values, and morality, such as democracy, equality, and individualism. The symbolic interactionists assume that everything within the social reality has some meanings attached to them. To comprehend the social reality or a given object within the social reality means to comprehend its meanings and significance. Social reality's meanings are born, grown, changed, and transformed in and through social interactions and communications between "I" and "we"—the individual and society. What is particularly significant for sociology, the symbolic interactionists argue, is to study the meanings of different social actions and institutions and how those meanings are interpreted and evaluated within the minds or the selves of individuals. The social reality will be much more visible and understandable if sociology explores how meanings created and shared by "we" are continuously interpreted, evaluated, and examined by the "I"—the "self."

Introduction

The structural-functional paradigm looks at society as structures and systems of human actions, institutions, and behavior. The proponents of structural-functionalism are curious about how social order and stability are possible. The conflict paradigm looks at society as a vast arena of social conflicts between and among different social groups based on such factors as race, gender, age, sexual orientation, religion, ethnicity, nationality, culture, and ideology. The proponents of the conflict paradigm are concerned with how social hierarchy, domination, exploitation, and oppression are crucial in the formation of power and social organization and how they drive social change and transformations. There is another perspective, or sociological eye, that is described as symbolic interactionism. The symbolic interactionists look at society as a set of meanings, symbols, and significance. According to the proponents of this perspective, a culture, or a social structure, is not like a physical thing that is visible, touchable, and observable. Social reality is not like physical reality. Instead, social reality is a social construction or a human construction shaped and expressed by mutually shared meanings and symbols. Human society is an ongoing process of meaning creation, meaning change, and meaning interpretation. The perspective of symbolic interactionism is deeply rooted in the idealistic or the subjectivist tradition of philosophy. Still, it began from such classical sociologists as Max Weber, Georg Simmel, and Karl Mannheim. The paradigm of symbolic interactionism has generated a considerable amount of theoretical, methodological, and empirical literature. This chapter will examine the core assumptions, analytical strategies, and some empirical research and examples of the paradigm of symbolic interactionism.

The Paradigm of Symbolic Interactionism: Philosophical and Scientific Legacies

The Philosophical Duality Between Objectivism and Subjectivism

The philosophical and scientific legacies of symbolic interactionism can be traced back to two distinctive traditions of thought and theorizing in philosophy and science: the philosophical duality between objectivism and subjectivism, particularly the philosophical discovery of the mind by French philosopher Rene Descartes, and the birth of cognitive science, which led to discoveries about the autonomy of the mind. Since the beginning of philosophy in ancient Greece and Athens about 2,500 years ago, there has been a debate about the nature of social reality—the heart of social facts, roles, behaviors, values, and institutions. There are two broad camps in philosophy: objectivism versus subjectivism, or materialism versus idealism, or realism versus nominalism. At the core of the debate is the curiosity about what governs a society—a social life or human social behavior. Are human social facts and events governed internally by the human mind, or is the human mind merely a reflection of the external, objective reality? How are the mind and society connected? How are the mind, body, brain, and behavior connected? Understanding this philosophical duality is at the core of all philosophical ideas and sociological theorizing about human society and human social facts and events. Advocates of the objectivist or materialist perspective believe the human mind is merely the reflection of the objective world. The human mind is not autonomous, and it has no inner capacity for reason, thoughts, and imagination. The human mind acts and thinks in a way that it is shaped, controlled, and dictated by the objective world's facts and events. The objectivists contend that the social world is external, binding, and constraining, such as the boundaries of law, work, politics, power, government, work, family, race, gender, roles, nations, culture, and ideology. The objectivists do not recognize or look at humans "as composed individuals who have selves. Instead, they assume human beings to be merely organisms with some kind of organization, responding to forces that play upon them" (Blumer, 2008, p. 249). Some of these forces are social systems, social structures, culture, status/position, social roles, customs, institutions, collective representation, social situations, social norms, and values. The objectivists assume that "the behavior of people as members of a *society* is an expression of the play on them of these kinds of factors or forces. The individuals who compose a human society are treated as media through which such factors operate, and the social action of such individuals is regarded as an expression of such factors" (Blumer, 2008, p. 249). The structural-functional and the conflict paradigms share some of the core notions of the philosophical perspective of objectivism. One of the most forceful expositions of the objectivist or the materialist viewpoint of philosophy is the Marxian theory of historical materialism and class conflict. For Marx, the mode of production and the class structure were the shapers and movers of the human mind and its manifestations in philosophy, ideology, culture, and social conflict. On the other hand, the symbolic interactionist paradigm is rooted in the subjectivist or the idealistic tradition of philosophy.

The subjectivist tradition goes back to the ancient Greek philosophies of Socrates, Plato, and Aristotle. The core of the subjectivist philosophy is that the human mind is an active, autonomous, and dynamic entity. Socrates, Plato, and Aristotle defined humans as moral, ethical, and intelligent beings. Socrates claimed that an unexamined life is not worth living. Plato said an ideal form of government could come through a marriage between knowledge and power. Aristotle believed that humans are born with innate passions for power and politics. Rene Descartes, a 17th-century French philosopher and scientist, is the father of the subjectivist tradition in modern philosophy and social science. Descartes theorized that the mind is an independent entity and is autonomous in its functions and operations. Descartes argued that the mind could think, reason, feel, experience, and imagine independent of any objective reality. The brain is the physical center of intelligence, but the mind is the center for human consciousness, creativity, self-reflection, and self-awareness. Descartes argued that modern science would not have been possible without the mind being an autonomous entity in the human brain. The reality of the physical world did not lead to the discovery of modern science and scientific theories. The theories related to the facts of the material world, such as Newton's theory of gravity, Einstein's theory of relativity, or DNA structure, are instead discovered by following intuitions, theorizing, and the imaginations of the mind. Descartes's famous dictum that "I think, therefore I am" is the central idea in the subjectivist tradition of modern philosophy (Descartes, 1999). Following the subjectivist tradition in philosophy, the proponents of the symbolic interactionist paradigm begin by assuming that sociology must study how the human mind works to make sense of the social world. The essence of sociology is to examine how humans create the objective social world by creating meanings, symbols, laws, culture, literature, music, and ideology and how social structures and social conflicts are seen, defined, symbolized, and interpreted by different groups and individuals in different spaces and at different times and ages.

The Birth of Cognitive Science and the Modern Discovery of the Mind

Descartes's discovery of the mind and subjectivism's role was remarkable, but it remained in the realm of philosophy. The modern scientific study of the nature of the mind and subjectivism's position began with the development of the science of psychoanalysis by Sigmund Freud in the late 19th century. Freud, an Austrian neurologist by training, was the first to theorize that the mind is composed of three regions: conscious (superego), subconscious (ego), and unconscious (id). Freud argued that human actions and behavior are primarily driven by the unconscious region of the mind, but they are culturally shaped and controlled by the conscious region for the sake of society and civilization (Freud, 2010/1999). The Freudian psychoanalysis and subjectivism came under serious theoretical attack in the wake of the rise of behaviorism in American psychology in the 1950s and 1960s. The paradigm of behaviorism, born through the works of John B. Watson in the 1920s and matured in the 1940s and 1950s through the works of B. F. Skinner, assumes that mind and mentalism cannot be scientifically studied and examined. The mind cannot be directly observed, and the development of scientific and empirical statements about human subjectivity is impossible. Skinner (2012), the principal founder of the behaviorist school in American psychology, said, "Direct observation of the mind comparable with the observation of the nervous system has not proved feasible. Introspective psychology no longer pretends to supply direct information about events which are the causal antecedents, rather than the mere accompaniments, of behavior" (p. 137). In the view of proponents of the behavioral paradigm, human behavior is objectivist in nature and is externally shaped and controlled. Human behavior is caused primarily as a response to external stimuli.

Modern cognitive science emerged as a challenge to the assumptions of the behaviorist paradigm and its complete negation of the role of the mind and subjectivity in shaping human behavior. Cognitive science was born in the 1950s, borrowing ideas from cognitive psychology, cognitive anthropology, and linguistics, and it matured in the 1970s and 1980s with the development of modern neurology, computer science, and the science of artificial intelligence (Bechtel & Graham, 1999). The core assumption of cognitive science is that the human mind is the source of human intelligence and behavior and that a science of the human mind is possible (Burmudez, 2020; Kolak et al., 2006). Cognitive science examines how the human mind works and how it makes sense of the social world. The mind generates concepts, abstractions, reasoning, mental images, and metaphors, and it thinks and solves problems. There is a broad consensus among cognitive scientists that the human mind works through models, schemas, representations, and computational algorithms. These processes are scientifically identifiable, understandable, and provable. The evolution of cognitive science provided a significant impetus for developing the sociological paradigm of symbolic interactionism in the 1970s and 1980s.

The Roots of Subjectivism in Sociology: Max Weber, Georg Simmel, George H. Mead, and Charles H. Cooley

Max Weber: Theory of Social Action

The classical sociology of the 19th century contained the seeds of both the objectivist and subjectivist traditions of thoughts and ideas. The objectivist tradition was represented by Marx's theory of historical materialism and class conflict and Durkheim's theories of collective consciousness and social facts as "things." This objectivist tradition later in the 20th century gave impetus to the development of the structural-functional and the conflict perspectives. The subjectivist tradition in classical sociology was represented mainly by Max Weber's theory of social action, Simmel's theory of society as a process of association, Mead's functional view of the mind, and Cooley's theory of self and society. In the middle of the 20th century, the paradigm of symbolic interactionism emerged, drawing theoretical inspiration from these sources of subjectivism in developing a science of society. The perspective of symbolic interactionism draws major theoretical inspiration from Weber's formulation of sociology as a science of social action. Weber argued that subjectivism (i.e., the meaning of human activities or the human mind) can be legitimately studied by following the canons of the scientific method. For Weber, the core of sociology is the study of the subjectively and rationally imputed meaning of social actions.

Weber argued that all social facts and events and social institutions and organizations are bundles of individual actions, and all personal stories are expressed in terms of meanings and symbols. All unique meanings are created in society's context, but they can take different forms with a different sense of justifications. The meanings of some actions may be justified on the grounds of traditional customs and cultures, such as the respect and deification of a charismatic authority like Martin Luther King Jr., Gandhi, Mandela, or Abraham Lincoln. The meanings of some actions may be effectual and justified on the grounds of emotional attachments. The meanings of some actions may be based on values, such as the observance of Christmas, Hanukkah, or Ramadan, which are justified on religious grounds. The meanings of some activities, Weber contended, may also be explained on the grounds of science, reason, and rationality. Weber described these meanings as instrumental rationality—purposes that are rational, deliberate, and calculative. For example, a bureaucracy is based on an examination, written rules, specialization, division of labor, and hierarchy. Weber (1992) conducted major historical studies on world religions and examined their believers' themes and meanings. His research on the development of modern rational capitalism in the West has been particularly significant. Weber (2010/1992) theorized that modern rational capitalism was born in the West during the 19th century, particularly in northern European countries, primarily because of the beliefs and meanings of the Calvinist ethics in Protestantism. The Protestants, believing in Calvinism, Weber argued, developed a unique cultural mentality of applying science, reason, and rationality for "this-worldly" economic growth and materialism, and they cherished the meaning that this-worldly richness was a sign of salvation in the "other world." Weber thus generalized that modernity was born in the West primarily because of its unique cultural mentality of growth, change, and progress justified on religious grounds. Therefore, for Weber, the task of sociology involved the study of the rationally imputed meanings of social actions of individuals through the methods of interpretation, introspection, and comprehension—the methods collectively described by Weber as "verstehen." Weber's (2017) theory of social action and his method of verstehen provided a significant impetus for sociology to explore and understand the subjective dimensions of social and cultural life following the canons of the scientific method.

Georg Simmel: Theory of Sociation

Georg Simmel is another classical sociologist who made subjectivism—the study of the individual mind and how it controls and regulates social interactions—the core of sociological analysis. Social facts and events and social organizations and institutions, for Simmel, are not like rocks and stones. A society, Simmel (1972) argued, is born in and through human interactions and human associations, and all human interactions and associations are consciously driven. A society is not just "out there." It is also inside the minds of individuals who consciously participate in and create different structures or forms of interactions (Wolff, 1950). We, as individuals, Simmel theorized, internalize social rules, norms, and values. Still, the process of internalization is deliberately and consciously guided and orchestrated by our subjectivity—our self and the mind. The internalization of social norms and values by individuals, Simmel described, "explains the dual character of the moral command: that on the one hand, it confronts us as an impersonal order to which we simply have to submit, but that on the other, no external power, but only our most private and internal impulses, imposes it on us" (Simmel, 1959, as quoted in Ritzer, 2000, p. 157). Individuals have mental capacities and individual minds, Simmel contended, and are not "simply enslaved by external factors" (Ritzer, 2000, p. 158). The paradigm of symbolic interactionism further expands this notion of human subjectivity in creating a society and the continuity of the chronicle of human stories.

Charles H. Cooley: Theory of Self and Society

Charles H. Cooley, as discussed in Chapter 4, was one of the early pioneers of the study of the relationships between self and society that were expanded in his three volumes of work published in the first two decades of the 20th century: *Human Nature and the Social Order* (1902), *Social Organization* (1909), and *Social Processes* (1918/2013). Cooley's central theoretical curiosity was about how individuals and society are connected. How does an individual become social, and how is society possible? He theorized that self and society are twin-born, we know one as immediately as we know the other, and that the notion of a separate, independent ego is an illusion (Cooley, 1909/1937, p. 5). He further affirmed that the "antithesis of society versus the individual is false and hollow" (Cooley, 1902, p. 42). A child, for Cooley, is not born with a self. The self grows as a child begins to communicate with their significant others, most likely, Cooley said, from the age of 2. This birth of the self is the birth of the imagination of "I" about the social world within which the child is born and begins to grow. "Very soon," Cooley (1909) argued, "the mind begins to discriminate personal impressions, and to become naively self-conscious and naively conscious of society" (p. 8). From early childhood, the social self begins to evolve because a child starts to become aware, "in a reflective way, of the group and his social relation to it. He does not say 'I', nor does he name his mother, his sister, his nurse, but he has images and feelings out of which these ideas will grow" (Cooley, 1909, p. 8). When a child begins to grow, their human mind, or self-reflective capacity, also begins to be widened. "Later comes the more reflective consciousness," Cooley (1909) said, "which names both himself and other people and brings a fuller perception of the relations which constitute the unity of this small world. And so on to the most elaborate phases of self-consciousness and social consciousness. Self and society go together as phases of a common whole" (pp. 8–9). The human mind of an individual, or the social consciousness of an individual, according to Cooley (1909), has three interconnected dimensions. The first is that an individual has a sense of self-consciousness—meaning "what I think of myself" (p. 12). Second, an individual has a sense of social consciousness—meaning "what I think of other people" (Cooley, 1909, p. 12). Third, an individual has a sense of public consciousness—meaning a collective view of the social milieu. Cooley (1902) said, "I conclude, therefore, that the image which people have of one another are the *solid facts of society* and that to observe and interpret these must be a chief aim of sociology" (p. 121).

George H. Mead: Functional Theory of the Mind

In the 1930s George H. Mead of the Chicago School of Sociology made many enduring contributions to the study of human subjectivity—the study of relationships between self and society. Mead (1934) elaborated his theory of the mind and human self in his book *Mind, Self, and Society*. For Mead, as it was for Cooley, the human mind and self are social constructions. A human is not born with a mind. The mind grows and evolves as the individual begins to interact with the social world. Mead theorized that the mind is not a passive physical entity inside the human brain. The mind is not like a blank slate that passively stores external information. The human mind, for Mead, is an active, living, and dynamic entity. It grows and evolves by actively participating in the social world—the world of human acts and interactions. The mind becomes an active and vibrant entity by participating in the social world of ceaseless interactions and creating and understanding the meanings of the social world expressed in terms of language, symbols, and gestures. The external social world does not enter the mind with some preconceived meanings and significance of social facts and events. Rather, the mind creates the meaning of the social world by its active and continuous engagement with the social world. A human mind is a meaning-creating entity. The mind, for Mead, "is the presence in the behavior of significant symbols. It is the internalization within the individual of the social process of communication in which meaning emerges" (Morris, 1934, p. xxii). The social world interpreted and mediated inside the mind is not a physical thing but a set of symbols and meanings. Mead's core theoretical argument is that the mind does not create society; society makes the mind. By actively participating with the social world and developing a unique reflexive capacity, the mind internalizes the values, meanings, and significance of the social world. Mead (1934) contended: "Reflexiveness, then, is the essential condition within the social process, for development of the mind" (p. 134). It is through the process of reflexiveness that an individual learns the attitudes of others toward them and adjusts their opinions toward others. "It is by means of reflexiveness—the turning back of the experience of the individual upon himself—the whole social process is thus brought into the experience of the individuals involved in it; it is by such means, which enable the individual to take the attitudes of others toward himself, that the individual is able consciously to adjust himself to that process" (Mead, 1934, p. 134).

The Paradigm of Symbolic Interactionism: Key Assumptions

The subjectivist tradition in philosophy—particularly of Rene Descartes, the birth of cognitive science, and the classical sociological tradition of subjectivism expanded by Weber, Simmel, Cooley, and Mead—created the contexts for the birth of the paradigm of symbolic interactionism and various forms of subjectivist and qualitative research in sociology during the 20th century. Structural functionalism and the conflict theory present an objectivistic explanation of social reality. The paradigm of symbolic interactionism does not deny the objective nature of social reality, but it is built on the assumption that the objective world of social reality is created by the subjective world of the human mind and human consciousness. For symbolic interactionism, the understanding of this process of how the objective world of social reality is created by the human mind and consciousness and through the lived experience of everyday life is the mission of sociology. The paradigm of symbolic interactionism was fathered by sociologist Herbert Blumer (1993/1966). Blumer made the study of the meanings of social actions the central point of sociological analysis. He theorized that humans act and behave universally in terms of meanings of different physical products, life situations, and social life and events. A chair, for example, is a physical object, but it has many meanings attached to it. In India, traditionally, an individual from a lower caste is not supposed to sit on a chair in front of a Brahmin. A chair is a symbol of power and prestige in most cultures. For Muslim women, the hijab has a meaning attached to it but one that might not be understandable to people of other religions. For Hindus in India, the River Ganges carries a tremendously sacred and symbolic meaning. For Muslims, the Qur'an is a highly holy text. In Pakistan, demeaning of the Qur'an, either physically or verbally, is considered blasphemy and is punishable by death. Humans act and behave, attaching meanings to all social categories and hierarchies such as race, gender, age, class, and status. The first premise of symbolic interactionism, therefore, is that humans are meaning-creating beings. "Human beings," Blumer (2008) said, "act toward things on the basis of the meanings that the things have for them. Such things include everything that human beings note in his world—physical objects, such as tress and chairs; other human beings such as a mother or a store clerk; categories of human beings such as friend or enemies; institutions, as a school or a government; [and] guiding ideas such as individual independence or honesty" (p. 2).

The second premise of symbolic interactionism is that meanings are socially and culturally born and created. We create meanings as we interact with other human beings in society. Human social life is the source of the creation of the meaning of human things, ideas, values, beliefs, and institutions. Meanings do not emerge in a social vacuum. The meaning of a thing is not intrinsic to the thing that is observed. It also does not grow from the inner psychological and perceptual world of the observer. "Symbolic interactionism," Blumer (1993) described, "sees meanings as social products, as creations that are formed in and through the defining activities of people as they interact" (p. 393). The third premise of symbolic interactionism is that meanings are born and created through a process of interpretation. We develop, follow, and interpret the meanings of our actions through a process of introspection—a conscious and deliberate discourse with our mind and the selves (Table 7.1). In creating meaning and interpretations, we also consciously evaluate in our mind the situation within which we act and behave. "Interpretation," Blumer (1993) noted, "should not be regarded as a mere automatic application of established meanings but as a formative process in which meanings are used and revised as instruments, for the guidance and formation of action" (p. 296).

TABLE 7.1 Symbolic Interactionism: Key Assumptions

Humans are acting, thinking, and meaning-creating beings. The human mind is an active and dynamic entity. Human actions and behaviors are not, as Freud described, propelled by the unconscious region of the mind. Human actions and behaviors are also not, as the structuralists represent, merely set responses to external social factors and forces.

Humans have selves. Human actions and behaviors are mostly self-directed, self-controlled, and self-evaluated. One, for example, is conscious of their race, gender, age, class, socioeconomic status, beliefs, and profession. The "average" human being is conscious of the social and cultural order or disorder within which they live.

Social interaction is the core of the beginning of the birth of the human self and the human conception of social order. We make sense of the social world in our minds and through social interactions with others. Society exists in my mind, and my "self" is conscious of society's existence because I interact with others. A child who is severely autistic, for instance, who does not have a typical notion of "self," and who is not capable of interacting with others in a social way, will not have a sense of social order. "Interaction is a social form of communication" (Blumer, 1966, p. 13).

Human actions and behavior are guided by the meanings they attach to them. Different social facts and events and various social institutions and organizations have no physical shapes or forms. They are just a bundle of human meanings. Even physical objects, such as a stone or a tree, can have abstract meanings to humans. One of sociology's tasks is to examine how the meanings of different social facts and events are formed and created.

The meanings of different social facts and events are socially created in the context of social interactions and social rules, norms, customs, beliefs, traditions, laws, culture, and ideology. The meaning of social facts and events and social ideas and institutions "must be seen as social creations—as being formed in arising out of the process of definition and interpretation as this process takes place in the interaction of people" (Blumer, 1966, pp. 11–12).

The meaning of social facts and events, however, are not fixed and unchangeable. "Nothing is more apparent than that objects in all categories can change their meaning … from the standpoint of symbolic interactionism human group life is a process in which objects are being created, affirmed, transformed, and cast aside" (Blumer, 1966, p. 12). With changes in the meanings of social facts and events over time, actions and behaviors of people "necessarily change in line with changes taking place in their world of objects" (Blumer, 1966, p. 12).

The creation of meanings of different facts and social events in our minds and the self, and the nature of change and transformations in our social actions and behavior, are based on interpretations, dialogues, and discourses within our mind and the self about how others define and describe those meanings. Thus, one subjectively, consciously, and actively creates their sense of the social world and interpret and construct its multifaceted meanings and significance.

The Paradigm of Symbolic Interactionism: Key Analytical Strategies

The symbolic interactionists argue that the study of the meaning of objects should be the core of sociological analysis. Blumer (1966) cautions that "to ignore the meaning of the things toward which people act is seen as falsifying the understanding. To bypass the meaning in favor of factors alleged to produce the behavior is seen as grievous neglect of the meaning in the formation of behavior" (p. 3). The meanings of objects are mutually and intersubjectively understood, and they are social creations. Blumer (1966) further explained that "the meanings of objects for a person arises fundamentally out of the way they are defined to him by others with whom he interacts. Out of a process of mutual indication, common objects emerge—objects that have the same meaning for a given set of people and are seen in the same manner by them" (p. 11). The proponents of symbolic interactionism seek to examine how meanings of different objects grow and evolve and how they are shared in common. The world of social reality, the symbolic interactionists argue, is composed of three categories of objects: physical (e.g., a stone, river, flag, building, or monument); social (e.g., race, gender, class, culture, ideology); and abstract (e.g., democracy, justice, equality, privacy). The meanings of these objects are socially created, sustained, changed, and transformed. The study of the nature of social organizations and institutions, social roles and processes, social progress and problems, and crimes and chaos are essentially the study of their meanings to different groups and how they are interpreted, conflicted, and changed from time to time (see Table 7.2).

TABLE 7.2 Symbolic Interactionism: Key Analytical Strategies

Select your problem of research and investigation. It could be a problem of democracy, or divorce, or deviance. Determine the time and space of the problem under study.
Examine the meaning of the problem under investigation and how it is understood and interpreted by different individuals, groups, and classes.
Explore how different individuals, groups, and classes attach different meanings to the same problem under investigation (e.g., Black Lives Matter, #MeToo, and gay rights movements or the Proud Boys organization).
Look into the language, metaphors, symbols, and signs through which meanings are shared, expressed, and articulated.
Inquire how the meanings of the problem under investigation have changed over time (e.g., how the meanings of divorce, same-sex marriage, or cohabitation have changed over time and how those changes, in turn, have altered our culture, law, politics, and ideology).
Use different interpretive and qualitative methods to examine people's experiences, such as ethnomethodology, biographical analysis, conversational analysis, phenomenological research, and action research.
Explore how public debates, disputes, and discourses reflect competing meanings and significance of physical, social, moral, and ethical "objects" and how they lead to social change and transformations.

The Paradigm of Symbolic Interactionism: Selected Theories and Schools of Thought

Peter L. Berger: Social Construction Reality

The perspective of the social construction of reality school of thought, developed by American sociologist Peter L. Berger, is a branch of symbolic interactionism. The social construction of reality is rooted in the philosophical tradition of phenomenology fathered by German philosopher Edmund Husserl in the early 20th century. Phenomenology is the study of human experience or the human mind and consciousness. How the external and the objective world of things and events are received, experienced, interpreted, and negotiated by our consciousness is the core of the philosophy of phenomenology. The starting point of human understanding, for phenomenology, is the study of human subjectivity—the human mind and its growth and functions in the context of the objective realities of life. The central notion in the social construction of reality theory is that the human social world is both objective and subjective (Berger, 1963/ 1966). We live in society, but society also lives in us. The different social boundaries or social structures and systems—such as family, work, school, power, politics, law, and culture—are socially and humanly created. They are objective, coercive, and enforceable. Once the social structures are created through the institutionalization of rules, laws, norms, and values, we—human beings—become habituated to live and remain within the boundaries of those social structures and systems. We usually do not think about those boundaries, generally do not challenge them, and naturally do not break them. Those boundaries define, describe, dictate, and legitimate our everyday roles and relations. As Berger describes: "To be located in society means to be at the intersection point of specific social forces. Commonly one ignores these forces at one's peril. One moves within the society within carefully defined systems of power and prestige. And once one knows how to locate oneself, one also knows that there is not an awful lot one can do about this" (Berger, 1963, p. 67).

However, social reality, the proponents of social construction theory argue, is also subjective in nature. We humans create our social boundaries—our systems and structures—by applying our values, virtues, and volitions. We are not born social, but we are made social; we learn to live with others in society. "The individual, however, is not born as a member of society. He is born with a predisposition towards sociality, and he becomes a member of society. In the life of every individual, therefore, there is a temporal sequence, in the course of which he is inducted into participation in the societal dialectic" (Berger & Luckmann, 1966, p. 149). By learning to be social, we continuously create and recreate our boundaries of social life—the limits of family, work, school, power, politics, law, ideology, and culture. In our ordinary, everyday life, we consciously and unconsciously construct the social reality that, in turn, becomes objective, unavoidable, uncontrollable, and irresistible—the fact that is external but binding and constraining. This subjective construction of social life for humans is not only socially but also biologically imperative. "Man is biologically predestined to construct and to inhabit a world with others. This world becomes for him the dominant and definite reality. Its limits are set by nature, but once constructed, this world acts back upon nature. In the dialectic between nature and the socially constructed world, the human organism itself is transformed" (Berger & Luckmann, 1966, p. 204). For the social constructionists, sociology is the science of the social construction of reality. The crux of sociology is to examine how we in our everyday life and experiences create the boundaries of our own "enslavement" and the four walls of our "imprisonment" (Berger, 1963). What are the social institutions, patterns of interactions, and social and cultural process through which we create and replicate the social reality? For the construction of the institution of family, for example, the conventional process is that we fall in love, we date, we decide to live together, we propose to each other, we go to church and a court of law to get married, we celebrate our marriage with others, and we then set up a family. Thus, a family is a social construction. But once a family is constructed, legalized, and legitimated, it gets a life of its own. It becomes a social force and an objective and unavoidable boundary for our actions and behavior. "The world of everyday life is not only taken for granted as reality by the ordinary members of society in the subjectively expressive conduct of their lives. It is a world that originates in their thoughts and actions and is maintained as real" (Berger & Luckmann, 1966, p. 33).

Erving Goffman: Society as Drama

In his famous pastoral comedy *As You Like It*, William Shakespeare (1623/1998) wrote, "All the world's a stage, and all the men and women merely players" (2.7.139-141). Shakespeare's metaphor represents symbolic interactionism, which is considered a significant theoretical discovery. Based on the assumptions of symbolic interactionism, sociologist Erving Goffman (1963a/1963b/1959) established a theoretical tradition describing society as a drama and social reality as a domain of theatrical performance. One of the assumptions of symbolic interactionism is that "I"—the self—acts and behaves based on the individual's interpretation of how the social reality unfolds in front of them, how they are judged or misjudged by society, and whether the individual is positively or negatively profiled by the "we"—the others. Goffman extended this assumption on the act of interpretation of the social reality by the self through the development of a theatrical model. Goffman theorized that we are like actors on a stage engaged in the dramaturgical performance of our social life in public. Individuals, in their engagement with ordinary social life, much as actors in a drama, according to Goffman, evaluate the audience, judge the audience's perspective about them, and accordingly act and control the management of impressions that the audience is continuously making about them.

One of the central assumptions of Goffman's theory is that social reality is more comprehensible if we look at it from the perspective of dramatization or role-playing. A social structure becomes real only when it is created and sustained through role-playing. The institution of family, for instance, becomes real when husband and wife play their socially expected and desirable roles. A bureaucracy becomes a social reality when individuals working within a bureaucracy play their assigned functions according to the bureaucratic norms of command and control, respect for hierarchy, and adherence to the specialization and division of labor. Goffman further theorized that social reality is double and fractured. There is a front stage of social reality and a backstage of social reality. The front stage is formal, structured, and artificial and is controlled by collective norms, values, and expectations. In the front stage, as in school, work, or a dating situation, we are continuously engaged in impression management. In the front stage, we want to act, conform, and manipulate others' impressions about us. "When the individual presents himself before others," Goffman (1959) said, "his performance will tend to incorporate and exemplify the officially accredited values of the society, more so than does his behavior as a whole" (p. 35). The front stage of reality is a stage of performance and impression management. Goffman (1959) said: "I have been using the term 'performance' to refer to all activity of an individual which occurs during a period marked by his continuous presence before a particular set of an observer" (p. 22). The backstage of social reality, for Goffman, is informal, and it belongs to us. In the backstage, we are not manipulating others, and we are not acting. In the backstage, we are, instead, with our own "selves." The front stage is a cognitive domain of acting and impression management, and the backstage is a cognitive domain of reflection and self-evaluation. Others control the front stage, and the backstage is controlled by me. The self and society are, thus, the two sides of the same social reality. The objective dimension of society (i.e., the structures, systems, controls, hierarchy, and dominations) is inseparable from society's subjective dimensions—the existence of an active and dynamic mind and the self. The objective reality of society—the front stage—becomes "real" by the self-interpreting of its multifaceted meanings and its role-playing for impression management.

Harold Garfinkle: Ethnomethodology

The perspective of symbolic interactionism has three postulates: (1) all objects have meanings; (2) meanings are created through communications and interactions, and (3) actions and behavior of individuals are based on their active and conscious interpretations of the meanings of objects. Based on these postulates' core ideas, Harvard sociologist Harold Garfinkle developed a sociological theory and a method known as ethnomethodology. It is based on the assumption that the structure of the social world or the structure of social reality is a set of rules, norms, and meanings. It is a pattern of habituated acts and actions. The rules, norms, meanings, and the patterns of behavior in a given social reality, such as an office, a courtroom, a restaurant, or a family, are not always made and governed by science and rationality or by the way sociologists would like them to be governed. They are rather made and governed by ordinary knowledge, common-sense knowledge, and folk theories of the members who participate in the creation of those settings of social realities. The essence of sociology and sociological research, the proponents of the ethnomethodological perspective contend, is the study of how and with what methods a social reality is created, sustained, and transformed by ordinary people using ordinary knowledge. In other words, it is the study of how objective social reality is subjectively made and constructed every day by ordinary people with ordinary knowledge. The essence of sociology is to explore and understand social reality, Garfinkle (1967) argued, in terms of how its "members' actual, ordinary activities consist of methods to make practical actions, practical circumstances, common sense knowledge of social structures, and practical sociological reasoning" (p. viii).

Symbolic Interactionism in Action

Black Lives Matter: Perceptions of Competing Meanings

In 2012, a 17-year-old, unarmed, Black adolescent named Trayvon Martin was shot and killed by a neighborhood watch volunteer, George Zimmerman, in Sanford, Florida. This was the immediate context of the birth of the Black Lives Matter movement in 2013 by three African American women—Alicia Garza, Patrisse Cullors, and Opal Tometi. These three women formed the virtual movement after Zimmerman was found not guilty of second-degree murder in the death of Martin. The movement became more galvanized in the context of the 2014 police killings of Eric Garner in New York City and Michael Brown in Ferguson, Missouri; the 2015 police killings of Walter Scott in North Charleston, South Carolina, Freddie Gray in Baltimore, Maryland, and Meagan Hockaday in Oxnard, California; the 2016 police killings of Deborah Danner in New York City and Alton Sterling in Baton Rouge, Louisiana; and the 2020 police killing of George Floyd in Minneapolis, Minnesota. The Black Lives Matter (BLM) movement began with the immediate goal of ending police brutality. Still, its meanings are much broader, and they are embedded in the historical struggles of ending Black oppression in America that began with the end of the Civil War in 1865. Black Lives Matter, in a sense, is the reincarnation of the meanings of the 1955 Montgomery bus boycott led by Rosa Park; the Civil Rights Act of 1957; the Greensboro, North Carolina, sit-in of 1960; the Freedom Rides of 1961; the March on Washington and Martin Luther King Jr.'s *I Have a Dream* speech, both in 1963; the Civil Rights Act of 1964; and the Selma to Montgomery march of 1965. Historically, all these movements targeted Black oppression and systemic racism in America. Their core appeal was to create new laws and build new norms and institutions for political and economic equalities for Black citizens. The Black Lives Matter movement demands reforms in criminal justice, the end of mass incarceration, and the end of police brutality. In a more pragmatic way, it demands new police accountability, police ethics, and police philosophy. In a more fundamental way, however, Black Lives Matter is a cultural movement for ending the dehumanization of Black individuals and recognizing Black humanity (see Table 7.3).

The earlier civil rights movements for ending racial inequality were led by Black leaders and elders, such as Frederick Douglass, Rosa Parks, Martin Luther King Jr., John Lewis, Jessie Jackson, and the Rev. Al Sharpton. The Black Lives Matter movement, however, is more of a movement of the young, college-educated, and urban digital tribe. It is primarily a movement of Generation Z from across various races, groups, and classes. The BLM movement's modern meanings are becoming increasingly universal—the demand for a world of equality, respect, and dignity for all—regardless of race, age, gender, gender identity, sexual orientation, or disability—both at home and abroad. It is a message to protest against the rise of a new political culture of "ultrarights"—the rise of new political regimes that uphold the values of racism, divisiveness, nativism, localism, authoritarianism, and bigotry—in America and many other countries in Europe, Asia, Africa, and Latin America.

The Black Lives Matter movement, however, is not perceived by many other groups, particularly the White adherents of the right-wing political ideology, in the same way. They perceive it as a violent movement, particularly against the police and law enforcement. In response to BLM, some extreme right-wing political groups have created alternative movements, such as White Lives Matter (WLM) and All Lives Matter (ALM). These groups are spreading a Black-on-White crime narrative, galvanizing movements to glorify and protect Confederate symbols and monuments, and claiming that the BLM movement is "orchestrating what they call a 'white genocide' (Viets, 2016, para. 1). The flyers from the Texas-based Aryan Renaissance Society (ARS) "includes the ARS logo, a lightning bolt and runic symbol drawn over a phoenix—a Greek mythological bird that arises from a tragic death, representing, according to ARS, the 'Strength, Defiance, Perseverance, and Nobility' of the 'Aryan Spirit'" (Viets, 2016, para. 6).

FIGURE 7.1   I Can't Breathe

A recent study by the Pew Research Center observed that "two-thirds of U.S. adults say they support the [BLM] movement, with 38% saying they strongly support it. This sentiment is particularly strong among black Americans, although majorities of white (60%), Hispanic (77%) and Asian (75%) Americans express at least some support" (Parker et al., 2020, p. 2). The study also noted that "Americans are talking to family and friends about race and racial equality: 69%, including majorities across racial and ethnic groups, say they have done so in the last month. And 37% of those who use social networking sites say they have posted or shared content related to race or racial equality on these sites during this period" (Parker et al., 2020, p. 3). The Black Lives Matter movement creates a new cultural space for dialogues and interpretations of how to address race relations in America. In the past, the primary method of solving the race issue in America was through politics and policymaking at the top levels of government. In the Black Lives Matter context, a new grassroots cultural renaissance for racial equality seems to be dawning on the horizon of American consciousness. The 2020 Pew Research Center study observed that about 56% of Americans believe that grassroots mass mobilization, protest, and rallies can be effective "to help black people achieve equality. ... More say working directly with black people to solve problems in their local communities (82%), bringing people of different racial backgrounds together to talk about race (74%), and working to get more black people elected to office (68%) would be at least somewhat effective tactics" (Parker et al., 2020, p. 4).

TABLE 7.3 Black Lives Matter: Perceptions of Meanings and Interpretations

Those in Favor of BLM Movement	Those Opposed to BLM Movement
BLM means the end of oppression BLM means the end of exploitation BLM means the end of dehumanization BLM means the end of discrimination BLM means the end of the reincarnation of Jim Crow BLM means the end of *Plessey v. Ferguson* philosophy BLM signifies Martin Luther King Jr.'s *Dream* speech BLM means the realization of the Civil Rights Act BLM means the end of police brutality BLM demands criminal justice reforms BLM demands mass incarceration Introduce reforms for police accountability End discriminatory sentencing BLM means restore equal justice BLM means the end of systemic racism BLM means racial equality	May incite political violence May incite violence against law enforcement May spread hateful message May spread a message of divisiveness May resort to reverse racism May create alternative political responses "White Lives Matter" or "All Lives Matter" May fuel unpatriotic political views

Confederate Monuments: The Stones, Bricks, and Symbols Have Meanings

The symbolic interactionist perspective begins with the assertion that everything we have and everything we do as social beings, and all facets of our thoughts and ideas, have meanings and significance. Even physical objects, such as stones, bricks, pebbles, trees, and rivers, have significant social meanings. Those meanings are socially created, changed, and transformed. Most of the time, these meanings are commonly shared, and they function as glue to social cohesion. Sometimes, those meaning are also the source of social conflict, divisiveness, violence, and even death and destruction. The socially imputed meanings of different objects are historical, cultural, religious, and ideological. It is through the study of the meanings of those physical objects for different groups and classes that sociologists make sense of the pleasures and the pains, the triumphs and the tragedies of the culture, the progress, and the history of a society. In America, the Confederate monuments and symbols have remained a significant source of social and racial conflict since the end of the Civil War in 1865. (Newson, 2020; Landrieu, 2019; Levinson, 2018). A study conducted by the Southern Poverty Law Center (2019) found that there are 780 Confederate monuments in America. There are also 103 public K–12 schools, three colleges, 80 counties and cities, and 10 military bases named for Confederates scattered throughout the nation, particularly in the southern states. The Confederate monuments and symbols began to be built in the days following the Civil War, but their growth and expansion accelerated after the birth of the Jim Crow era, based on the philosophy behind *Plessy v. Ferguson* (1896), when the U.S. Supreme Court justified the constitutionality of the doctrine of "separate but equal" (Chafe et al., 2014).

Since the days of Jim Crow, the ideas and meanings behind the Confederate monuments and symbols have remained deeply controversial, contentious, and conflicting. It would appear that America is sharply divided across many lines—by race/ethnicity, White versus non-White; by state, northern versus southern; by cultural landscape, Bible Belt (socially conservative and dominated by evangelical Protestants) versus Northern Belt (socially liberal and culturally modernist); and by political affiliation, mostly Republicans in the South and primarily Democrats in the North. For the White evangelical Christians of the South who believe in social conservatism, the Confederate signs and symbols represent the preservation and glorification of Southern history and its heritage. They are for the remembrance of those who died for the "noble" cause of protecting slavery and the progress of Southern culture and civilization. For them, the South and slavery were indivisible. Confederate President Jefferson Davis was sharply opposed to the abolition of slavery. Confederate General Robert E. Lee is believed to have said, "The blacks are immeasurably better off here than in Africa, morally, socially & physically. The painful discipline they are undergoing is necessary for their instruction as a race, & I hope it will prepare & lead them to better things. How long their subjugation may be necessary is known & ordered by a wise Merciful Providence" (USA Today Network, 2020, p. 5). Lee was a staunch advocate of White colonialism and imperialism. He believed that White superiority was genetically determined (USA Today Network, 2020). For the supporters of the Confederate signs and symbols, the 13th amendment has brought forth the destruction of Southern history and its heritage (Seabrook, 2018).

The Confederate signs and symbols, for Black Americans, on the other hand, are symbols of the justification and glorification of slavery and savagery. They are the stark reminders of the days of Black subjugation by slaveholders. They remind Black Americans of the physical, economic, sexual, and social exploitation White slave owners perpetrated against slaves for centuries. The Confederate monuments are in stones and bricks, but their continued presence speaks volumes. The fact that they have not been removed seems to justify and even glorify the days of enslaving and lynching Black people. For Black Americans, the 13th Amendment has been the beginning of their emancipation and the recognition of their humanity and civilization. The amendment, the era of reconstruction, the Civil Rights Act of 1954, and the Civil Rights Act of 1964 all indicate that America should be free of all Confederate monuments, signs, songs, and symbols. For many, it is thought that it is well past the time that America should live up to its own founding declarations concerning equality, and these Confederate symbols are in direct opposition to these ideals.

From the middle of the second decade of the 21st century, America was suddenly plunged into a new crisis of race relations. New debates have emerged about the meanings and significance of the Confederate signs and symbols and the justification for their use and display in public places. This recent debate and new mobilization began in the immediate context of the slayings of nine Black people in a Bible study class in the Emanuel African Methodist Episcopal Church in Charleston, South Carolina, by 17-year-old Dylann Roof in June 2015. Roof was described as having been indoctrinated by the ideals of White supremacy. This attack occurred 2 years after the formal launch of the Black Lives Matter movement in 2013. Four years after Black Lives Matter's birth, a more fundamental shift in American politics came, in 2017, with the ascendency in political power of a right-wing political regime. With the ascendency of an administration based on the ideology of "America First," the country's divisiveness began to be further widened with respect to race relations in general and the Confederate symbols and signs in particular. In this context, Black Lives Matter is further expanding its grassroots support base. There has also begun a massive mobilization of different ultraright groups to advance America-First ideology. The "Unite the Right" rally organized by different ultraright groups in August 2017 in Charlottesville, Virginia, to protest the removal of a statue of Robert E. Lee violently clashed with the supporters of the Black Lives Matter movement. The Charlottesville clash claimed the life of one woman. How these two competing camps with two conflicting ideologies will shape the stability or the volatility of American statecraft in the coming decades will remain an intriguing question for interactionist sociologists.

"YOU WANT A CONFEDERATE MONUMENT? MY BODY IS A CONFEDERATE MONUMENT."

Caroline Randall Williams

Vanderbilt University

"I am a Black Southern woman. And of my immediate white male ancestors, all of them were rapists. My very existence is a relic of slavery and Jim Crow.

...

And I have another privilege of knowing a lot of my family history. I've known the stories. I am the daughter of two Black people. I am the granddaughter of four Black people. I am the great-granddaughter of eight Black people. I have the privilege of knowing my great-grandmother.

But she knew her white father. She knew her white father who had raped her Black mother and in such a violent way that her mother lost her mind. And so my great-grandmother was raised by her grandmother, who'd been born a slave to the family of the son who raped her daughter and made her raise her own grandchild, right?

And my great-grandmother lived till I was 17 years old, and she was a really important part of my life. And so looking at her light skin, knowing her story, what she'd seen and lived through, I thought, 'This skin is the color of that. This skin is the color of those rapes.'

> ...
>
> But because I have that white blood, I get to use my brownness as a weapon against white supremacy because, as I wrote in the piece, I am proof. I am proof of what they did. I am proof that they are not who they think they are, who they say they are, who they are remembered to be.
>
> ...
>
> What is a monument but a standing memory, an artifact to make tangible the truth of the past? My body and blood are a tangible truth of the South and its past. The Black people I come from were owned by the white people I come from. The white people I come from fought and died for their lost cause. And I ask you now: Who dares to tell me to celebrate them? Who dares to ask me to accept their mounted pedestals?"

Source: MSNBC (July 2, 2020). Transcript into: "My Body is a Monument." www.msnbc.com

Change and Transformations in Marriage and Family in Modern America

The total population of the United States is about 330 million (November 2020), and is composed of about 84 million families. The U.S. Census Bureau defines a family "as a group of two people or more (one of whom is the householder) related by birth, marriage, adoption, and residing together; all such people (including related subfamily members) are considered as members of one family" (Duffin, 2019, p. 1). In 2019, the average size of a family was 3.4. In 2019, there were about 62 million married couples in the United States. The Census Bureau (2020) defined a married couple as "a husband and wife enumerated as members of the same household. The married couple may or may not have children living with them. The expression 'husband-wife' or 'married-couple' before the term 'household,' 'family,' or 'subfamily' indicates that the household, family, or subfamily is maintained by a husband and wife" (Marital Status section).

Family in America is one of the social institutions that is going through many significant changes and transformations. There is scarcely any facet of the institution of marriage and family that has not been undergoing radical shifts in terms of meanings and significance since the middle of the 20th century (see Table 7.4). In 1990, America's marriage rate was 9.8 marriages per 1,000 people (Curtin & Sutton, 2020). In 2018, it fell to 6.8 marriages per 1,000 people, the "lowest level in the 118 years covered by the new report and the lowest recorded since 1867, the first year for which federal government data on national marriages is available" (Gavin, 2020, para. 5). A 2010 survey on marriages in America found that 44% of Americans ages 18–29 and 41% ages 31–49 believe that the institution of marriage is becoming obsolete (Statista Research Department, 2011). A recent report published by the National Center for Health Statistics similarly observed that "adults in the United States are increasingly postponing marriage, and that a record number of current youth and young adults are projected to forego marriage altogether" (Curtin & Sutton, 2020, p. 1). Of all developed countries, America has one of the highest divorce rates, "with roughly 45% of marriages expected to end through a divorce" (Brown & Lin, 2012, p. 1). A study by the Pew Research Center noted there is an emerging new age of "gray divorce" in America (Horowitz et al., 2019). In 2015, for every 1,000 married persons ages 50 and older, ten divorced—up from five in 1990, according to data from the National Center for Health Statistics (Curtin & Sutton, 2020) and United States Census Bureau (2020). "Among those ages 65 and older, the divorce rate has roughly tripled since 1990, reaching six people per 1,000 married persons in 2015" (Pew Research Center, March 9, 2017, p. 1).

While many are becoming skeptical about the traditional meaning of marriage and divorce, more Americans are opting for cohabitation. A study on marriage and cohabitation in America by the Pew Research Center observed that "as more U.S. adults are delaying marriage—or foregoing it all together—the share who have ever lived with an unmarried partner has been on the rise. Amid these changes, most Americans find cohabitation acceptable, even for couples who don't plan to get married" (Horowitz et al., 2019, p. 1). The study found that "young adults are particularly accepting of cohabitation—78% of those ages 18 to 29 say it's acceptable for an unmarried couple to live together, even if they don't plan to get married—but majorities across age groups share this view" (Horowitz et al., 2019, p. 2). Two of the major concomitant developments from these trends are the rise of unwed motherhood and single parenting. According to the Centers for Disease Control and Prevention (Daugherty & Copen, 2016) data, 40.2% of U.S. children born in 2015 were born to unmarried mothers. "In 1940, 3.8 percent of the babies born in the United States were born to unmarried women. In 1992, it exceeded 30 percent for the first time, hitting 30.1 percent. And, in 2015, it was 40.2 percent" (Jeffrey, 2016, paras. 4–5). According to the U.S. Census Bureau, about 27% of children in America live with single parents. Custodial Mothers and Fathers and Their Child Support cited a 2015 report, released by the U.S. Census Bureau every 2 years, showing there are about 13.6 million single parents in the United States today and that those parents are responsible for raising 22.4 million children. "This number represents approximately 27% of children under 21 in the U.S. today" (Wolf, 2020, para. 3). A report from the Centers for Disease Control and Prevention, titled "Trends in Attitudes about Marriage, Childbearing, and Sexual Behavior" in America, noted that "from 2002 to 2011–2013, there was an increase in the percentages of men and women who agreed with premarital cohabitation, nonmarital childbearing, the right for gay and lesbian adults to adopt children, same-sex sexual relations, and premarital sex for those aged 18" (Daugherty & Copen, 2016, p. 1). The report further added, "There was no change in the percentages of men and women who agreed with premarital sex for those aged 16. There was no change from 2006–2010 to 2011–2013 in attitudes regarding marriage, cohabitation and the risk of divorce, the necessity of having children for one's happiness, and raising children in a cohabiting union" (Daugherty & Copen, 2016, p. 1).

Four sets of factors are primarily responsible for the shifting nature and meaning of family and marriage in America: law, technology, economy, and culture. Since the 1960s, the U.S. Supreme Court has made a series of decisions that enlarged the boundaries of women's reproductive freedom, marital freedom, and sexual freedom in general. Some of these decisions include *Griswold v. Connecticut* in 1965, *Eisenstadt v. Baird* in 1972, *Roe v. Wade* in 1973, *Romer v. Evans* in 1996, *Lawrence v. Texas* in 2003, and *Obergefell v. Hodges* in 2015. The *Griswold* and the *Eisenstadt* decisions decriminalized the use of contraceptives by married and unmarried women. *Roe v. Wade* decriminalized abortion. The *Obergefell* ruling legalized same-sex marriage. In 1969, California Governor Ronald Reagan signed a no-fault divorce law for California. By the 1980s, no-fault divorce law was enacted in all 50 states. This has sharply increased the rate of divorce in America from the beginning of the 1990s. Technologically, advent of the birth control pill in 1965 (the pill received approval of the Food and Drug Administration that same year) and emergence of the technology of in vitro fertilization and the freezing of human eggs further enlarged the boundaries of women's reproductive freedom. Traditionally, the lack of economic freedom of women contributed to marital stability, and traditionally, human work was physical. As a result of the advent of the modern knowledge economy, the rise of digital society, growth of the service economy, and the expansion of women's education, more women are now working outside the home, and their boundaries of economic freedom have vastly enlarged. This has led to a demand for more equality and quality of life and happiness in marital relations and brought many challenges to the institution of patriarchy (Amato et al., 2009; Cherlin, 2010). The legal, technological, and economic forces in many complex ways have, in turn, been affected by the advent of the modern culture of individualism, equality, human rights, sexual freedom, and love and romanticism.

Family and marriage core meanings have been changing from control to freedom, domination to equality, reproduction to love and romanticism, and sex within marriage bonds to freedom of love, sex, and intimacy (Giddens, 1993/1997). The traditional norms of collective controls by parents, relatives, and communities on sexual and marital regulations are becoming increasingly obsolete. The sexual and marital behaviors, traditionally perceived as deviance, now are legally acceptable, politically "correct," and culturally legitimate. Modern work and technology have opened a new horizon of freedom and equality. Concerning the advent of the contemporary culture of individualism, sociology, from the beginning of its classical time in the 19th century, was concerned about the weakening of family and marriage, the "death of community" (Nisbet, 2010), and the advent of the "homeless mind" (Berger et al., 1973). The symbolic interactionist sociologists will remain curious about the future directions of changes in America's family and marriage meanings and, in turn, their effects on the future of modernity in America.

TABLE 7.4 Changing Meanings of Marriage and Family in America

Family Functions and Issues	Before 1960	1960–2020
Family size	Large/five to eight children	Small/two to three children
Family type	Extended	Nuclear
Parental role	Authoritative	Liberal
Spousal role	Unequal	High demand for equality
Parent–child relations	Obedience and conformity	Autonomy/self-growth
Single parenting	Chance	Choice
Sex and marriage	Highly regulated	Loosely regulated
Childbearing	Social obligation	Elective
Cohabitation	Socially stigmatized	Social approval
Unwed motherhood	Socially stigmatized	High social tolerance
Teen pregnancy	Highly controlled	Loosely controlled

Abortion	Illegal	Legal (*Row v. Wade*)
Contraceptives for married women	Illegal	Legal (*Griswold v. C.T.*)
Contraceptives for unmarried women	Illegal	Legal (*Eisenstadt v. Bird*)
The technology of in vitro fertilization	Not available	Available
Surrogate mothering	Socially unacceptable	Socially acceptable
Alternative lifestyles	Socially stigmatized	Social tolerance
Same-sex marriage	Illegal	Legal (*Obergefell v. Hodges*)
The basis for divorce	Based on fault	No-fault divorce law
Rate of divorce	Low	High
Divorce	Socially stigmatized	High social tolerance
Love/sex/intimacy	Integrated/collective control	Separated/choice
Birth rate	Moderately high	Declined
Marriage rate	Moderately high	Very low (6.5 per 1,000)

Structural-Functionalism, Conflict Theory, and Symbolic Interactionism: A Comparative Look

Societies are not governed by the way science or sociologists would like them to be governed. Societies are ongoing processes of construction and deconstruction of social structures, roles, rules, laws, ideology, and culture. Sociology as a science is based on the assumption that the domain of society, much as the domain of nature or the domain of life and human organism, is governed by certain structures, rules, laws, forms, and patterns. Social life is not absolutely random and chaotic. The constitution of social life is understandable, predictable, and generalizable. As a science, sociology, therefore, seeks to theorize how society is formed and governed. What are the social forms and processes through which human societies grow, change, and evolve? What is the profile of human nature? And of more importance, how are individuals and society connected? Since the birth of sociology in the middle of the 19th century, there has been a considerable accumulation of concepts, ideas, and theories to capture the mysteries of social reality and to debunk the science of human lives and stories. Three paradigms or scientific perspectives dominate the field of sociology. In Chapters 5, 6, and 7, these paradigms have been discussed and examined. This concluding section of Chapter 7 takes a comparative look at the competing assumptions, areas of theorizing, the focus of theorizing, and the fundamental concepts of these three sociological paradigms. As mentioned in Chapter 2, science is much like searching for a black cat in a dark room. Science is a process of theorizing about the nature and the constitution of a given reality. The reality is never wholly captured and understood. But science keeps searching for the "truth" through theorizing, intuition, and imagination. The three sociological paradigms—the three sociological eyes—discussed in Chapters 5, 6, and 7 are, therefore, the three sets of discoveries by sociologists to observe and capture the social reality.

The structural-functional paradigm is based on the assumption that social life is a constellation of structures and systems. These structures have different forms and patterns. Our actions and behavior are shaped and controlled by systems and structures within which we live and grow. The cultural consensus is the glue that binds a system or a structure together. The conflict paradigm assumes that social systems and structures are always fragile because social conflicts between and among different human groups—race, gender, class, ethnicity, nationality, religion, culture, and ideology—are universal and inevitable. Social conflict is the driver and the shaper of social change and transformations. The proponents of the symbolic interactionist paradigm assume that social structures and systems, and social groups and communities, are nothing but bundles of meanings. Sociologists, therefore, should study how those meanings grow and change and how they shape and mold our behavior (see Table 7.5).

TABLE 7.5 The Sociological Paradigms: A Comparison

Paradigms	Assumptions	Areas of Theorizing	Focus of Theorizing	Major Sociologists
Structural-functional	Society as structure and systems Social order is possible through cultural consensus.	Structures Systems Norms and values Command Authority Functions	Systemic integration Systemic functions Whole-part relationships	Emile Durkheim Talcott Parsons Robert Merton Anthony Giddens
Conflict	Social conflict is universal. The social domain is a domain of power struggle.	Race conflict Gender conflict Class conflict Religious conflict Ideological conflict	Domination Oppression Exploitation Discrimination Dehumanization Extermination	Karl Marx Lewis Coser Ralph Dahrendorf Randall Collins C. Wright Mills
Symbolic interactionism	All objects—physical, social, and moral—have meanings. Meaning are created through social interactions.	Meanings Significance Ideas Norms Values Symbols Gestures	Meaning creation Social interaction Mind and the self Internalization Interpretation of meanings Symbols/gestures	Max Weber Georg Simmel Herbert Blumer Herbert Mead Charles Cooley

The concepts that the three paradigms have evolved and used as analytical tools are also very different. For the structural functionalists, the core ideas are hierarchy, control, authority, order, functions, and cultural consensus. The core concepts include domination, oppression, exploitation, discrimination, and dehumanization for the conflict theorists. On the other hand, the symbolic interactionists seek to explore the role of the mind and the self and the way meanings of different objects are created and expressed through language, symbols, and gestures (see Table 7.6).

TABLE 7.6 The Sociological Paradigms: Key Concepts

Structural Functionalism	Conflict Paradigm	Symbolic-Interactionist Paradigm
Structures	Social conflict	Mind
Systems	Racial conflict	Self
Social order	Gender conflict	Meanings
Social stability	Class conflict	Significance
Command	Role conflict	Social interactions
Control	Religious conflict	Internalization
Authority	Oppression	Interpretation
Hierarchy	Exploitation	Language
Roles and status	Domination	Symbols
Norms and values	Discrimination	Gestures
Functions/dysfunctions	Natural rights	Social construction of reality
Cultural consensus	Universal human rights	Ordinary knowledge
Homeostasis	Freedom	Ordinary experience

In examining a particular social reality in terms of a specific sociological paradigm, one needs to be aware of its assumptions and its core set of analytical categories. It could be misleading to talk about meanings and symbols and then examine them in terms of command and control or order and stability. Similarly, analysis of social conflicts could be misleading if the nature of domination and oppression between different competing groups are examined in terms of the need for social order and consensus. If a given social problem is examined from the three sociological paradigms (e.g., divorce or child abuse from the perspectives of structural functionalism, conflict theory, and symbolic interactionism [Tables 7.7 and 7.8]), one will need to proceed from three sets of assumptions and use three sets of analytical categories. The existence of multiple paradigms in science is not a sign of its weakness. There are various paradigms in all branches of science and in all scientific domains—nature, life, mind, and society. In physics, for example, the Newtonian paradigm is different from the relativistic paradigm of Einstein. Both the Newtonian and the relativistic paradigms are different from the theories and assumptions of quantum physics fathered by Max Planck, Werner Heisenberg, and Erwin Schrodinger.

TABLE 7.7 Divorce: From the Three Sociological Paradigms

	Divorce: Structural Functionalism
Power	Patriarchal men are less likely to believe in power equality between men and women.
Authority	There has been an increasing decline in male authority in modern culture.
Control	Dominating men are more likely to create stress in an equal spousal relationship.
	Divorce: The Conflict Paradigm
Domination	Divorce is more likely when women fight back against male domination.
Cultural conflict	Intercultural or interracial marriages are more vulnerable to divorce.
Role conflict	Working women experience role conflict, and role conflict generates marital stress.
	Divorce: Symbolic Interactionism
Meaning	The predominant meaning of modern marriage is not a reproduction but love and romanticism.
Symbols	Men and women have different perceptions about the material and nonmaterial symbols of love and affection.
Interpretation	Divorce is more acceptable and less stigmatized in modern societies. The changing meaning of marriage is associated with a high rate of cohabitation and unwed motherhood.

In biology, there are three major paradigms: molecular biology, developmental biology, and evolutionary biology. The core of the curiosity in biology is how genes and the environment are connected. In economics, supply-side economics is different from neo-Keynesian economics and institutional economics. One of the key points in paradigmatic differences in economics is the extent to which the free-market economy should be controlled and regulated by the government. In political science, some see the world from the perspective of realism, and some see the world of politics from the perspective of internationalism and globalism. The paradigmatic debate in political science centers on the idea of whether the politics of a nation should be guided from the standpoint of national interest or the contexts of global political realities. In psychology, the major paradigms are psychoanalysis, behaviorism, cognitive psychology, and evolutionary psychology. All fields of science are multiparadigmatic. Thomas Kuhn, who popularized the idea of paradigm in social science, argued that change from one paradigm to another paradigm in a field of science signifies its progress and vitality. In sociology, structural functionalism, the conflict perspective, and symbolic interactionism are three of the main viewpoints of observing the social world and understanding change and evolution in the whole variety of human social stories.

TABLE 7.8 Child Abuse: From the Three Sociological Paradigms

	Child Abuse: Structural Functionalism
Power	Parents believing in traditional patriarchal power are more likely to abuse their children.
Authority	In many traditional societies, children are perceived as properties of their parents, and absolute parental authority to control children is legitimate.
Control	An increasing challenge to parental control from children leads to child abuse.
	Child Abuse: The Conflict Paradigm
Domination	Many parents believe it is their right to dominate and discipline their children.
Class	Parents from lower socioeconomic status households are more likely to abuse their children.
Marital conflict	Dysfunctional families with marital conflict are more likely to abuse their children.
	Child Abuse: Symbolic Interactionism
Meanings	Many traditional parents do not see domination and controlling of a child as abuse.
Interpretation	Many parents have an internalized sense that children are their properties.
Symbols	Child abuse is physical, economic, sexual, and emotional.

Selected Questions, Essays, Assignments, and Quizzes

1. Symbolic interactionism as a sociological perspective has evolved from the subjectivist tradition in philosophy, particularly Rene Descartes's philosophy of the mind. Examine this statement and describe the starting point of analysis of social reality from the perspective of subjectivism.

2. In classical sociology, the subjectivist tradition was born through the writings of Max Weber and Georg Simmel. Describe and explain Weber's theory of social action and Simmel's idea of society as a process, focusing mainly on Weber's explanation of the rise of modern rational capitalism in the West.

3. The paradigm of symbolic interactionism is based on the assumption that all objects have meanings and meanings are socially created through human interactions and communications. There are rivers in all countries. Still, for the Indian Hindus, the river Ganges has a special meaning and significance. Based on internet research, write a short essay (three to four single-spaced pages, 12 pt. font) explaining the importance of the Ganges to the Hindus of India.

4. November 11 is Veterans Day in America. On every Veterans Day, the American president is expected to go to the Arlington Cemetery in Virginia. Develop a table or chart describing 10 sets of meanings of the Arlington Cemetery to all Americans.

5. September 11, 2001 is the day of great awakening for America's domestic and national security.

America's relation with the Muslim world has probably permanently changed after 9/11. Based on your internet research and class lectures, describe and explain the meaning and significance of 9/11 for all Americans and the way America's perception of the world has changed since that day.

6. Quiz: One of the core assumptions of symbolic interactionism is that our mind is an active and dynamic entity. We are not merely enslaved by external facts and events. We instead interpret them in our mind; we evaluate different responses, then we decide what to do and what not to do concerning a particular social event or a social reality. From your everyday life experience, describe an episode in which you really debated with yourself for quite some time how to respond to a particular episode. You can make a list (one or two single-spaced pages) of the internal dialogues you had with yourself with respect to that episode (e.g., Should I tell him? Should I keep quiet? Should I tell my mom?).

7. Many of America's social problems, such as single parenting, divorce, juvenile delinquency, child maltreatment, spousal violence, and fatherless homes, are growing because of the changing meanings and significance of the institutions of marriage and family. Based on your understanding of the perspective symbolic interactionism, related class lectures, and your internet research, write an essay (four or five single-space pages, 12 pt. font) describing how love, sex, intimacy, marriage, family, and children were perceived traditionally and how and why those traditional meanings are currently interpreted and perceived differently (develop a table or chart to answer this question).

8. The #MeToo movement is bringing some significant changes in relationships between men and women and in the governance of corporate America. Describe the changing nature and meanings of sexual harassment in the workplace, citing at least five related U.S. Supreme Court decisions made during the past 4 decades.

9. The Black Lives Matter (BLM) movement is not seen and perceived by Black Americans and White Americans in the same way. Based on class lectures and your related internet research, describe the competing meanings of BLM for Black Americans and White Americans. Describe and explain the alternative movements growing in response to BLM.

10. In recent years, America has plunged into a huge debate and discourses about Confederate symbols and monuments. The Civil War seems to be giving birth to a new culture war in America in the 21st century. Describe and explain the meaning of the Confederate symbols and monuments to the supporters of both sides of this issue (i.e., Black Americans and right-wing political groups).

References

Amato, P. R., Booth, A., Johnson, D. R., & Rogers, S. J. (2009). *How marriage in America is changing.* Harvard University Press.

Bechtel, W., & Graham, G. (Eds.) *A companion to cognitive science.* Wiley and Blackwell.

Berger, P. L. (1963). *Invitation to sociology: A humanistic perspective.* Anchor Books.

Berger, P. L., & Luckmann, T. (1966). *The social construction of reality: A Treatise in the sociology of knowledge.* Penguin Books.

Berger, P. L., Berger, B., & Kellner, H. (1973). *The homeless mind: Modernity and consciousness.* Random House.

Blumer, H. (2008). Society as symbolic interaction. In P. Kivisto (Ed.), *Social theory–Roots and branches: Readings* (pp. 246–253). Oxford University Press.

Blumer, H. (1993). The nature of symbolic interactionism. In J. M. Charon (Ed.), *The meaning of sociology* (pp. 344–396). Prentice-Hall.

Blumer, H. (1966). *Symbolic interactionism: Perspective and method.* Prentice-Hall.

Brown, S. F., & Lin, I. F. (2012). The gray divorce revolution: Rising divorce among middle-aged and older adults, 1990–2010. *Journal of Gerontology, 67*(6), 731–741.

Burmudez, J. L. (2020). *Cognitive science: An introduction to the science of the mind.* Oxford University Press.

Chafe, W. W., Gavins, R., & Korstad, R. (Eds.). (2014). *Remembering Jim Crow: African-Americans tell about life in segregated south*. New Press.

Cherlin, A. J. (2010). *The marriage-go-around. The state of marriage and the family in America today*. Vintage.

Cooley, C. H. (1902, 2012). *Human nature and the social order*. Hard Press Publishing.

Cooley, C. H. (1909). *Social organization: A study of the larger mind*. Schocket Books.

Cooley, C. H. (1918, 2013). *Social process*. Hard Press Publishing.

Curtin, S., & Sutton, P. (2020). *Marriage rates in the United States, 1900–2018*. Centers for Disease Control, National Center for Health Statistics. Retrieved from https://www.cdc.gov/nchs/data/hestat/marriage_rate_2018/marriage_rate_2018.htm on December 20, 2020.

Daugherty, J., & Copen, C. (2016). *Trends in attitudes about marriage, childbearing, and sexual behavior: The United States, 2002, 2006–2010, and 2011–2013*. Centers for Disease Control and Prevention, National Center for Health Statistics.

Descartes, R. (1999). *Discourses on methods and meditations on first philosophy* (D. A. Cress, Trans.). Hackett Publishing.

Duffin, E. (2019). *The number of families in the U.S. from 1960–2019*. Retrieved from statistica.com on December 20, 2020.

Freud, S. (1999). *The ego and the id* (The complete psychological works of Sigmund Freud). W. W. Norton.

Freud, S. (2010). *Civilization and its discontents*. W.W. Norton.

Garfinkle, G. (1967). *Studies in ethnomethodology*. Prentice-Hall.

Gavin, G. (2020). *U.S. marriage rate drops historic low*. U.S. News and World Report. Retrieved from https://www.usnews.com/news/healthiest-communities/articles/2020-04-29/us-marriage-rate-drops-to-record-low on December 20, 2020.

Giddens, A. (1991). *Modernity and self-identity: Self and society in the late modern age*. Stanford University Press.

Giddens, A. (1993). *The transformation of intimacy: Sexuality, love, and eroticism in modern societies*. Stanford University Press.

Goffman, E. (1959). *The presentation of self in everyday life*. Anchor Books: Doubleday.

Goffman, E. (1963). *Behavior in public places: Notes on the social organization of gathering*. Free Press.

Goffman, E. (1963). *Stigma: Notes on the management of spoiled identity*. Simon and Schuster.

Horowitz, J., Graf, N., & Livingston, G. (2019). *Marriage and cohabitation in the U.S.* Pew Research Center.

Jeffrey, T. (2016). *CDC: 40%+ of U.S. babies born to unmarried women for 8th straight year*. CNS News. Retrieved from https://www.cnsnews.com/news/article/terence-p-jeffrey/cdc-babies-born-unmarried-women-exceeded-40-8th-straight-year on December 20, 2020.

Kolak, D., Hirstein, W., & Waskan, J. (2006). *Cognitive science: An introduction to mind and brain*. Routledge.

Landrieu, M. (2019). *In the shadow of statues: A White southerner confronts history*. Penguin Press.

Levinson, S. (2018). *Written in stone: Public monuments in changing societies*. Duke University Press.

Mead, G. H. (1934). *Mind, self, and society: From the standpoint of social behaviorist*. University of Chicago Press.

Nisbet, R. (2010). *The quest for community: A study in the ethics of order and freedom*. Intercollegiate Studies.

Newson, A. (2020). *Cut in stone: Confederate monuments and theological disruption*. Baylor University Press.

Parker, K., Horowitz, J. M., & Anderson, M. (2020). *Amid protests, majorities across racial and ethnic groups express support for the Black Lives Matter movement*. Pew Research Center.

Pew Research Center. (March 9, 2017). *Led by Baby Boomers, divorce rates climb for America's 50+ population* (by R. Stepler). Retrieved from https://www.pewresearch.org/fact-tank/2017/03/09/led-by-baby-boomers-divorce-rates-climb-for-americas-50-population/ on December 20, 2020.

Ritzer, G. (2000). *Sociological theory* (5th ed.). McGraw-Hill.

Seabrook, L. (2018). *Confederate monuments: Why every American should honor Confederate soldiers and their memorials*. Sea Raven Press.

Shakespeare, W. (1998). *As you like it*. Project Gutenberg. (Original work published 1623)

Simmel, G. (1972). *On individuality and social forms* (D. N. Levine, Ed.). University of Chicago Press.

Skinner, B. F. (2012). *Science and human behavior*. Free Press.

Southern Poverty Law Center. (2019). *Whose heritage? Public symbols of the Confederacy*. Retrieved from https://www.splcenter.org/20190201/whose-heritage-public-symbols-confederacy on December 20, 2020.

Statista Research Department. (2011). *U.S. survey on marriage being obsolete in 2010*. Retrieved from https://www.statista.com/statistics/243900/respondents-thoughts-on-marriage-being-obsolete-in-the-united-states/ om December 20, 2020.

United States Census Bureau. (2020). *Current population survey: Subject definitions*. Retrieved from https://www.census.gov/programs-surveys/cps/technical-documentation/subject-definitions.html on December 20, 2020.

USA Today Network Report. (2020). *Confederate monuments: What the men honored by statues did and believed*. Retrieved from https://www.tennessean.com/in-depth/news/2020/07/30/confederate-monuments-robert-lee-jefferson-davis-statues/5535000002/ on December 20, 2020.

Viets, S. (2016). *Meet White Lives Matter: The racist response to Black Lives Matter movement*. Southern Poverty Law Center. Retrieved from https://www.splcenter.org/hatewatch/2016/03/18/meet-white-lives-matter-racist-response-black-lives-matter-movement on December 20, 2020.

Weber, M (1992). *The sociology of religion* (E. Fischoff, Trans.). Beacon Press.

Weber, M. (2010). *The Protestant ethic and the spirit of capitalism*. Oxford University Press.

Weber, M. (2017). *The methodology of social sciences* (E. A. Shils & H. A. Finch, Trans. and Eds.). Routledge.

Wolf, J. (2020). *Single parent statistics based on census data*. Retrieved from https://www.verywellfamily.com/single-parent-census-data-2997668 on December 30, 2020.

Wolff, K. (1950). *The sociology of Georg Simmel* (K. Wolff, Ed. and Trans.). Free Press.

Figure Credits

Fig. 7.1: Copyright © 2020 by Josh Hild. Reprinted with permission.

CPSIA information can be obtained
at www.ICGtesting.com
Printed in the USA
LVHW061203150722
723547LV00004B/27

9 781793 510495